Andrews McMeel Publishing
a division of Andrews McMeel Universal
1130 Walnut Street, Kansas City, Missouri 64106

www.andrewsmcmeel.com

24 25 26 27 28 TEN 10 9 8 7 6 5 4 3 2 1

ISBN: 978-1-5248-9027-8

Library of Congress Control Number: 2023951127

Editor: Lucas Wetzel
Art Director: Tiffany Meairs
Production Editor: Jennifer Straub
Production Manager: Chadd Keim

ATTENTION: SCHOOLS AND BUSINESSES
Andrews McMeel books are available at quantity discounts with bulk purchase for educational, business, or sales promotional use. For information, please e-mail the Andrews McMeel Publishing Special Sales Department: sales@amuniversal.com.

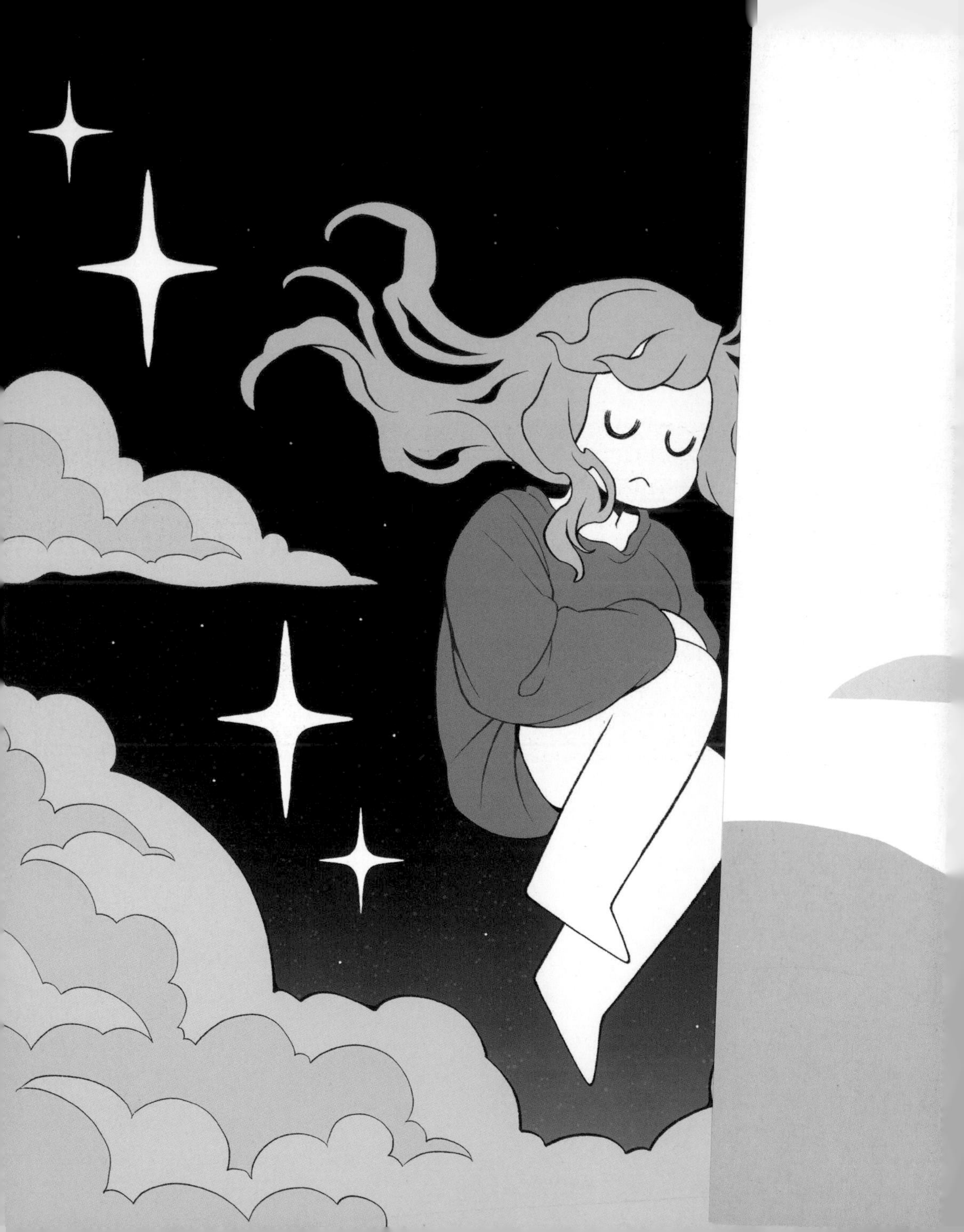

# LAVENDER CLOUDS

## COMICS ABOUT NEURODIVERGENCE AND MENTAL HEALTH

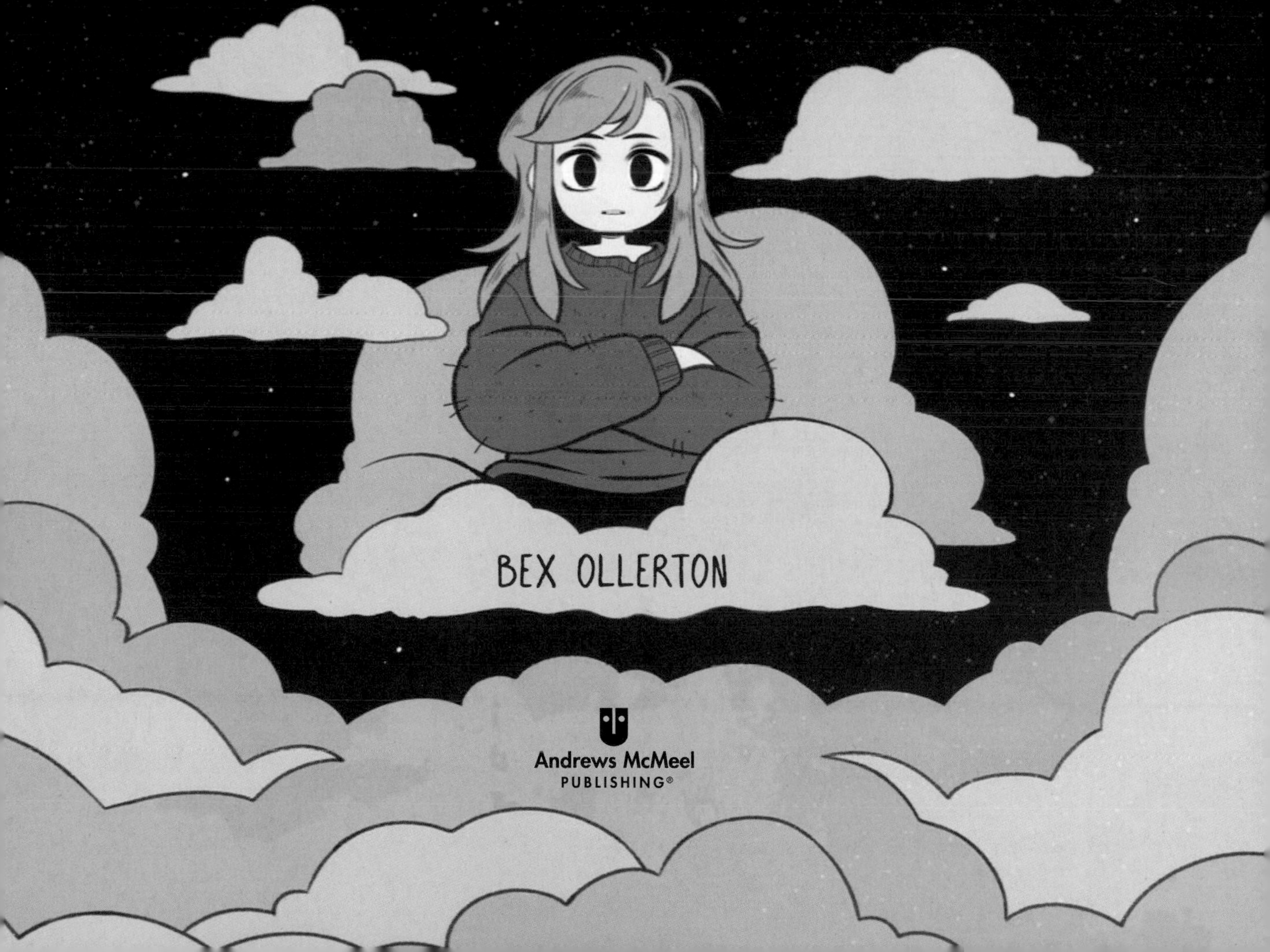

BEX OLLERTON

Andrews McMeel
PUBLISHING®

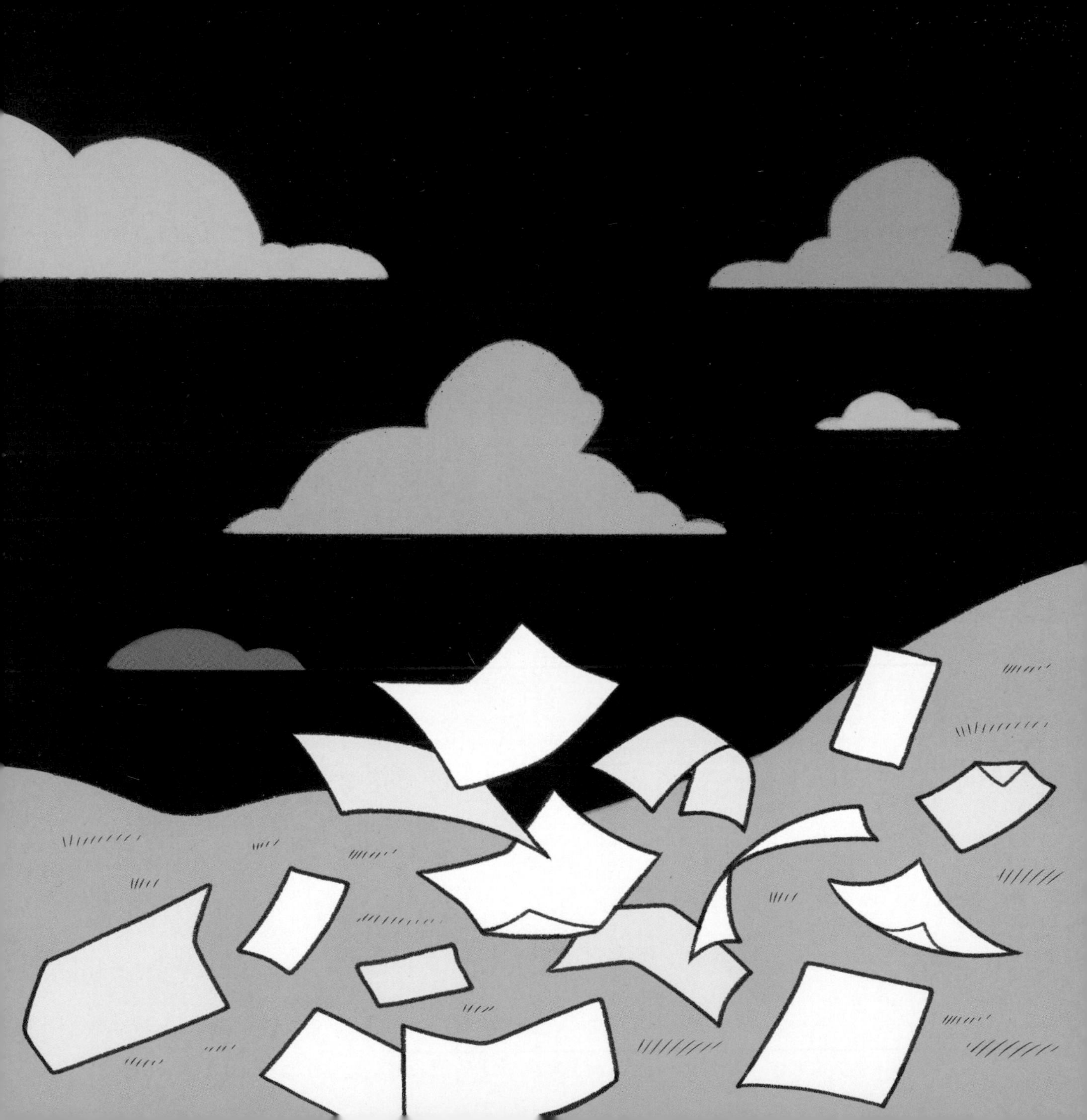

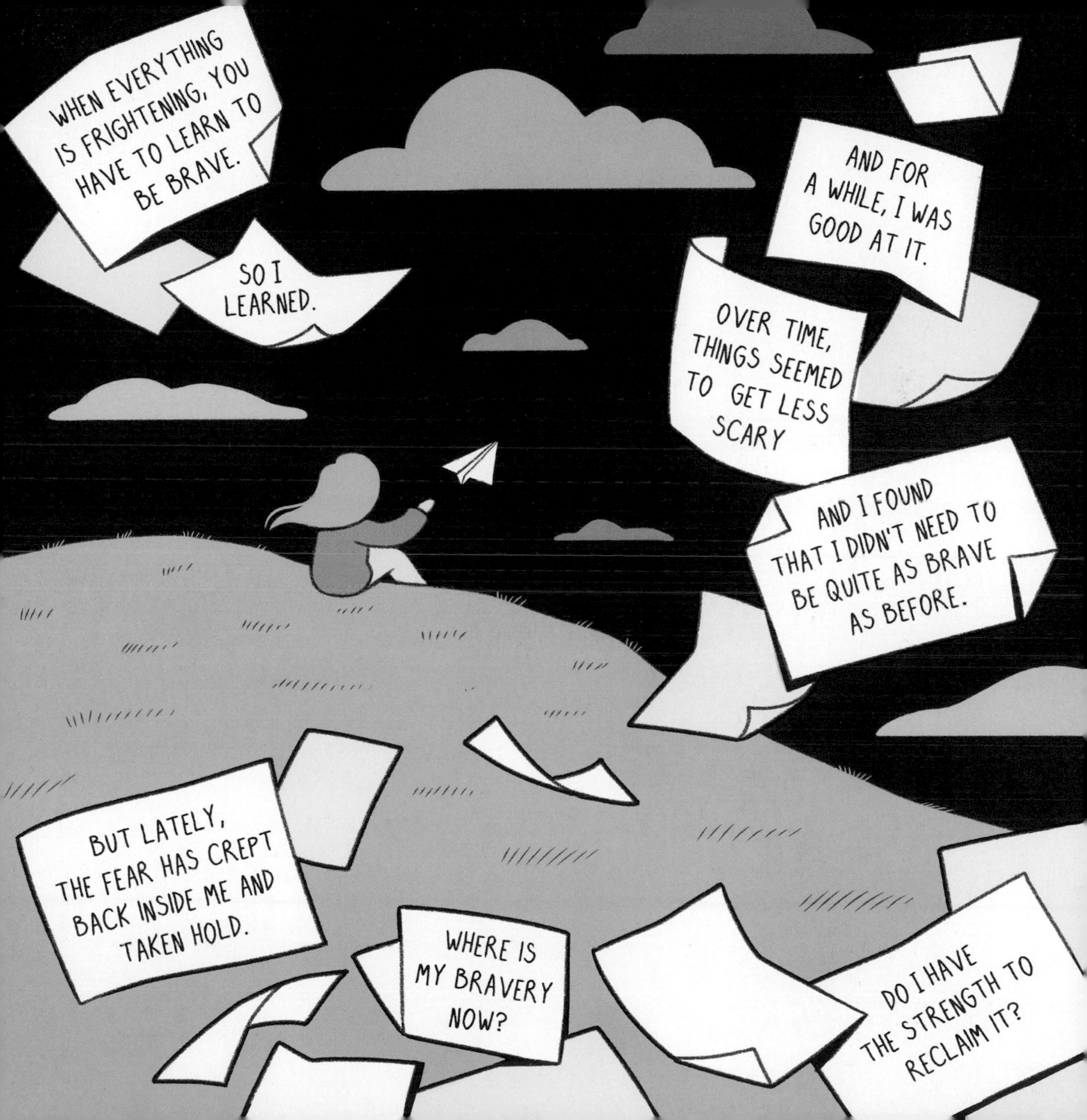
WHEN EVERYTHING IS FRIGHTENING, YOU HAVE TO LEARN TO BE BRAVE.
SO I LEARNED.
AND FOR A WHILE, I WAS GOOD AT IT.
OVER TIME, THINGS SEEMED TO GET LESS SCARY
AND I FOUND THAT I DIDN'T NEED TO BE QUITE AS BRAVE AS BEFORE.
BUT LATELY, THE FEAR HAS CREPT BACK INSIDE ME AND TAKEN HOLD.
WHERE IS MY BRAVERY NOW?
DO I HAVE THE STRENGTH TO RECLAIM IT?

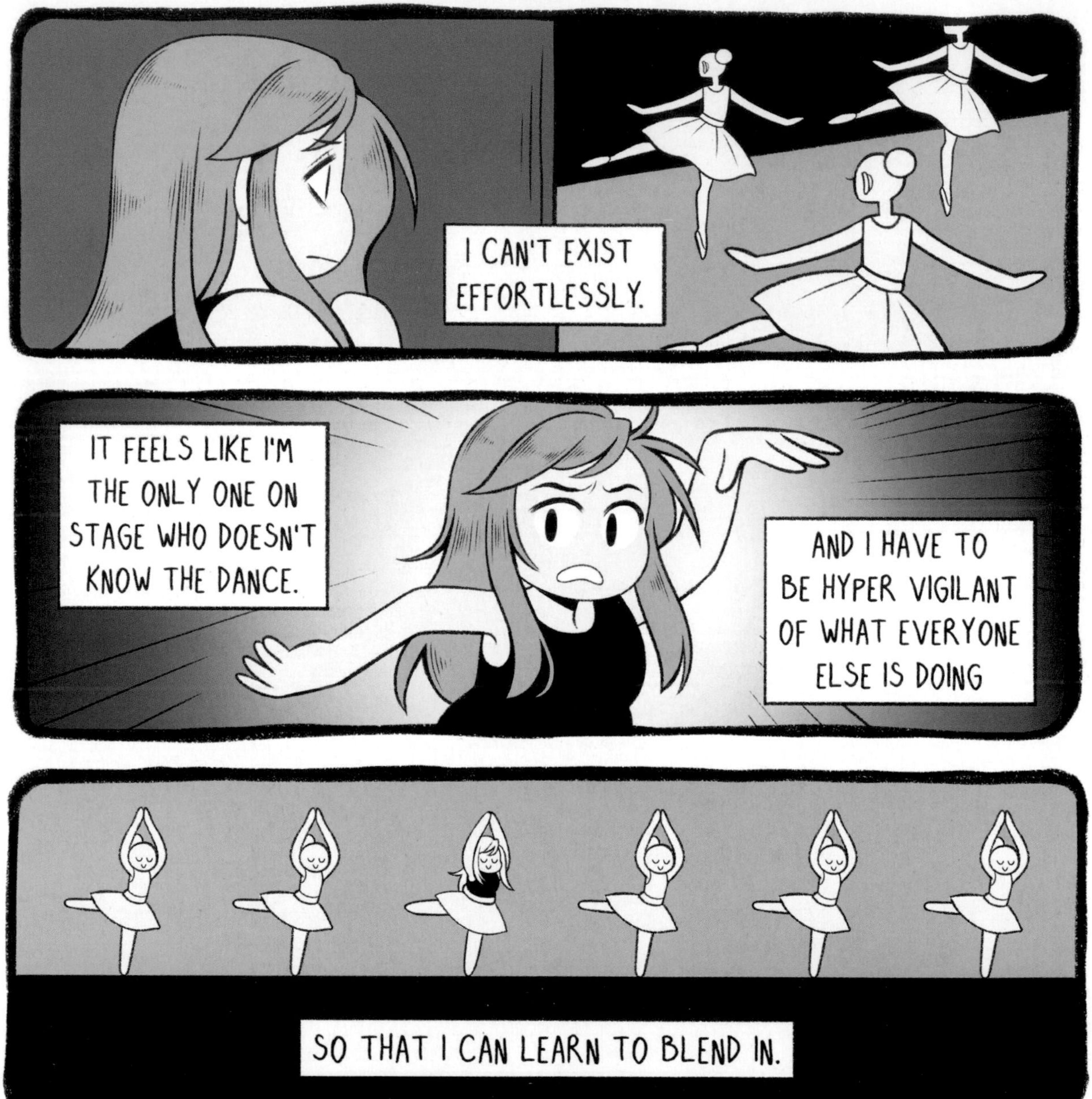
I CAN'T EXIST EFFORTLESSLY.
IT FEELS LIKE I'M THE ONLY ONE ON STAGE WHO DOESN'T KNOW THE DANCE.
AND I HAVE TO BE HYPER VIGILANT OF WHAT EVERYONE ELSE IS DOING
SO THAT I CAN LEARN TO BLEND IN.

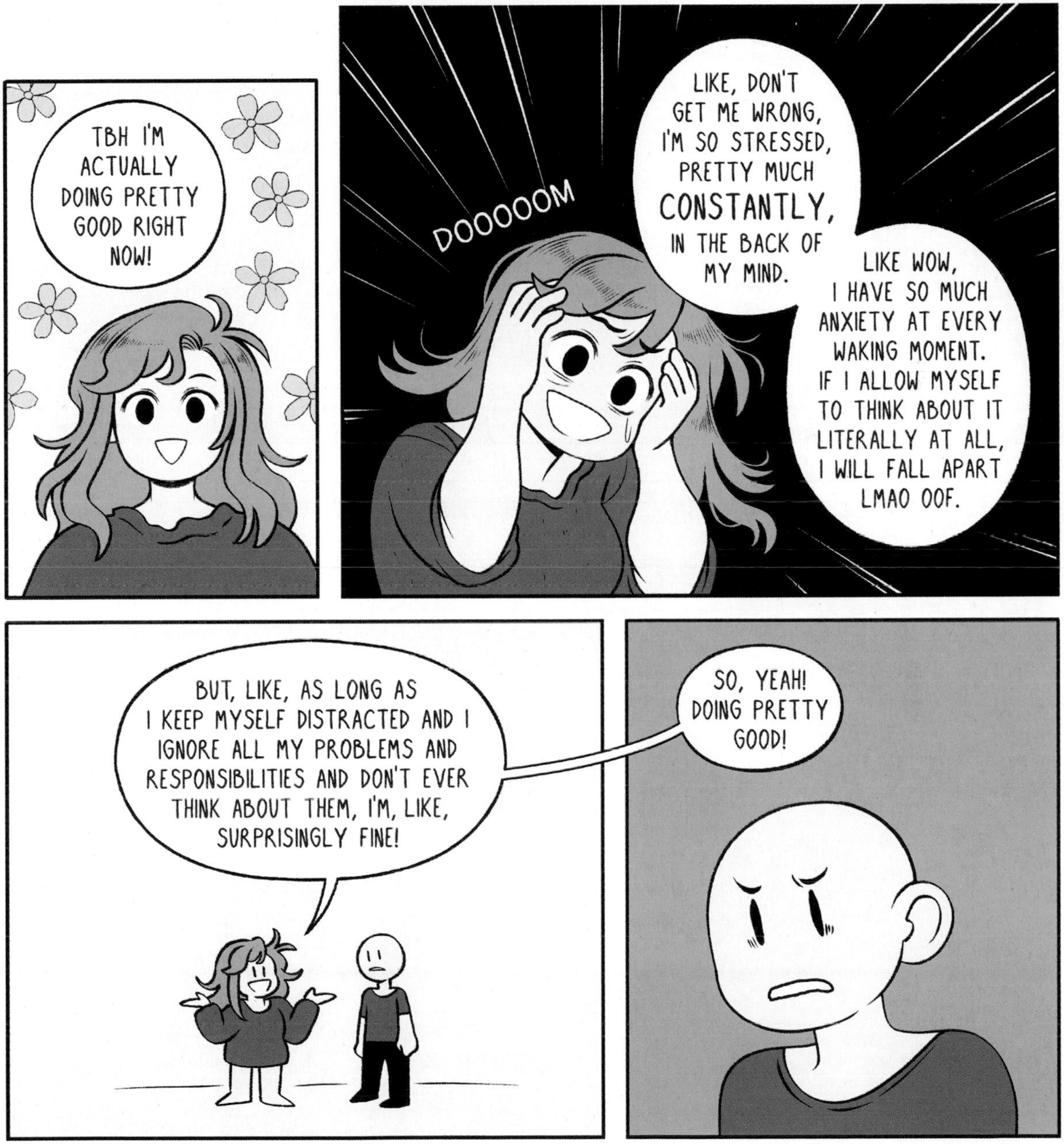
TBH I'M ACTUALLY DOING PRETTY GOOD RIGHT NOW!
DOOOOOM
LIKE, DON'T GET ME WRONG, I'M SO STRESSED, PRETTY MUCH CONSTANTLY, IN THE BACK OF MY MIND.
LIKE WOW, I HAVE SO MUCH ANXIETY AT EVERY WAKING MOMENT. IF I ALLOW MYSELF TO THINK ABOUT IT LITERALLY AT ALL, I WILL FALL APART LMAO OOF.
BUT, LIKE, AS LONG AS I KEEP MYSELF DISTRACTED AND I IGNORE ALL MY PROBLEMS AND RESPONSIBILITIES AND DON'T EVER THINK ABOUT THEM, I'M, LIKE, SURPRISINGLY FINE!
SO, YEAH! DOING PRETTY GOOD!

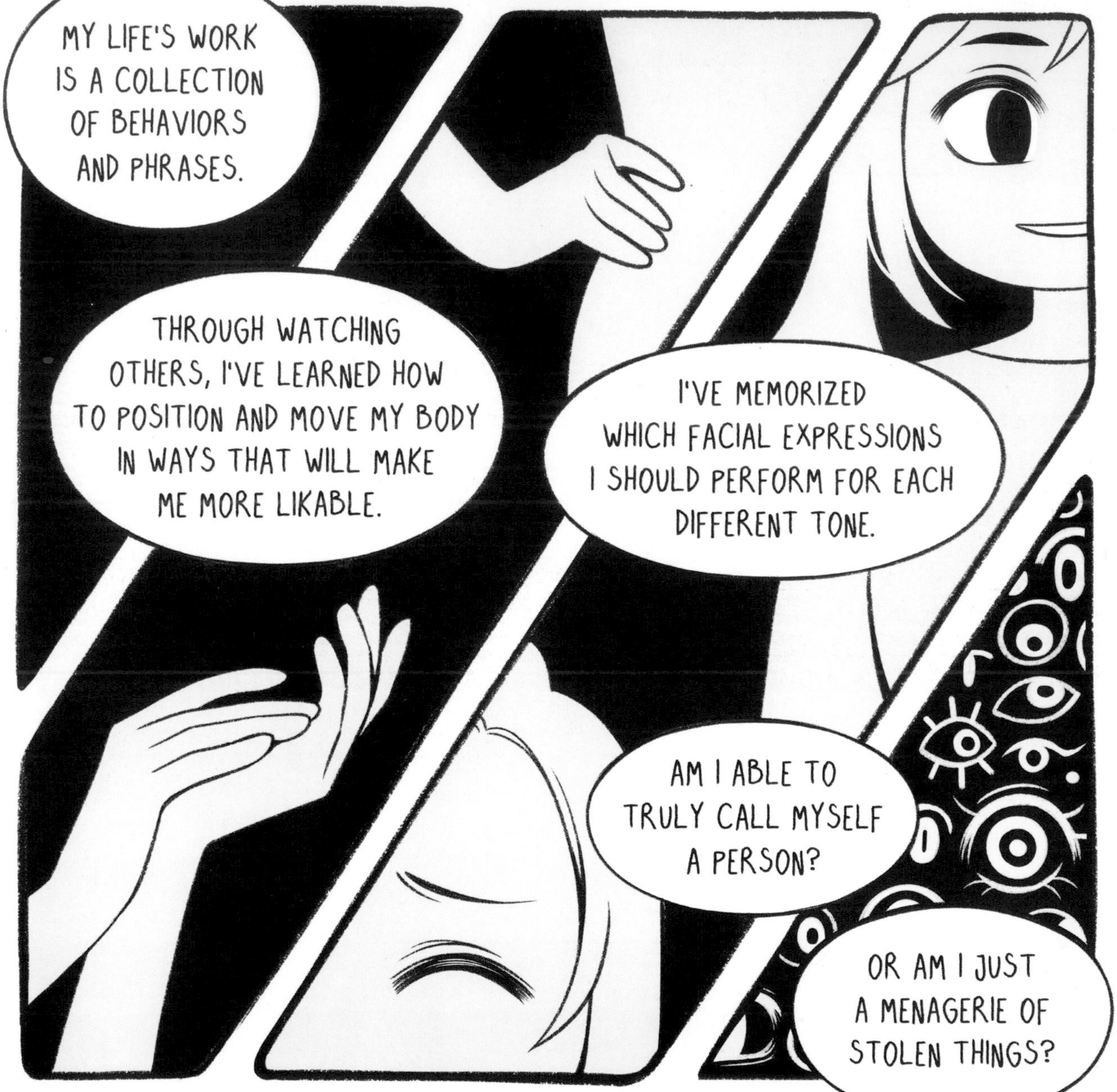
MY LIFE'S WORK IS A COLLECTION OF BEHAVIORS AND PHRASES.
THROUGH WATCHING OTHERS, I'VE LEARNED HOW TO POSITION AND MOVE MY BODY IN WAYS THAT WILL MAKE ME MORE LIKABLE.
I'VE MEMORIZED WHICH FACIAL EXPRESSIONS I SHOULD PERFORM FOR EACH DIFFERENT TONE.
AM I ABLE TO TRULY CALL MYSELF A PERSON?
OR AM I JUST A MENAGERIE OF STOLEN THINGS?

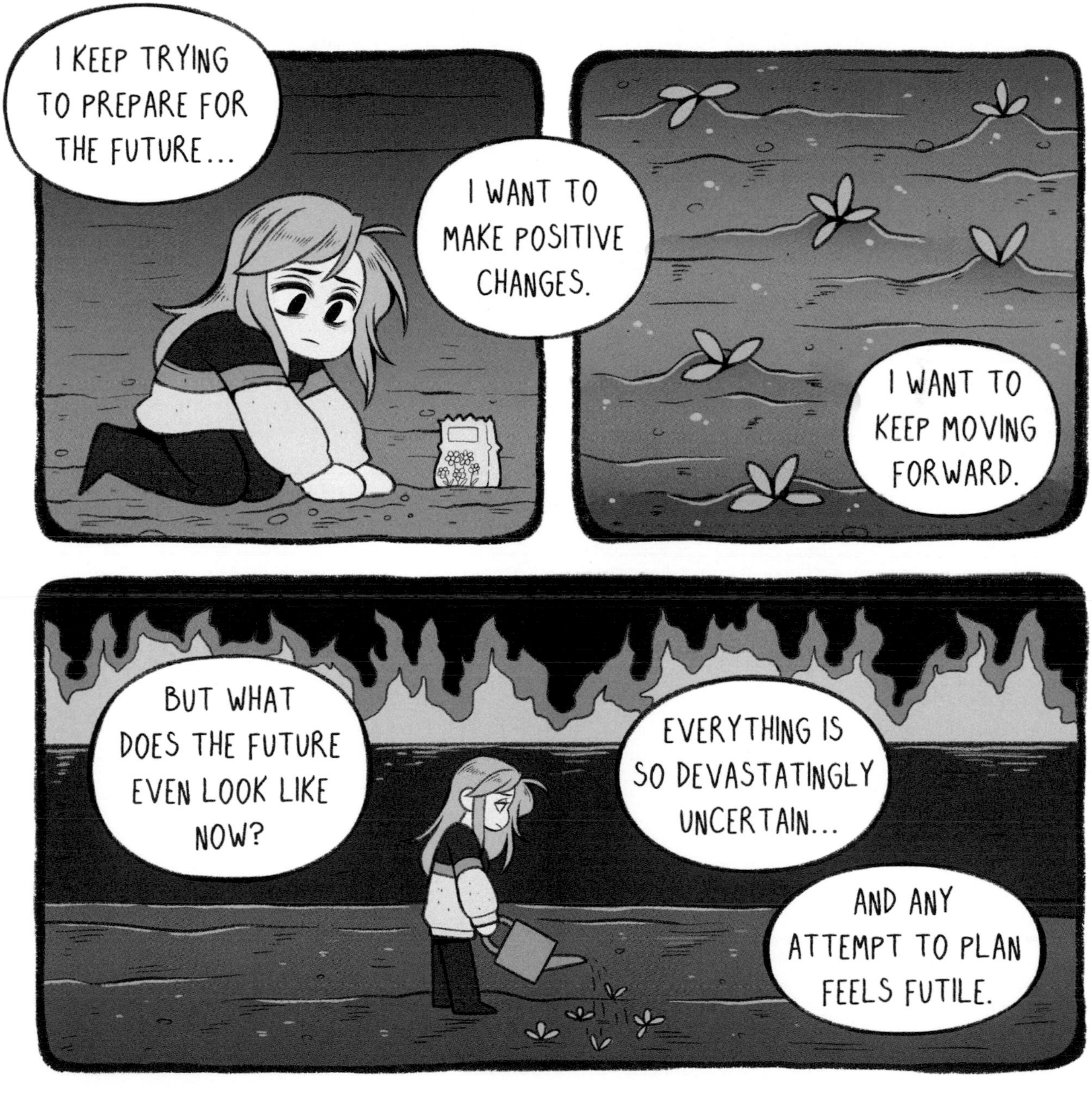
I KEEP TRYING TO PREPARE FOR THE FUTURE...
I WANT TO MAKE POSITIVE CHANGES.
I WANT TO KEEP MOVING FORWARD.
BUT WHAT DOES THE FUTURE EVEN LOOK LIKE NOW?
EVERYTHING IS SO DEVASTATINGLY UNCERTAIN...
AND ANY ATTEMPT TO PLAN FEELS FUTILE.

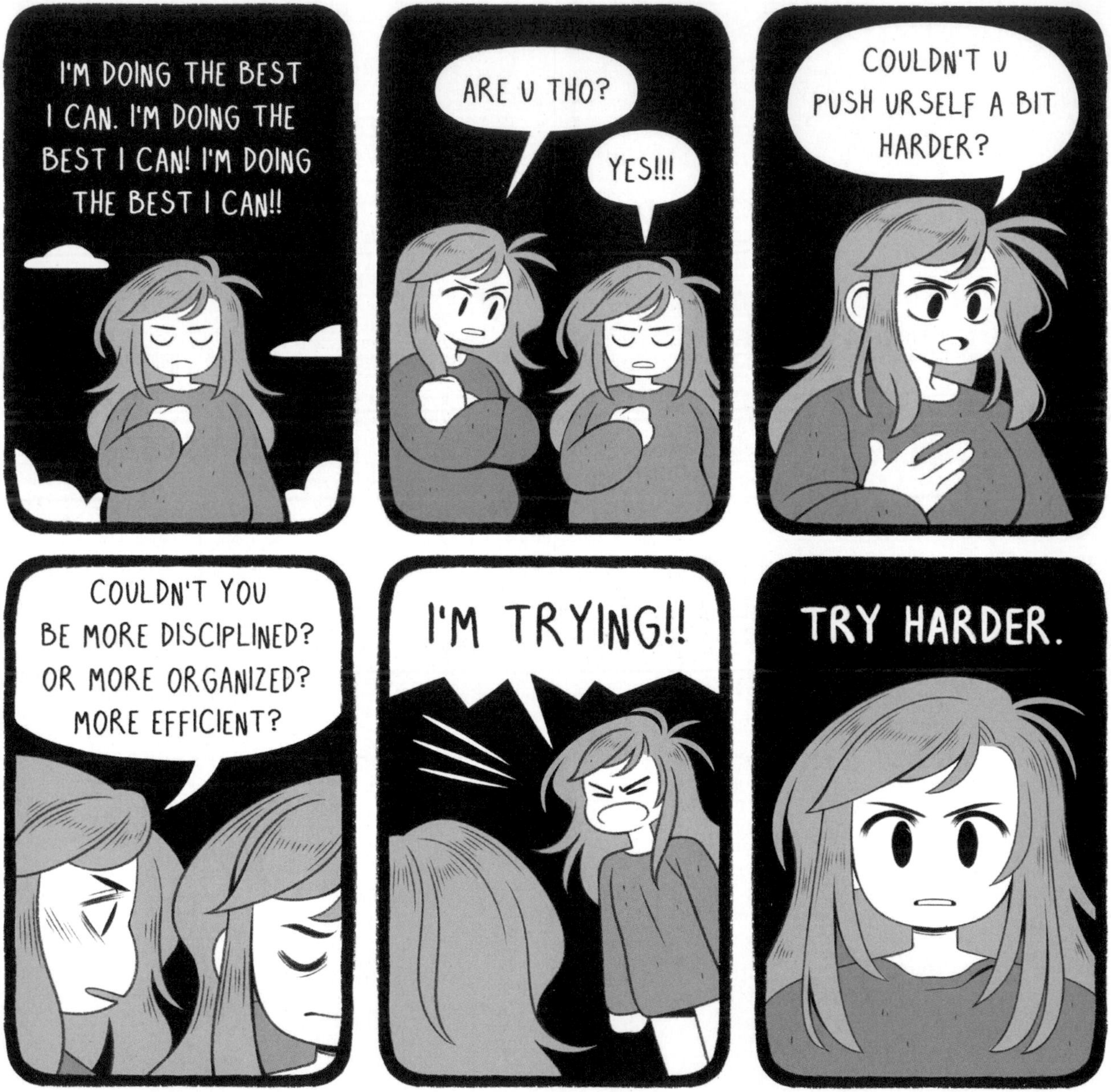
I'M DOING THE BEST I CAN. I'M DOING THE BEST I CAN! I'M DOING THE BEST I CAN!!
ARE U THO?
YES!!!
COULDN'T U PUSH URSELF A BIT HARDER?
COULDN'T YOU BE MORE DISCIPLINED? OR MORE ORGANIZED? MORE EFFICIENT?
I'M TRYING!!
TRY HARDER.

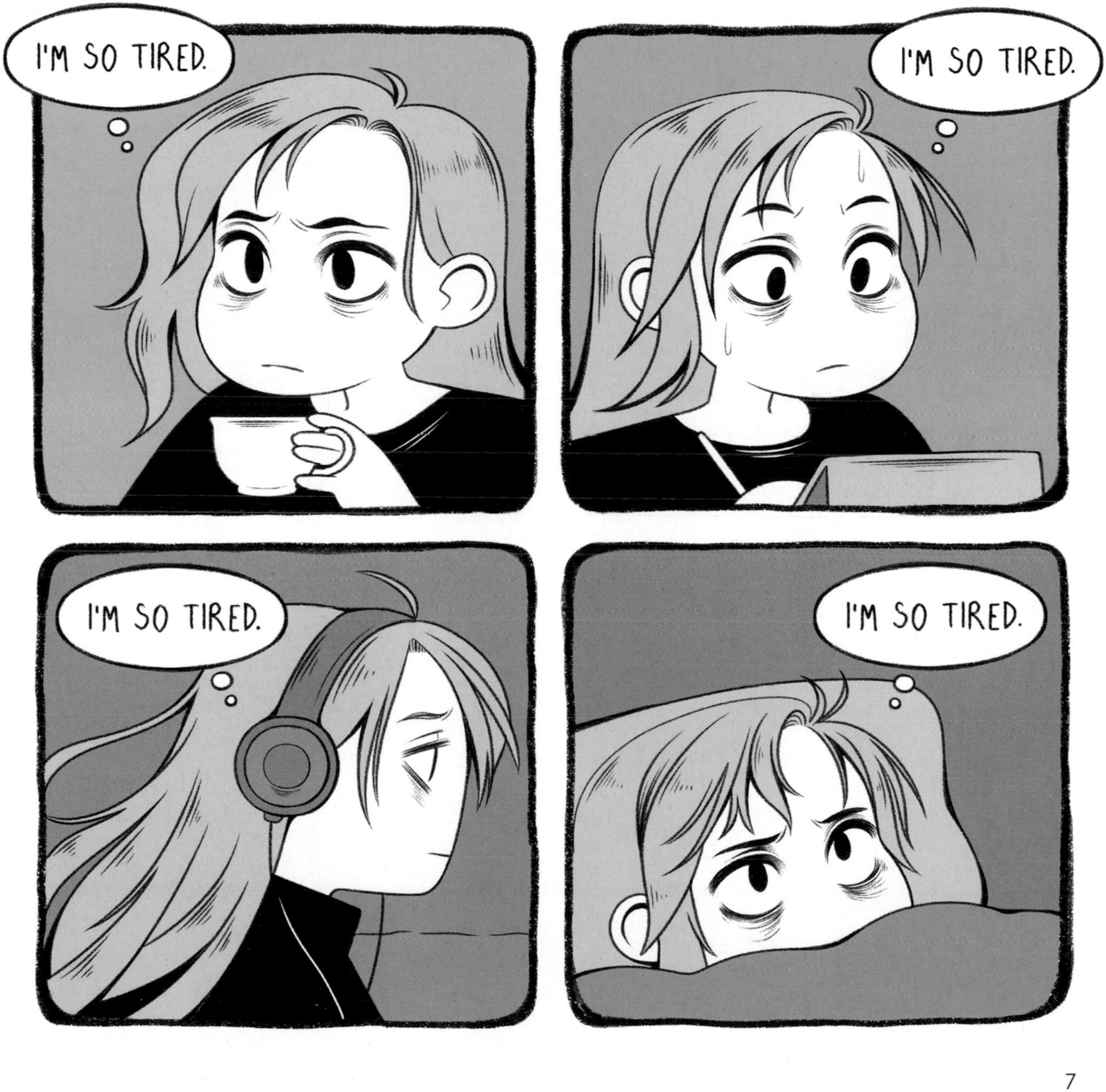
I'M SO TIRED.
I'M SO TIRED.
I'M SO TIRED.
I'M SO TIRED.

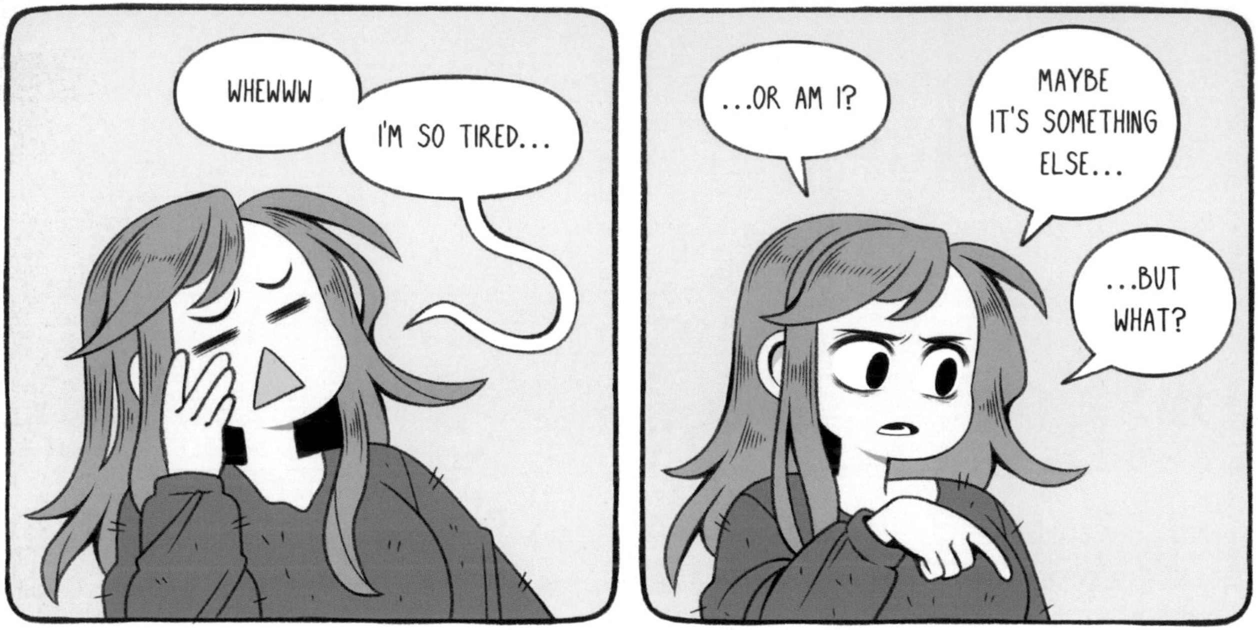
WHEWWW
I'M SO TIRED...
...OR AM I?
MAYBE IT'S SOMETHING ELSE...
...BUT WHAT?

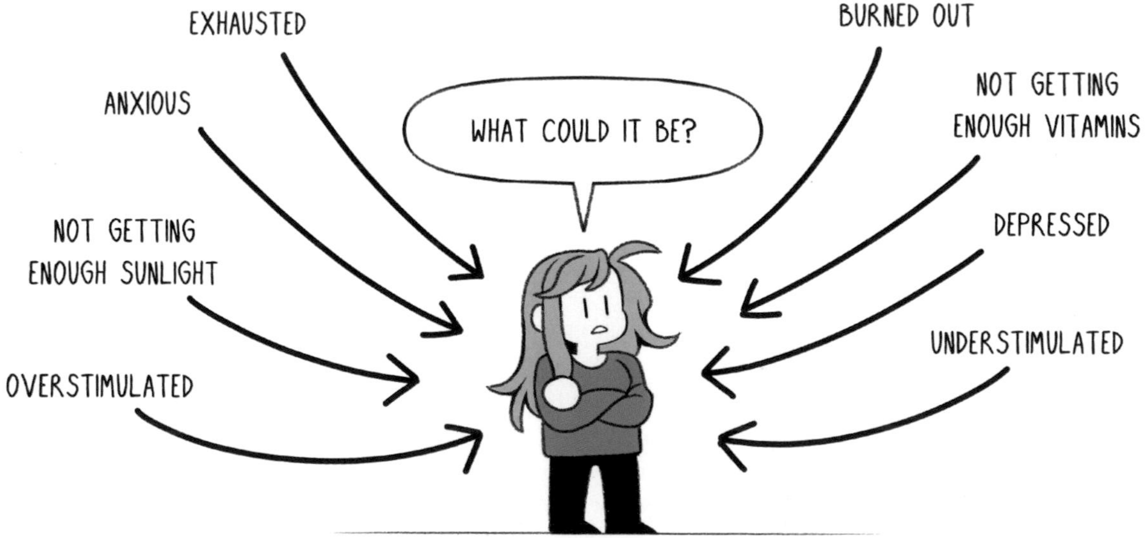
WHAT COULD IT BE?
EXHAUSTED
ANXIOUS
NOT GETTING ENOUGH SUNLIGHT
OVERSTIMULATED
BURNED OUT
NOT GETTING ENOUGH VITAMINS
DEPRESSED
UNDERSTIMULATED

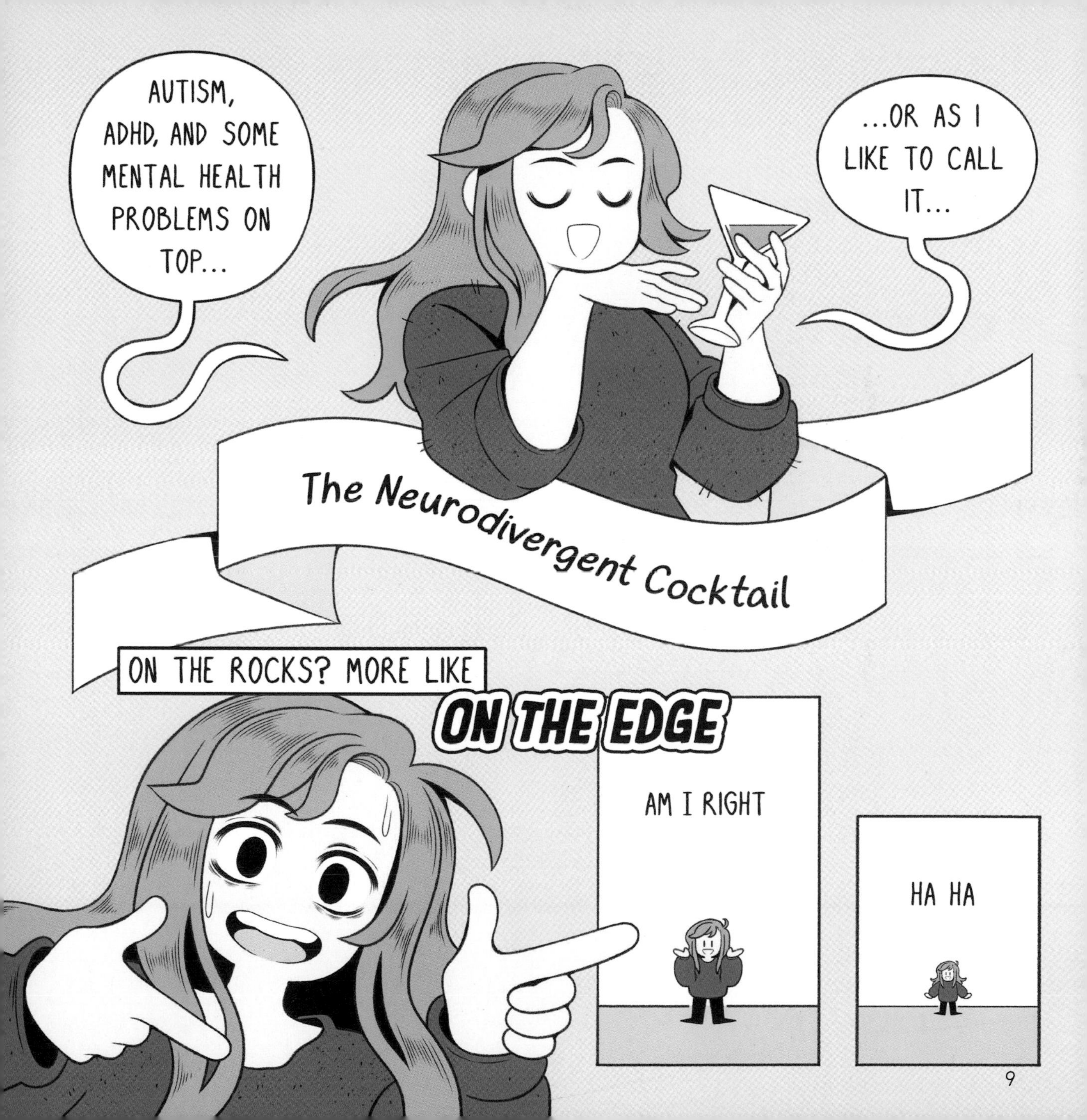
AUTISM, ADHD, AND SOME MENTAL HEALTH PROBLEMS ON TOP...
...OR AS I LIKE TO CALL IT...
The Neurodivergent Cocktail
ON THE ROCKS? MORE LIKE
ON THE EDGE
AM I RIGHT
HA HA

# WHICH TYPE OF NEURODIVERGENT ARE **YOU**?

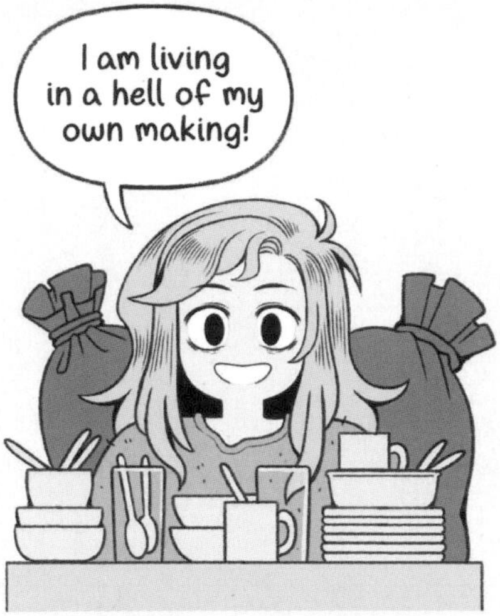
I am living in a hell of my own making!

THE TRASH POSSUM NEURODIVERGENT

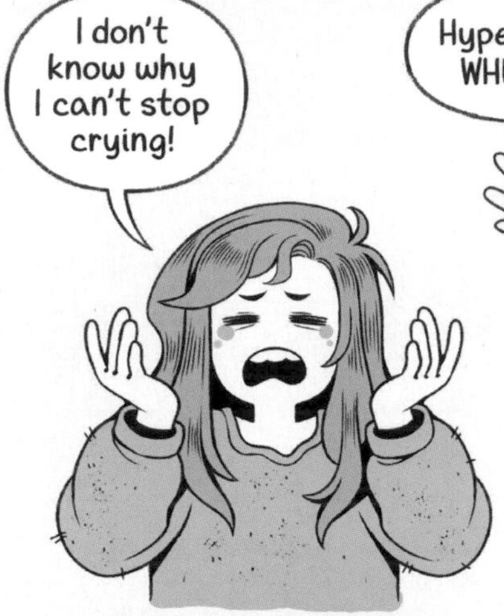
I don't know why I can't stop crying!

THE OVERWHELMED SOBBING NEURODIVERGENT

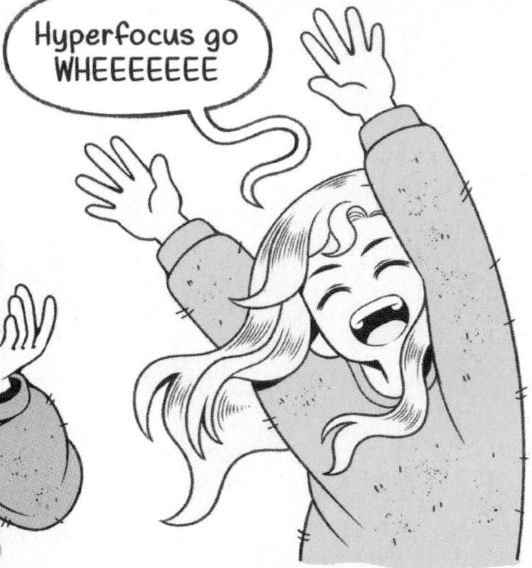
Hyperfocus go WHEEEEEEE

THE FERAL GOBLIN NEURODIVERGENT

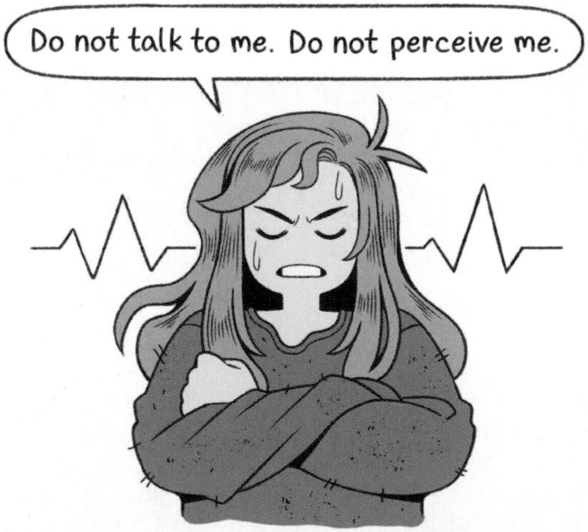
Do not talk to me. Do not perceive me.

THE SHUTDOWN AND SHUT-OUT NEURODIVERGENT

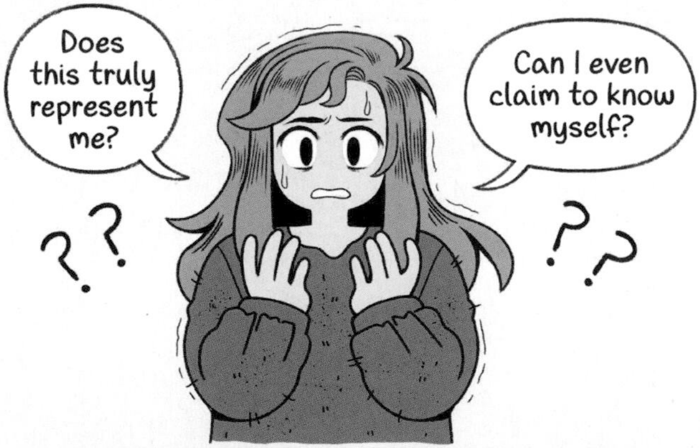
Does this truly represent me?
Can I even claim to know myself?
??
??

THE NEURODIVERGENT WHO OVERTHINKS WHICH TYPE OF NEURODIVERGENT THEY ARE, EVEN THOUGH THERE ARE NO STAKES.

# WHICH TYPE OF NEURODIVERGENT ARE **YOU**?

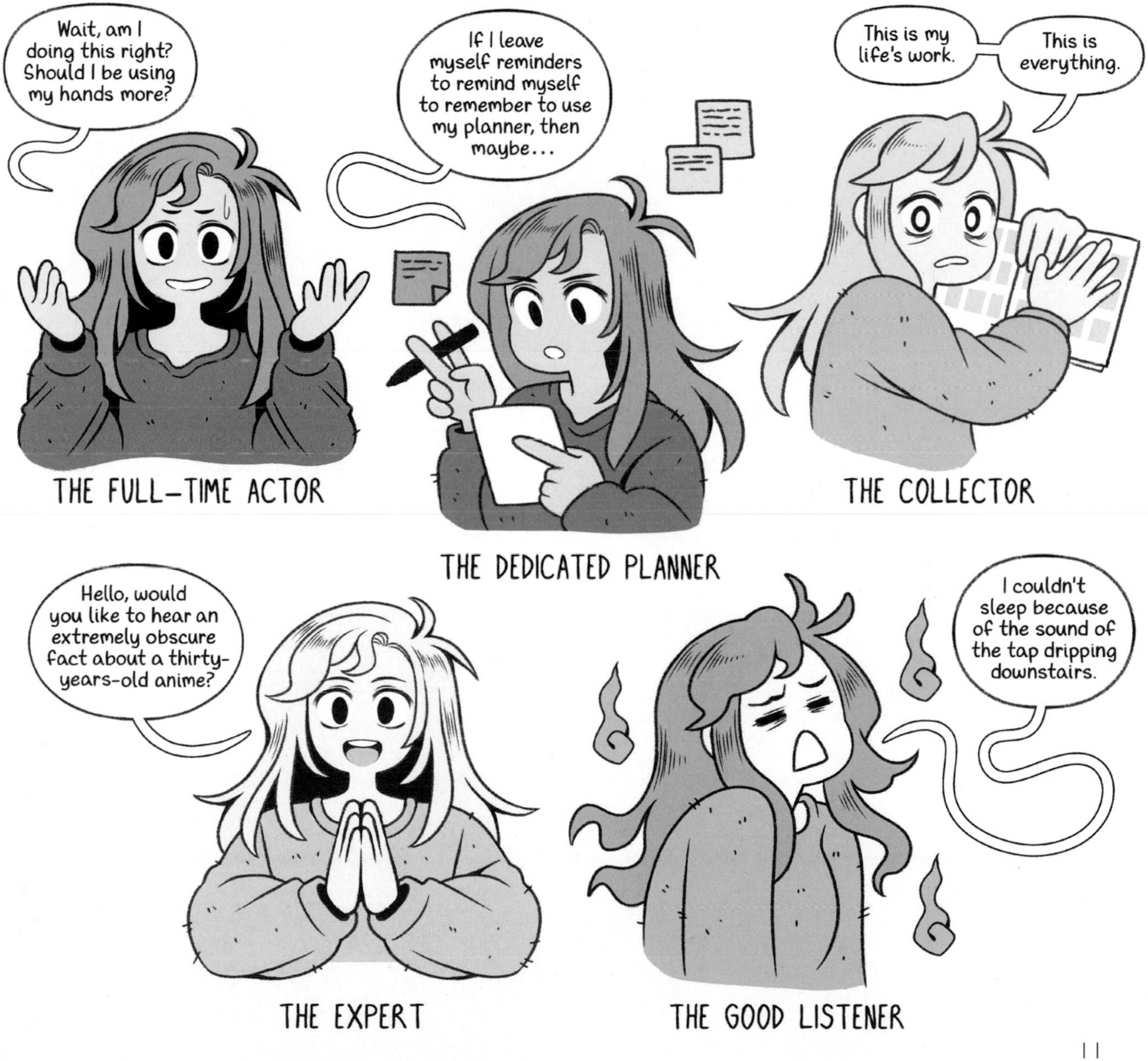
Wait, am I doing this right? Should I be using my hands more?
THE FULL-TIME ACTOR
If I leave myself reminders to remind myself to remember to use my planner, then maybe...
THE DEDICATED PLANNER
This is my life's work.
This is everything.
THE COLLECTOR
Hello, would you like to hear an extremely obscure fact about a thirty-years-old anime?
THE EXPERT
I couldn't sleep because of the sound of the tap dripping downstairs.
THE GOOD LISTENER

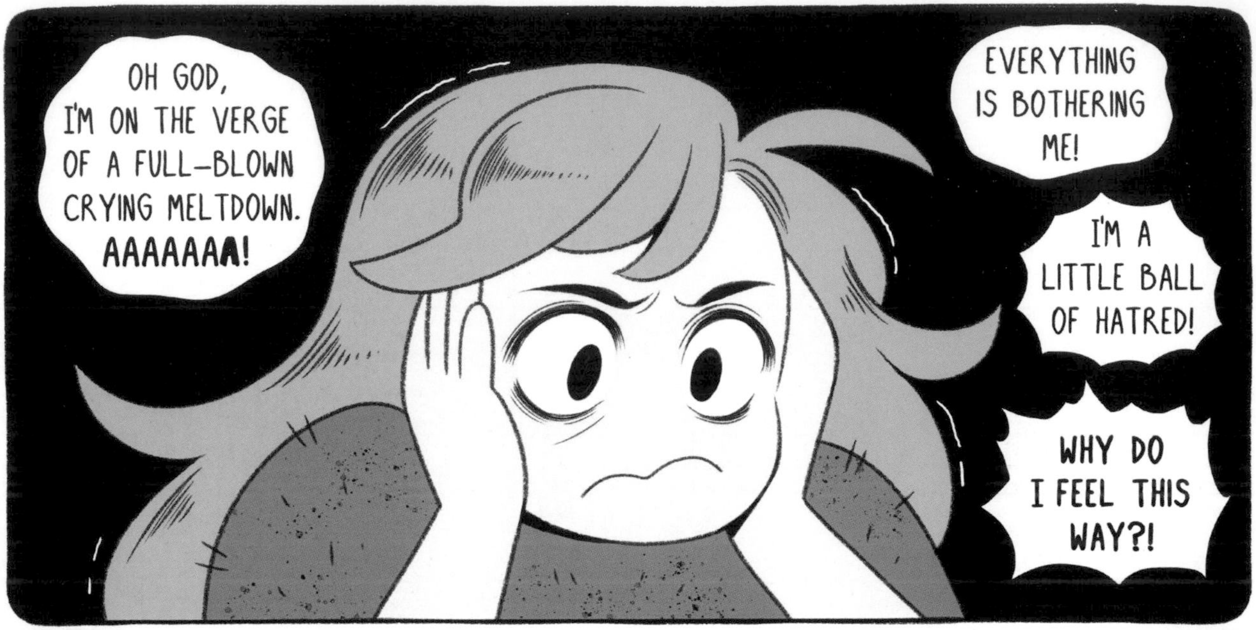
OH GOD, I'M ON THE VERGE OF A FULL-BLOWN CRYING MELTDOWN. AAAAAAA!
EVERYTHING IS BOTHERING ME!
I'M A LITTLE BALL OF HATRED!
WHY DO I FEEL THIS WAY?!

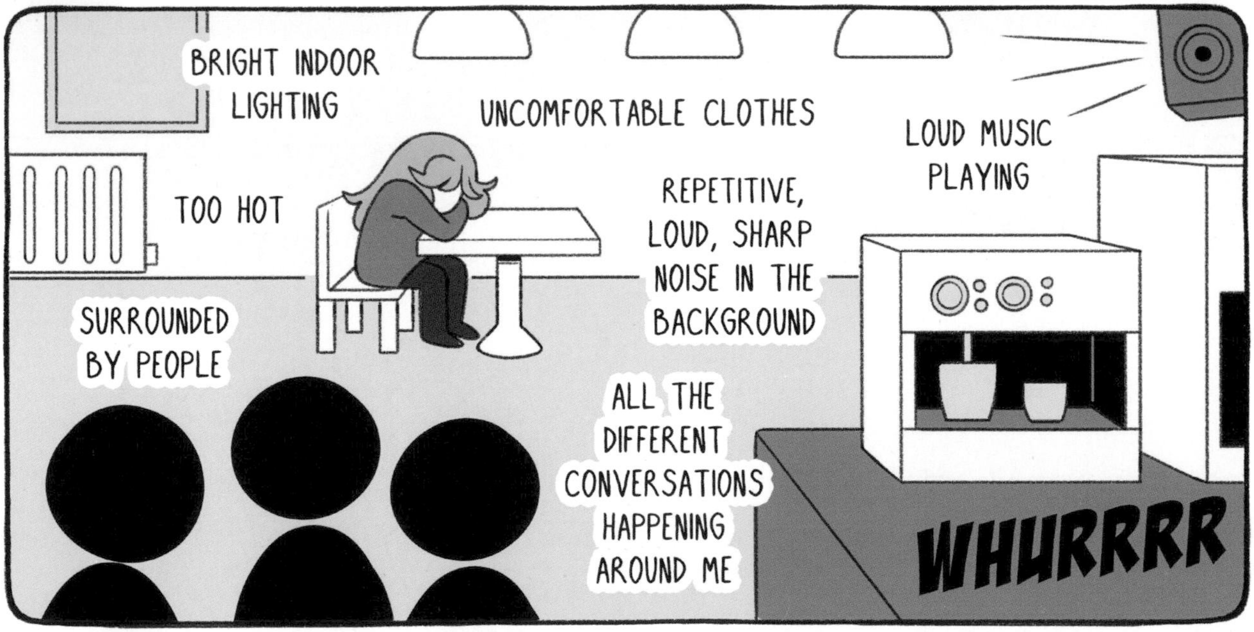
BRIGHT INDOOR LIGHTING
UNCOMFORTABLE CLOTHES
LOUD MUSIC PLAYING
TOO HOT
REPETITIVE, LOUD, SHARP NOISE IN THE BACKGROUND
SURROUNDED BY PEOPLE
ALL THE DIFFERENT CONVERSATIONS HAPPENING AROUND ME
WHURRRR

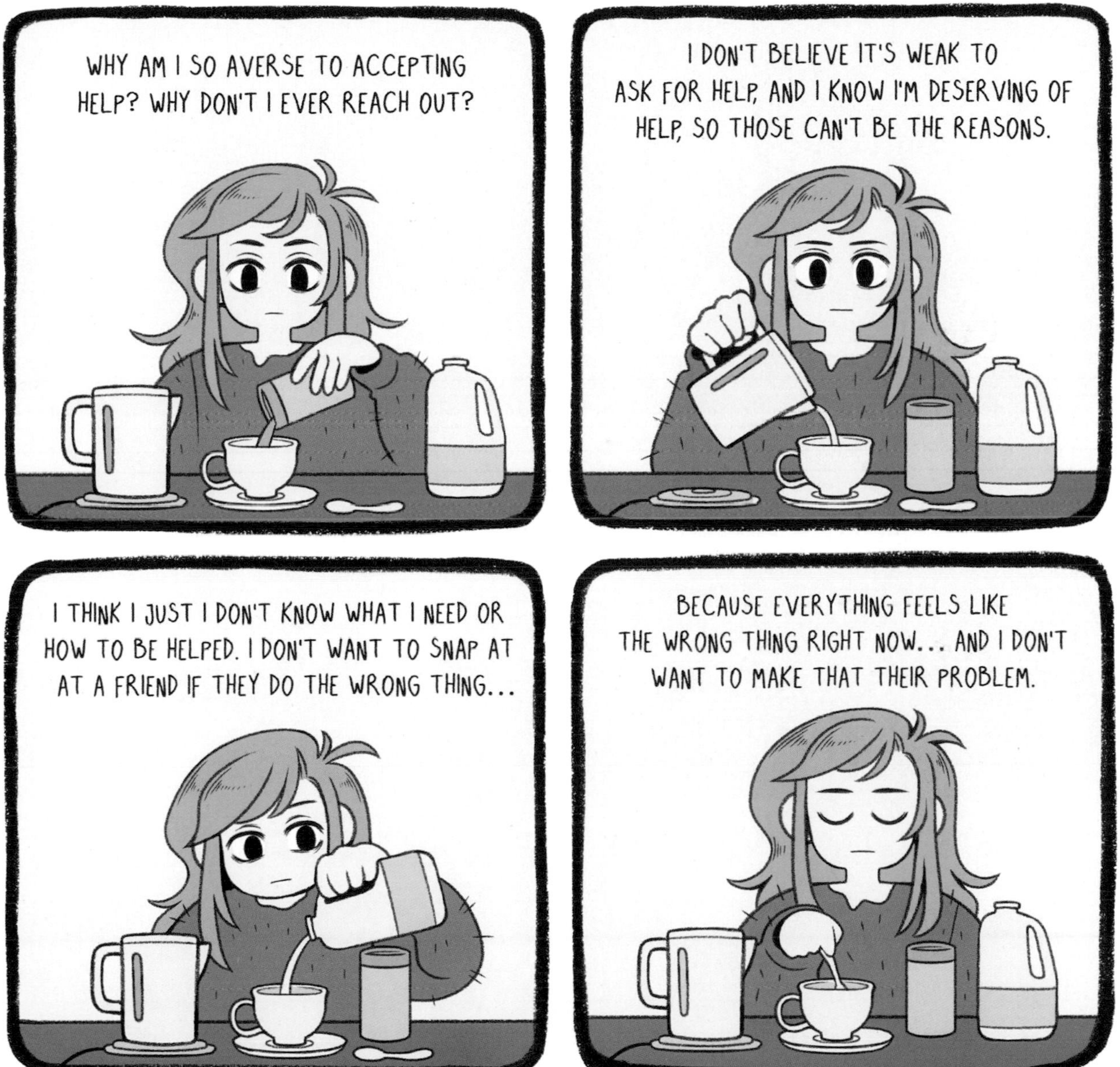
WHY AM I SO AVERSE TO ACCEPTING HELP? WHY DON'T I EVER REACH OUT?
I DON'T BELIEVE IT'S WEAK TO ASK FOR HELP, AND I KNOW I'M DESERVING OF HELP, SO THOSE CAN'T BE THE REASONS.
I THINK I JUST I DON'T KNOW WHAT I NEED OR HOW TO BE HELPED. I DON'T WANT TO SNAP AT AT A FRIEND IF THEY DO THE WRONG THING...
BECAUSE EVERYTHING FEELS LIKE THE WRONG THING RIGHT NOW... AND I DON'T WANT TO MAKE THAT THEIR PROBLEM.

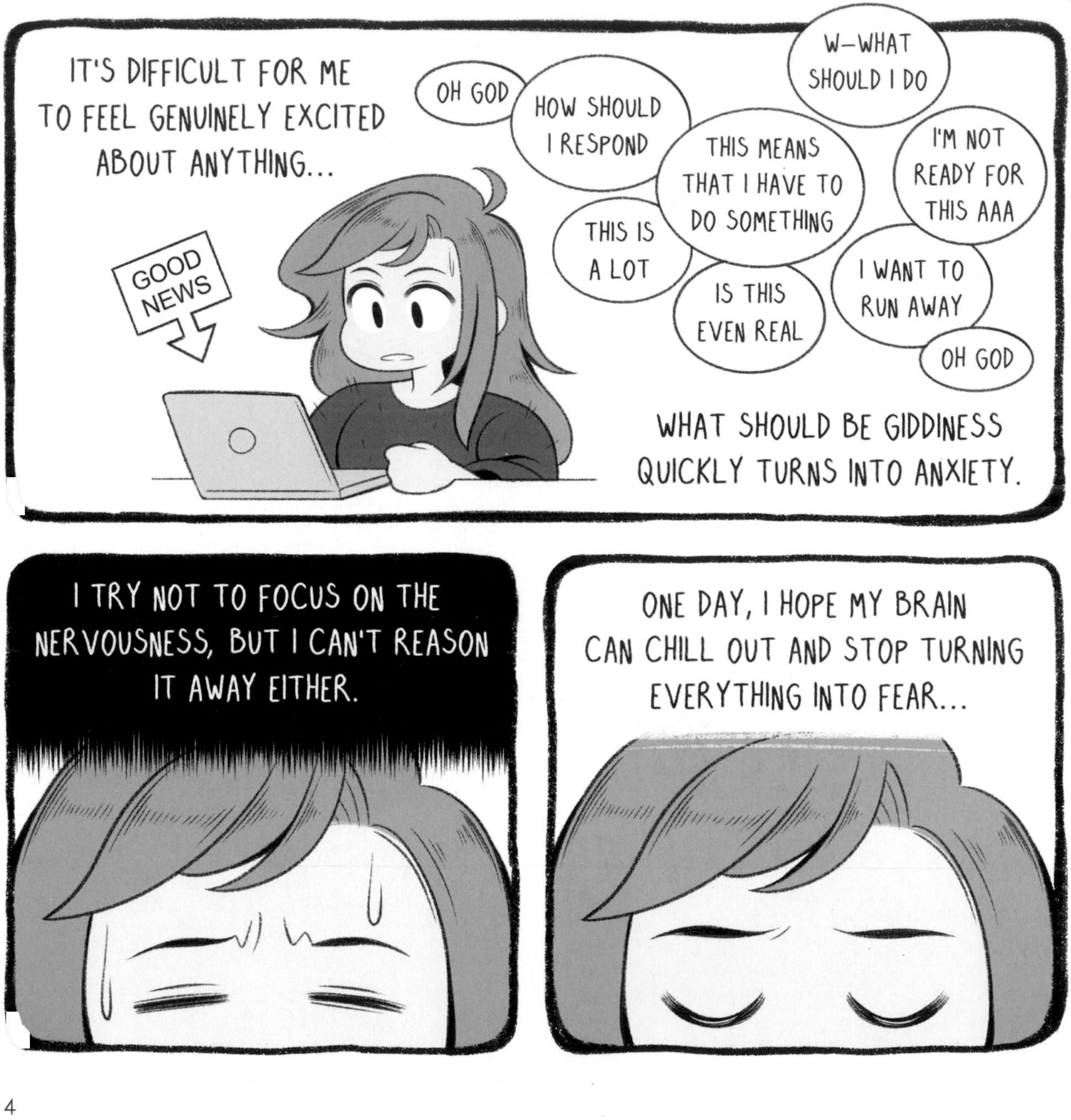
IT'S DIFFICULT FOR ME TO FEEL GENUINELY EXCITED ABOUT ANYTHING...
GOOD NEWS
OH GOD
HOW SHOULD I RESPOND
W—WHAT SHOULD I DO
THIS MEANS THAT I HAVE TO DO SOMETHING
I'M NOT READY FOR THIS AAA
THIS IS A LOT
IS THIS EVEN REAL
I WANT TO RUN AWAY
OH GOD
WHAT SHOULD BE GIDDINESS QUICKLY TURNS INTO ANXIETY.
I TRY NOT TO FOCUS ON THE NERVOUSNESS, BUT I CAN'T REASON IT AWAY EITHER.
ONE DAY, I HOPE MY BRAIN CAN CHILL OUT AND STOP TURNING EVERYTHING INTO FEAR...

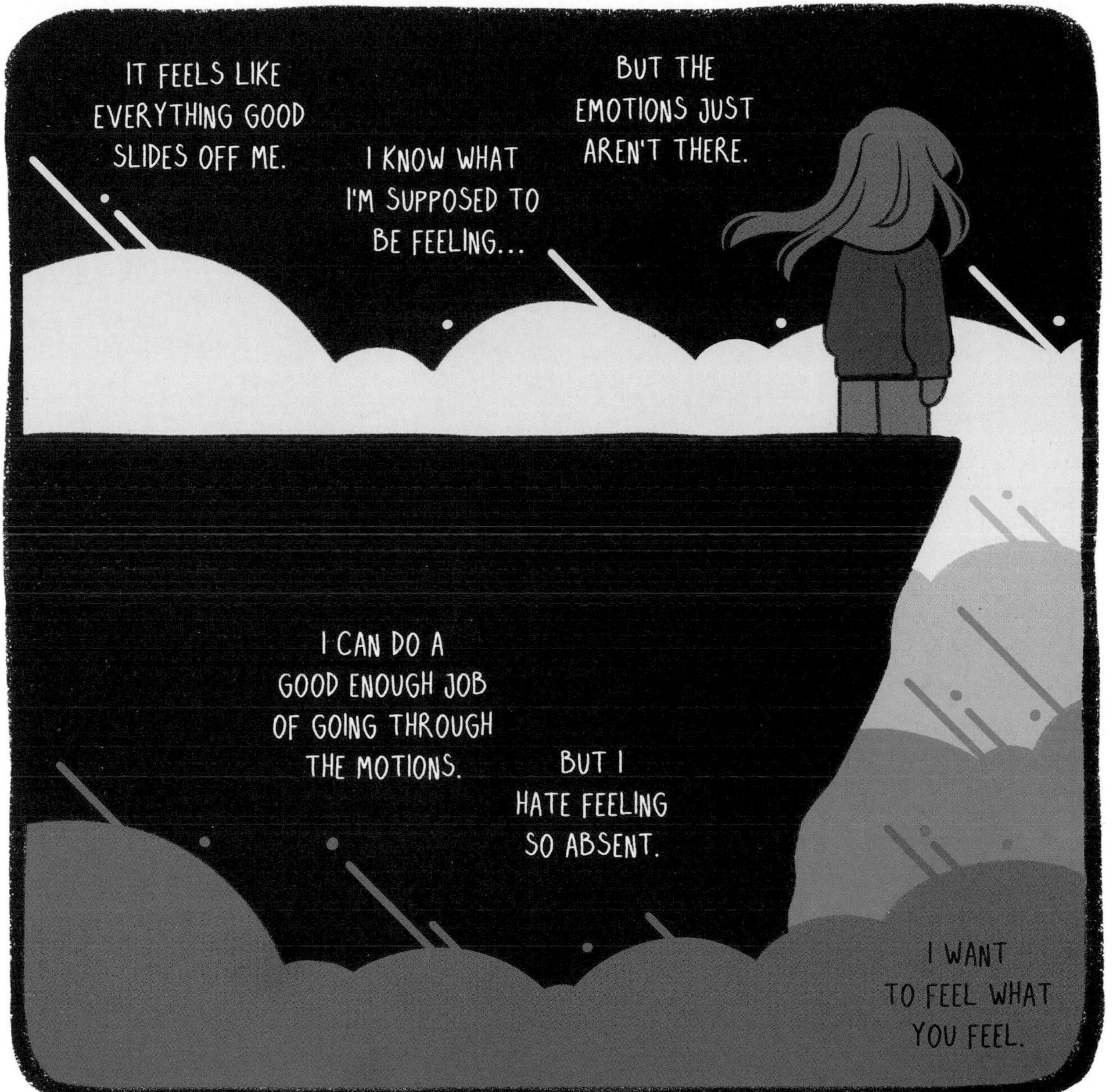
IT FEELS LIKE EVERYTHING GOOD SLIDES OFF ME.
I KNOW WHAT I'M SUPPOSED TO BE FEELING...
BUT THE EMOTIONS JUST AREN'T THERE.
I CAN DO A GOOD ENOUGH JOB OF GOING THROUGH THE MOTIONS.
BUT I HATE FEELING SO ABSENT.
I WANT TO FEEL WHAT YOU FEEL.

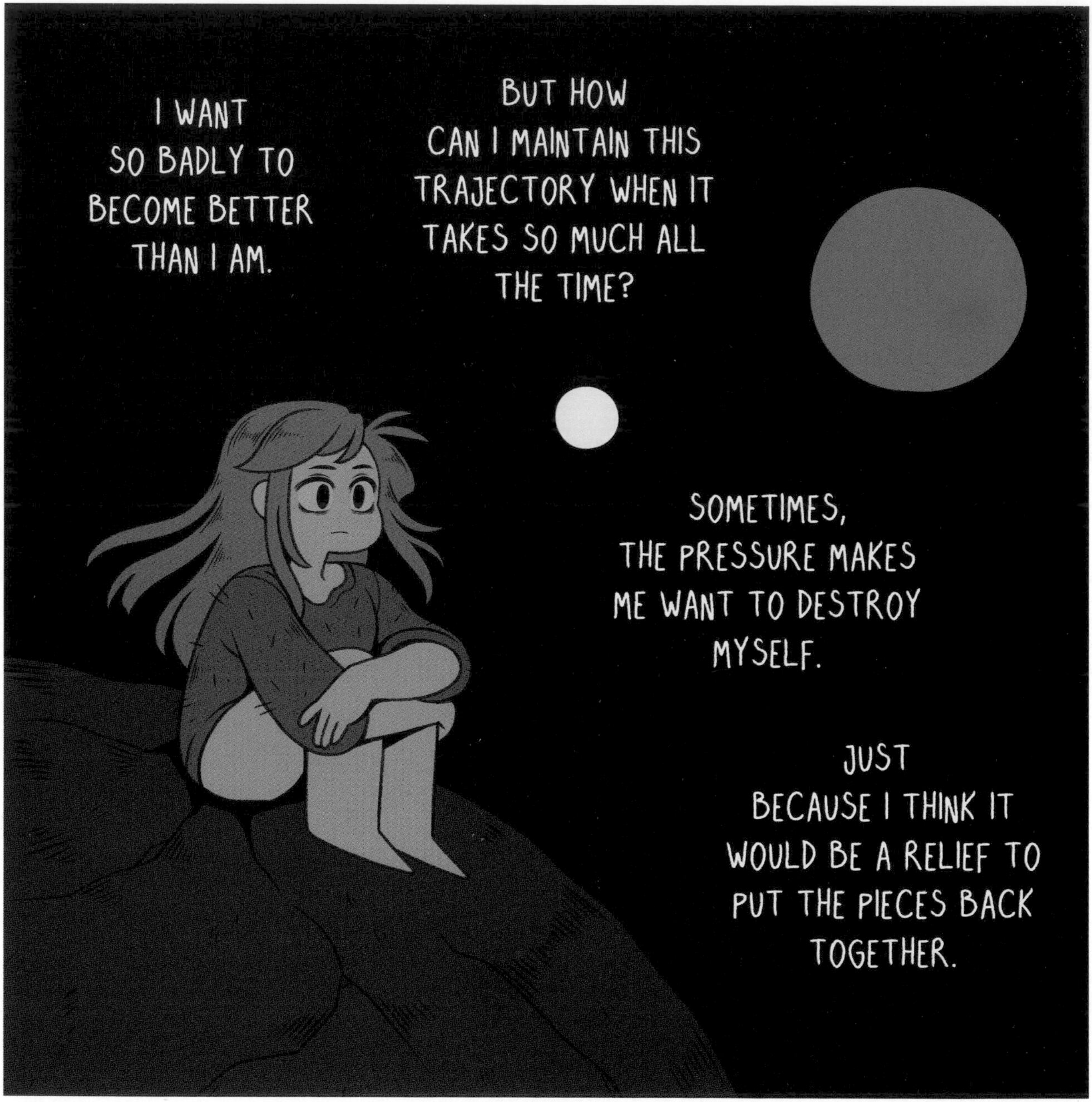
I WANT SO BADLY TO BECOME BETTER THAN I AM.
BUT HOW CAN I MAINTAIN THIS TRAJECTORY WHEN IT TAKES SO MUCH ALL THE TIME?
SOMETIMES, THE PRESSURE MAKES ME WANT TO DESTROY MYSELF.
JUST BECAUSE I THINK IT WOULD BE A RELIEF TO PUT THE PIECES BACK TOGETHER.

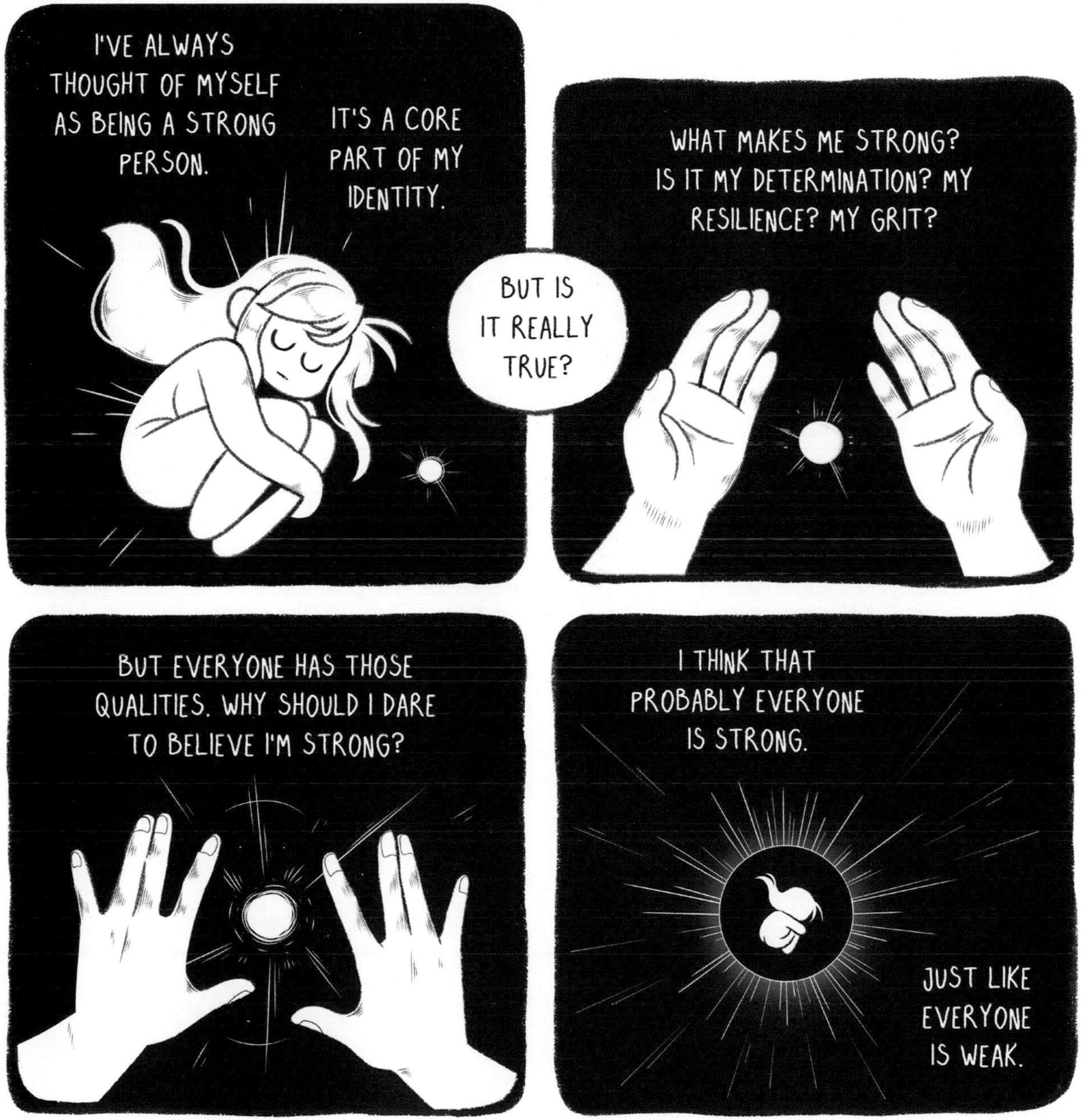
I'VE ALWAYS THOUGHT OF MYSELF AS BEING A STRONG PERSON.
IT'S A CORE PART OF MY IDENTITY.
BUT IS IT REALLY TRUE?
WHAT MAKES ME STRONG? IS IT MY DETERMINATION? MY RESILIENCE? MY GRIT?
BUT EVERYONE HAS THOSE QUALITIES. WHY SHOULD I DARE TO BELIEVE I'M STRONG?
I THINK THAT PROBABLY EVERYONE IS STRONG.
JUST LIKE EVERYONE IS WEAK.

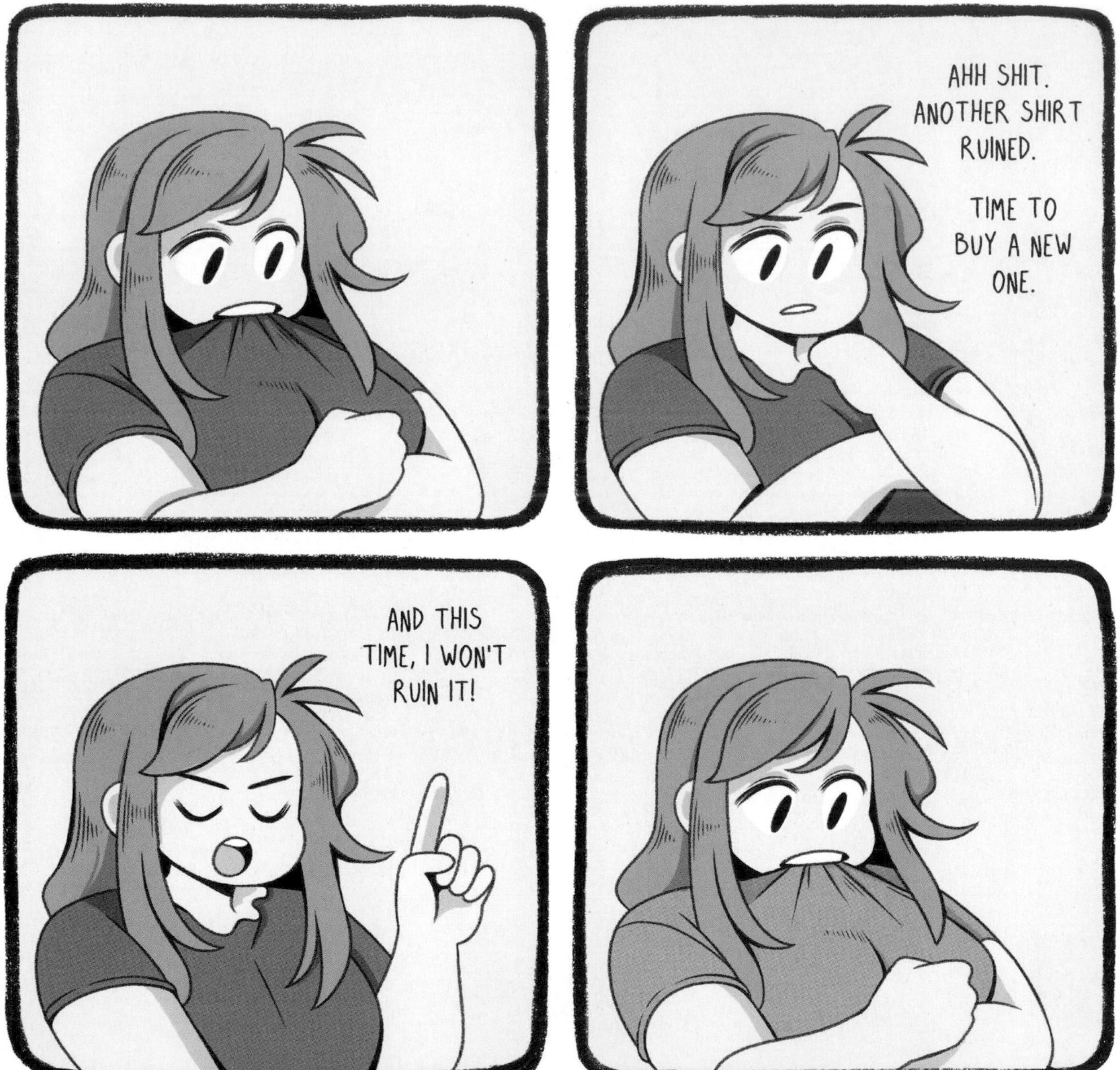
AHH SHIT. ANOTHER SHIRT RUINED.
TIME TO BUY A NEW ONE.
AND THIS TIME, I WON'T RUIN IT!

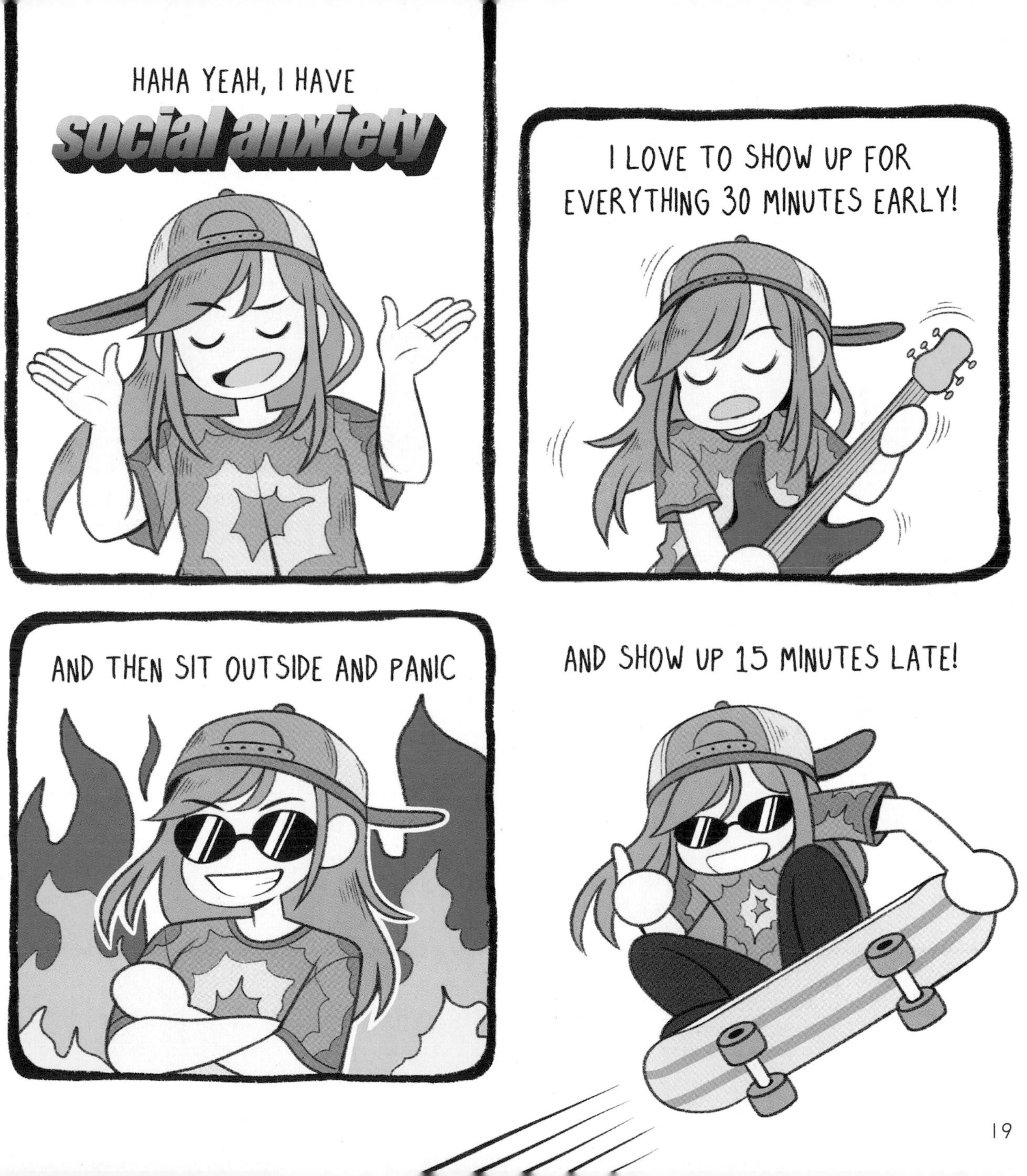
HAHA YEAH, I HAVE
social anxiety
I LOVE TO SHOW UP FOR EVERYTHING 30 MINUTES EARLY!
AND THEN SIT OUTSIDE AND PANIC
AND SHOW UP 15 MINUTES LATE!

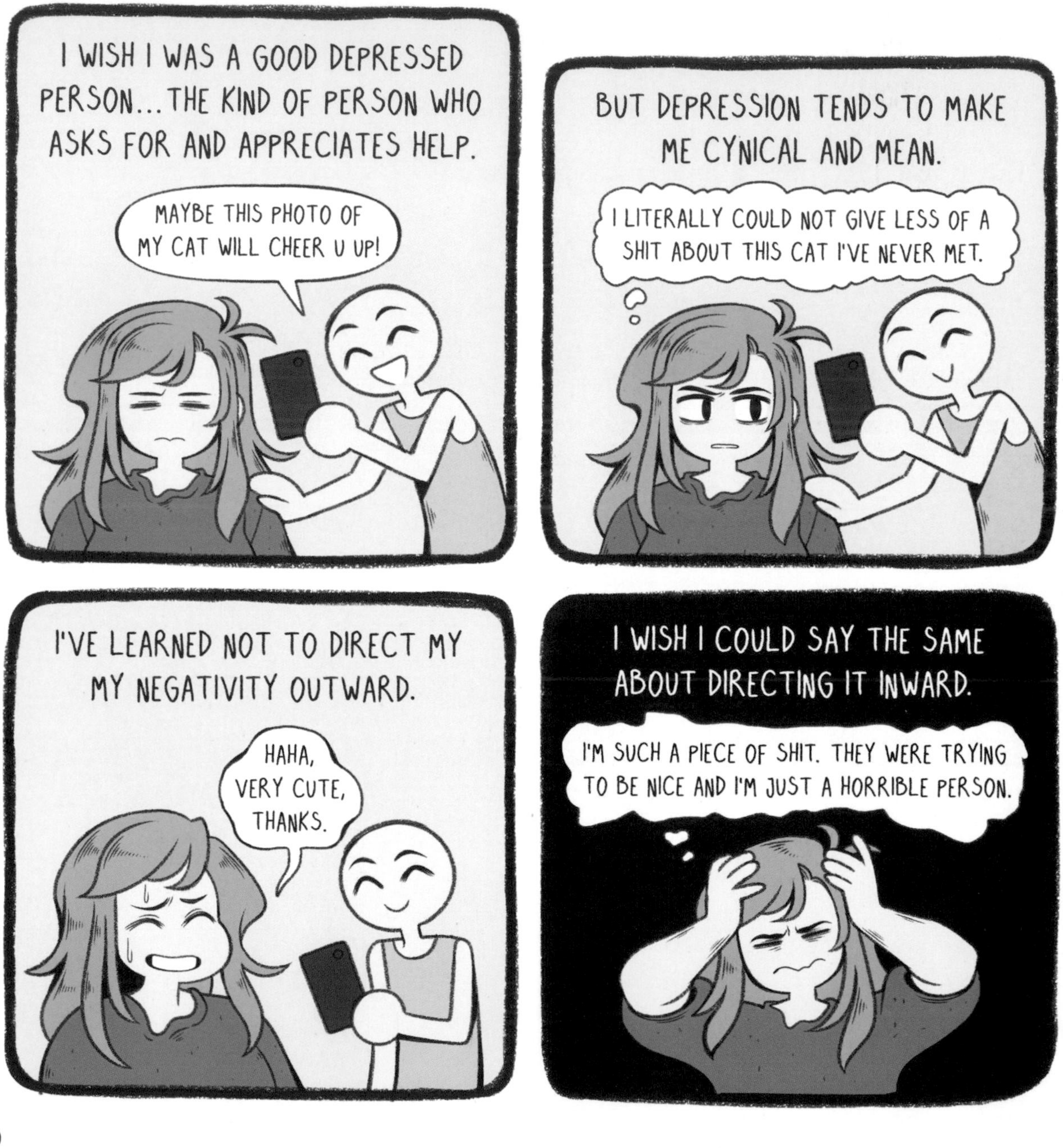
I WISH I WAS A GOOD DEPRESSED PERSON... THE KIND OF PERSON WHO ASKS FOR AND APPRECIATES HELP.
MAYBE THIS PHOTO OF MY CAT WILL CHEER U UP!
BUT DEPRESSION TENDS TO MAKE ME CYNICAL AND MEAN.
I LITERALLY COULD NOT GIVE LESS OF A SHIT ABOUT THIS CAT I'VE NEVER MET.
I'VE LEARNED NOT TO DIRECT MY MY NEGATIVITY OUTWARD.
HAHA, VERY CUTE, THANKS.
I WISH I COULD SAY THE SAME ABOUT DIRECTING IT INWARD.
I'M SUCH A PIECE OF SHIT. THEY WERE TRYING TO BE NICE AND I'M JUST A HORRIBLE PERSON.

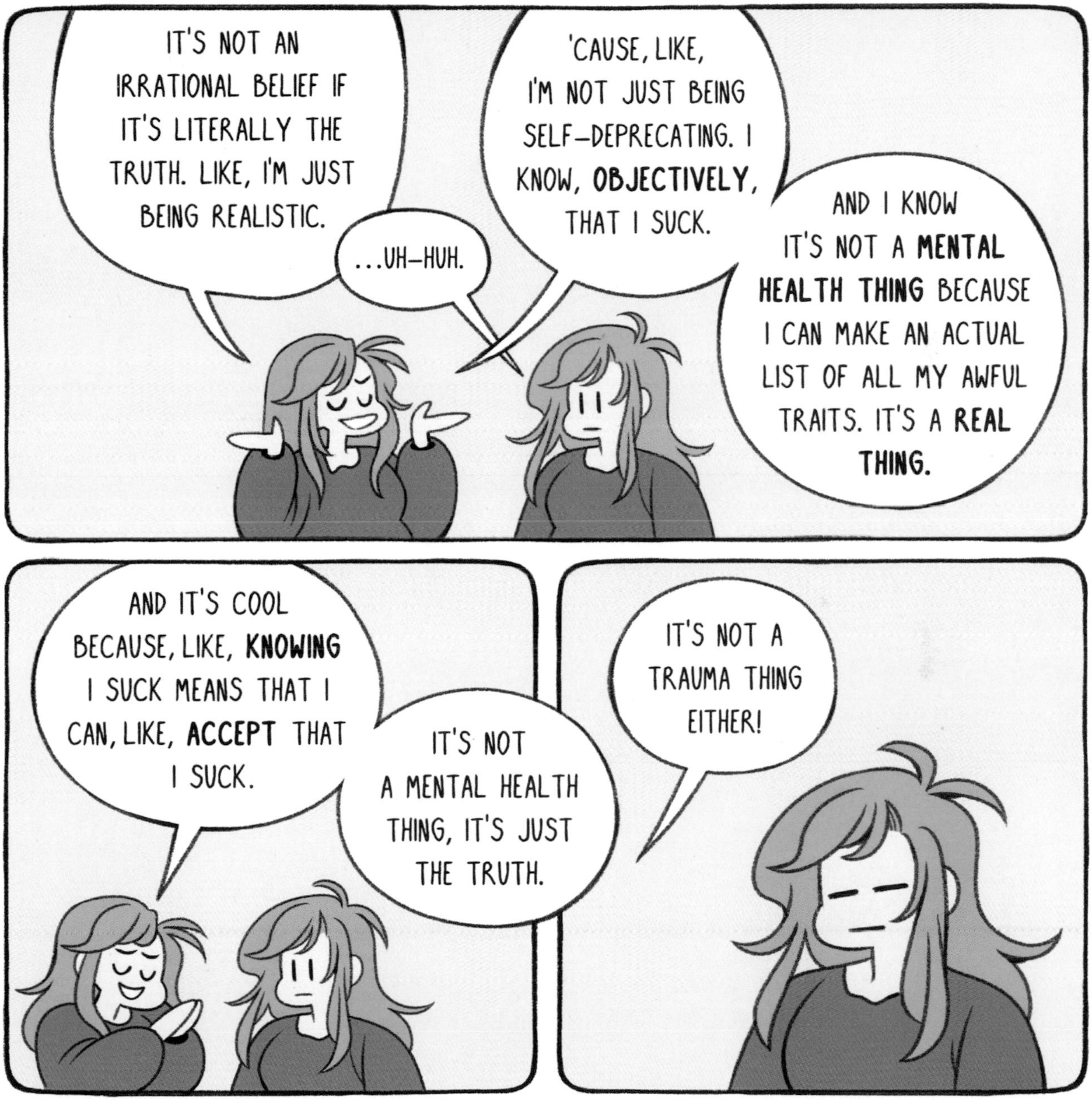
IT'S NOT AN IRRATIONAL BELIEF IF IT'S LITERALLY THE TRUTH. LIKE, I'M JUST BEING REALISTIC.
...UH-HUH.
'CAUSE, LIKE, I'M NOT JUST BEING SELF-DEPRECATING. I KNOW, **OBJECTIVELY**, THAT I SUCK.
AND I KNOW IT'S NOT A **MENTAL HEALTH THING** BECAUSE I CAN MAKE AN ACTUAL LIST OF ALL MY AWFUL TRAITS. IT'S A **REAL THING.**
AND IT'S COOL BECAUSE, LIKE, **KNOWING** I SUCK MEANS THAT I CAN, LIKE, **ACCEPT** THAT I SUCK.
IT'S NOT A MENTAL HEALTH THING, IT'S JUST THE TRUTH.
IT'S NOT A TRAUMA THING EITHER!

I CAN BE VERY HOT AND COLD WHEN IT COMES TO OTHER PEOPLE. I'M EASILY HURT BUT QUICK TO FORGIVE, AND I DON'T LIKE THIS ABOUT MYSELF.

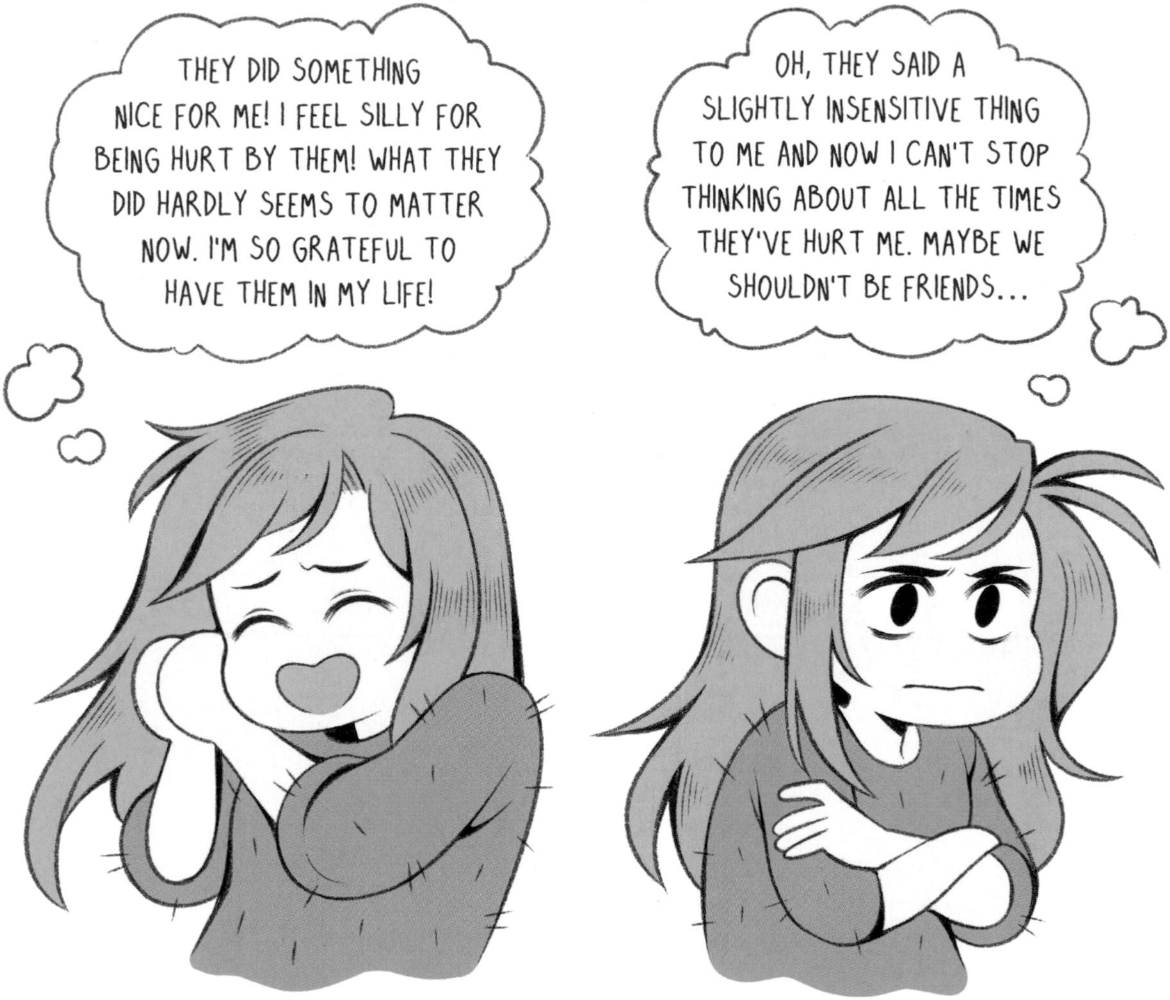
THEY DID SOMETHING NICE FOR ME! I FEEL SILLY FOR BEING HURT BY THEM! WHAT THEY DID HARDLY SEEMS TO MATTER NOW. I'M SO GRATEFUL TO HAVE THEM IN MY LIFE!
OH, THEY SAID A SLIGHTLY INSENSITIVE THING TO ME AND NOW I CAN'T STOP THINKING ABOUT ALL THE TIMES THEY'VE HURT ME. MAYBE WE SHOULDN'T BE FRIENDS...

REASONING AWAY THESE EMOTIONS IS EXHAUSTING, BUT I TRY MY BEST TO BE LESS EMOTIONALLY IMPULSIVE AND FOCUS ON THE FULL PICTURE.

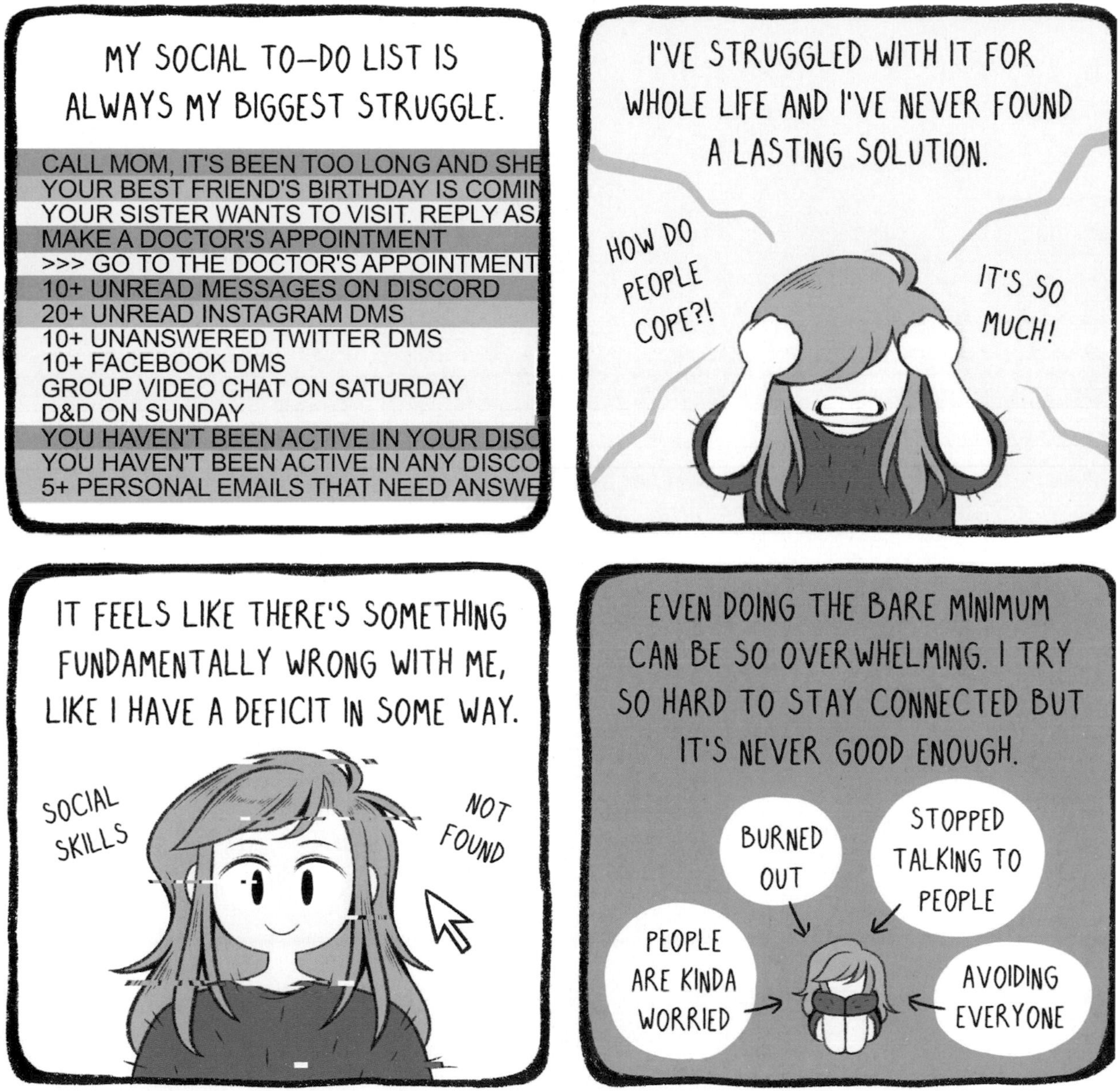
MY SOCIAL TO-DO LIST IS ALWAYS MY BIGGEST STRUGGLE.
CALL MOM, IT'S BEEN TOO LONG AND SHE
YOUR BEST FRIEND'S BIRTHDAY IS COMIN
YOUR SISTER WANTS TO VISIT. REPLY AS
MAKE A DOCTOR'S APPOINTMENT
>>> GO TO THE DOCTOR'S APPOINTMENT
10+ UNREAD MESSAGES ON DISCORD
20+ UNREAD INSTAGRAM DMS
10+ UNANSWERED TWITTER DMS
10+ FACEBOOK DMS
GROUP VIDEO CHAT ON SATURDAY
D&D ON SUNDAY
YOU HAVEN'T BEEN ACTIVE IN YOUR DISC
YOU HAVEN'T BEEN ACTIVE IN ANY DISCO
5+ PERSONAL EMAILS THAT NEED ANSWE
I'VE STRUGGLED WITH IT FOR WHOLE LIFE AND I'VE NEVER FOUND A LASTING SOLUTION.
HOW DO PEOPLE COPE?!
IT'S SO MUCH!
IT FEELS LIKE THERE'S SOMETHING FUNDAMENTALLY WRONG WITH ME, LIKE I HAVE A DEFICIT IN SOME WAY.
SOCIAL SKILLS
NOT FOUND
EVEN DOING THE BARE MINIMUM CAN BE SO OVERWHELMING. I TRY SO HARD TO STAY CONNECTED BUT IT'S NEVER GOOD ENOUGH.
BURNED OUT
STOPPED TALKING TO PEOPLE
PEOPLE ARE KINDA WORRIED
AVOIDING EVERYONE

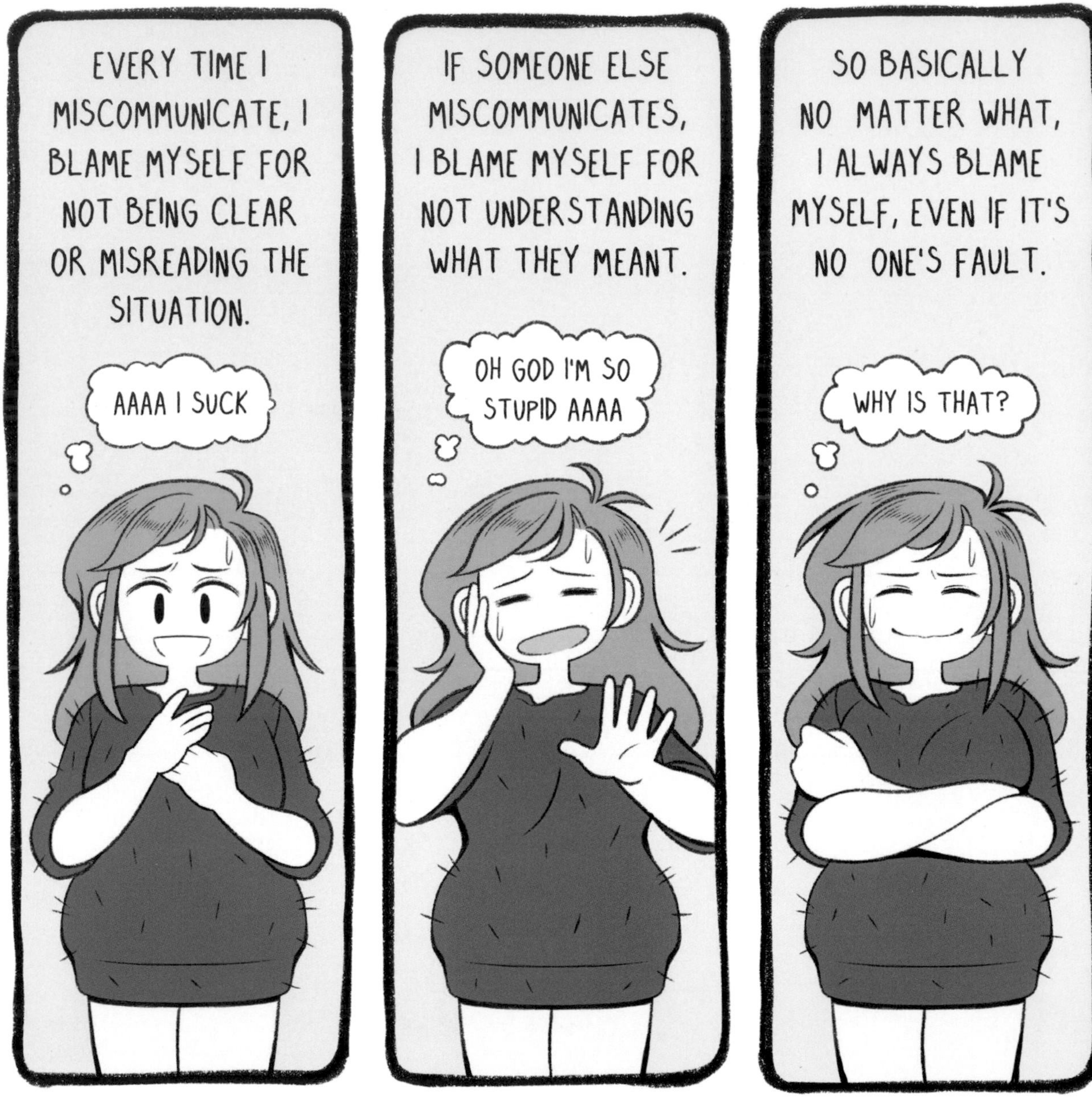
EVERY TIME I MISCOMMUNICATE, I BLAME MYSELF FOR NOT BEING CLEAR OR MISREADING THE SITUATION.
AAAA I SUCK
IF SOMEONE ELSE MISCOMMUNICATES, I BLAME MYSELF FOR NOT UNDERSTANDING WHAT THEY MEANT.
OH GOD I'M SO STUPID AAAA
SO BASICALLY NO MATTER WHAT, I ALWAYS BLAME MYSELF, EVEN IF IT'S NO ONE'S FAULT.
WHY IS THAT?

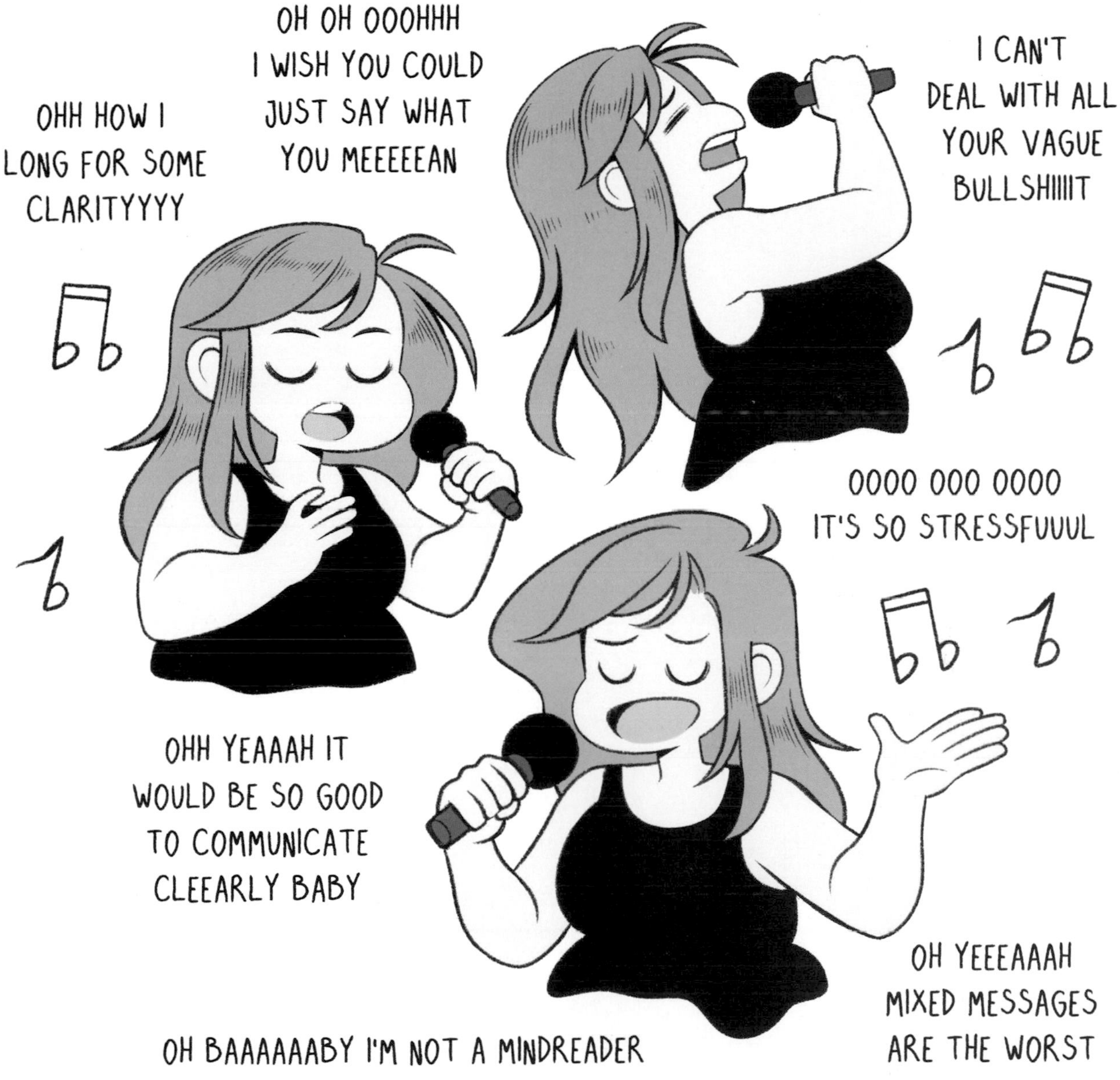
OHH HOW I LONG FOR SOME CLARITYYYY
OH OH OOOHHH I WISH YOU COULD JUST SAY WHAT YOU MEEEEEAN
I CAN'T DEAL WITH ALL YOUR VAGUE BULLSHIIIIT
OOOO OOO OOOO IT'S SO STRESSFUUUL
OHH YEAAAH IT WOULD BE SO GOOD TO COMMUNICATE CLEEARLY BABY
OH BAAAAAABY I'M NOT A MINDREADER
OH YEEEAAAH MIXED MESSAGES ARE THE WORST

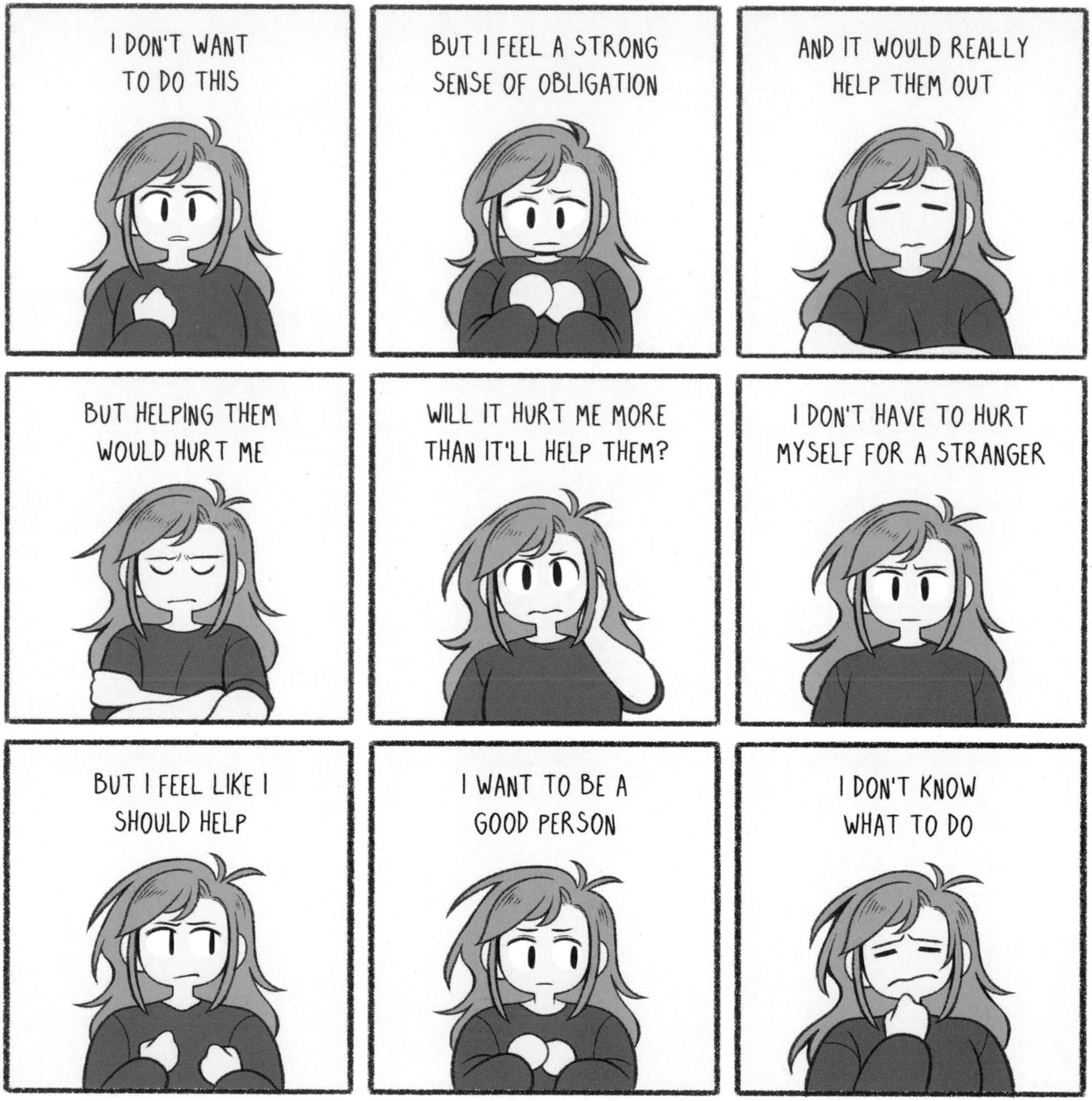
I DON'T WANT TO DO THIS
BUT I FEEL A STRONG SENSE OF OBLIGATION
AND IT WOULD REALLY HELP THEM OUT
BUT HELPING THEM WOULD HURT ME
WILL IT HURT ME MORE THAN IT'LL HELP THEM?
I DON'T HAVE TO HURT MYSELF FOR A STRANGER
BUT I FEEL LIKE I SHOULD HELP
I WANT TO BE A GOOD PERSON
I DON'T KNOW WHAT TO DO

I'M NOT RESPONSIBLE
FOR YOUR BEHAVIOR.

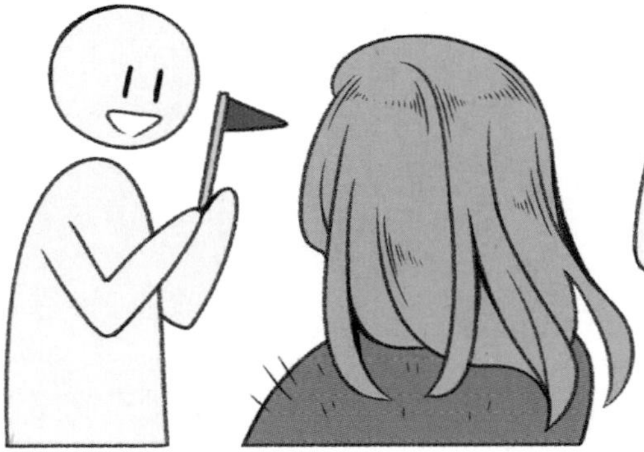

I DON'T OWE YOU A CHANCE
TO EXPLAIN YOURSELF.

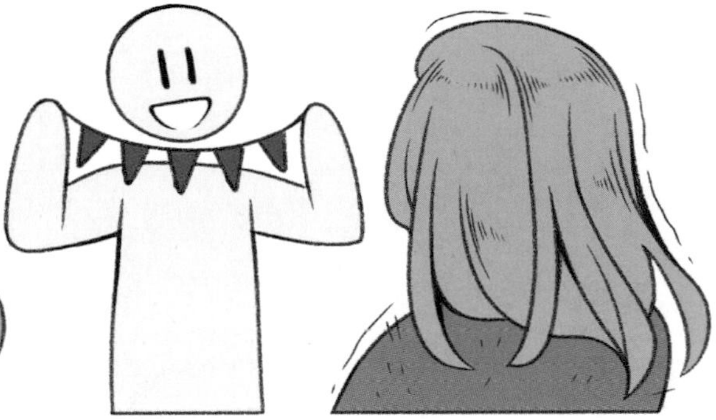

I DON'T OWE YOU A ONE-ON-ONE
TUTORIAL ON HOW TO NOT MAKE
PEOPLE UNCOMFORTABLE.

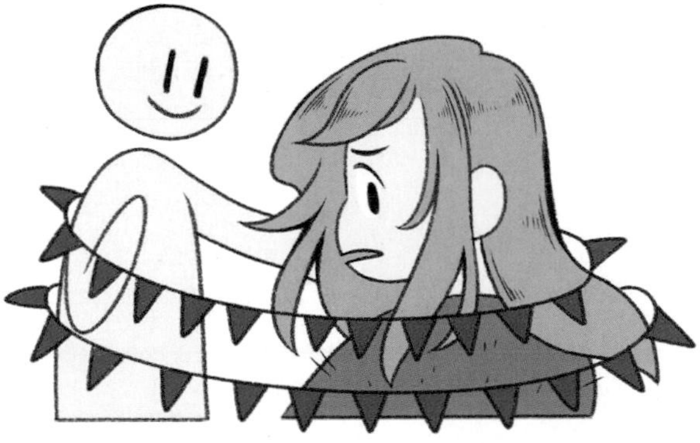

I DON'T HAVE TO WASTE MY TIME
ON YOUR ATTEMPTS TO CONVINCE
ME THAT I'M WRONG TO BE HURT.

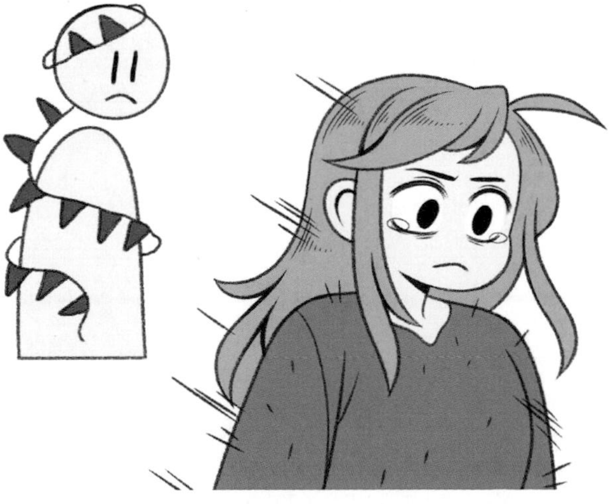

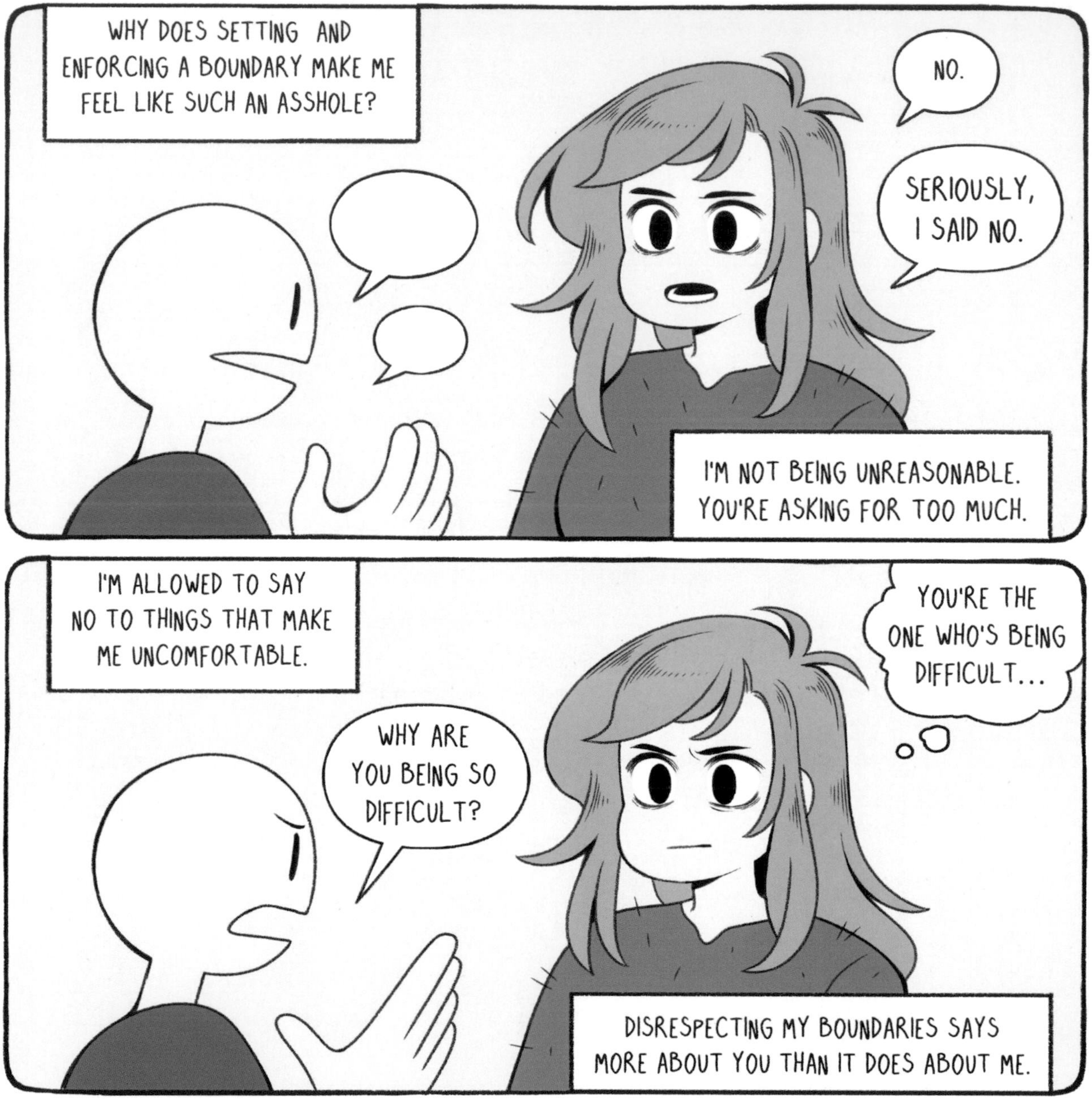
WHY DOES SETTING AND ENFORCING A BOUNDARY MAKE ME FEEL LIKE SUCH AN ASSHOLE?
NO.
SERIOUSLY, I SAID NO.
I'M NOT BEING UNREASONABLE. YOU'RE ASKING FOR TOO MUCH.
I'M ALLOWED TO SAY NO TO THINGS THAT MAKE ME UNCOMFORTABLE.
YOU'RE THE ONE WHO'S BEING DIFFICULT...
WHY ARE YOU BEING SO DIFFICULT?
DISRESPECTING MY BOUNDARIES SAYS MORE ABOUT YOU THAN IT DOES ABOUT ME.

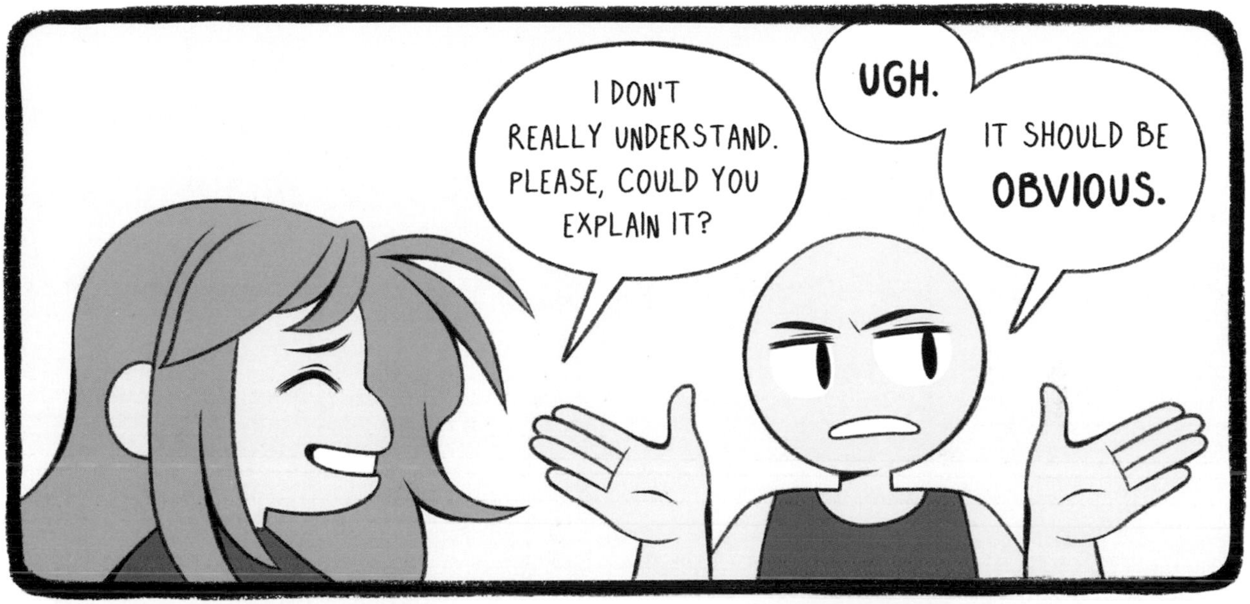
I DON'T REALLY UNDERSTAND. PLEASE, COULD YOU EXPLAIN IT?
UGH.
IT SHOULD BE **OBVIOUS.**

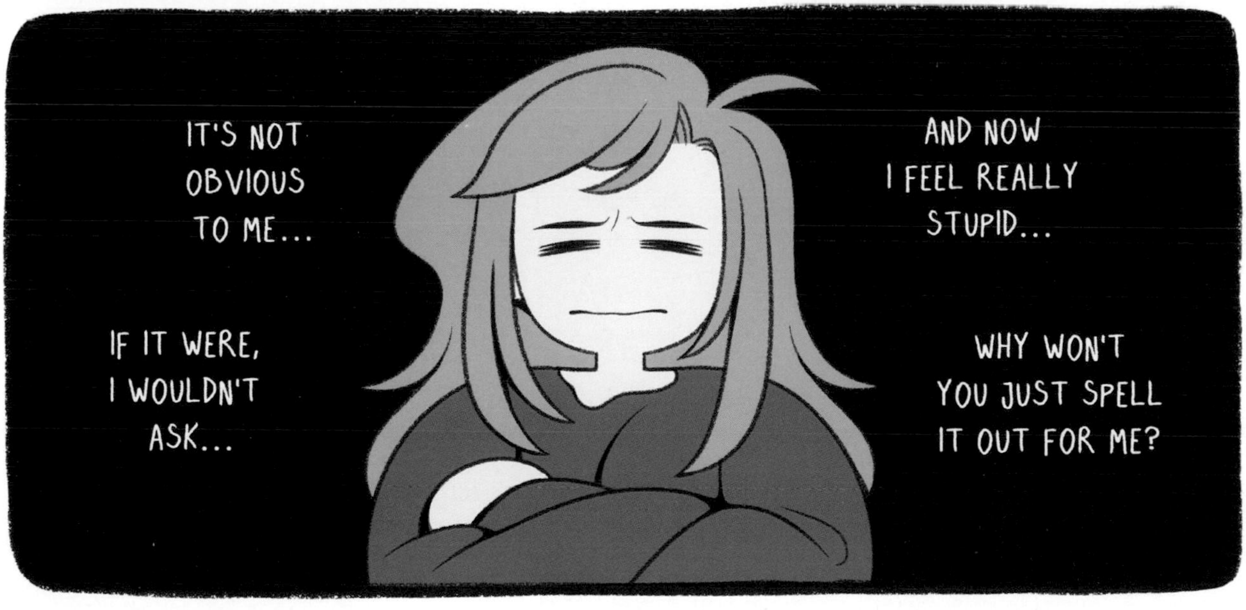
IT'S NOT OBVIOUS TO ME...
IF IT WERE, I WOULDN'T ASK...
AND NOW I FEEL REALLY STUPID...
WHY WON'T YOU JUST SPELL IT OUT FOR ME?

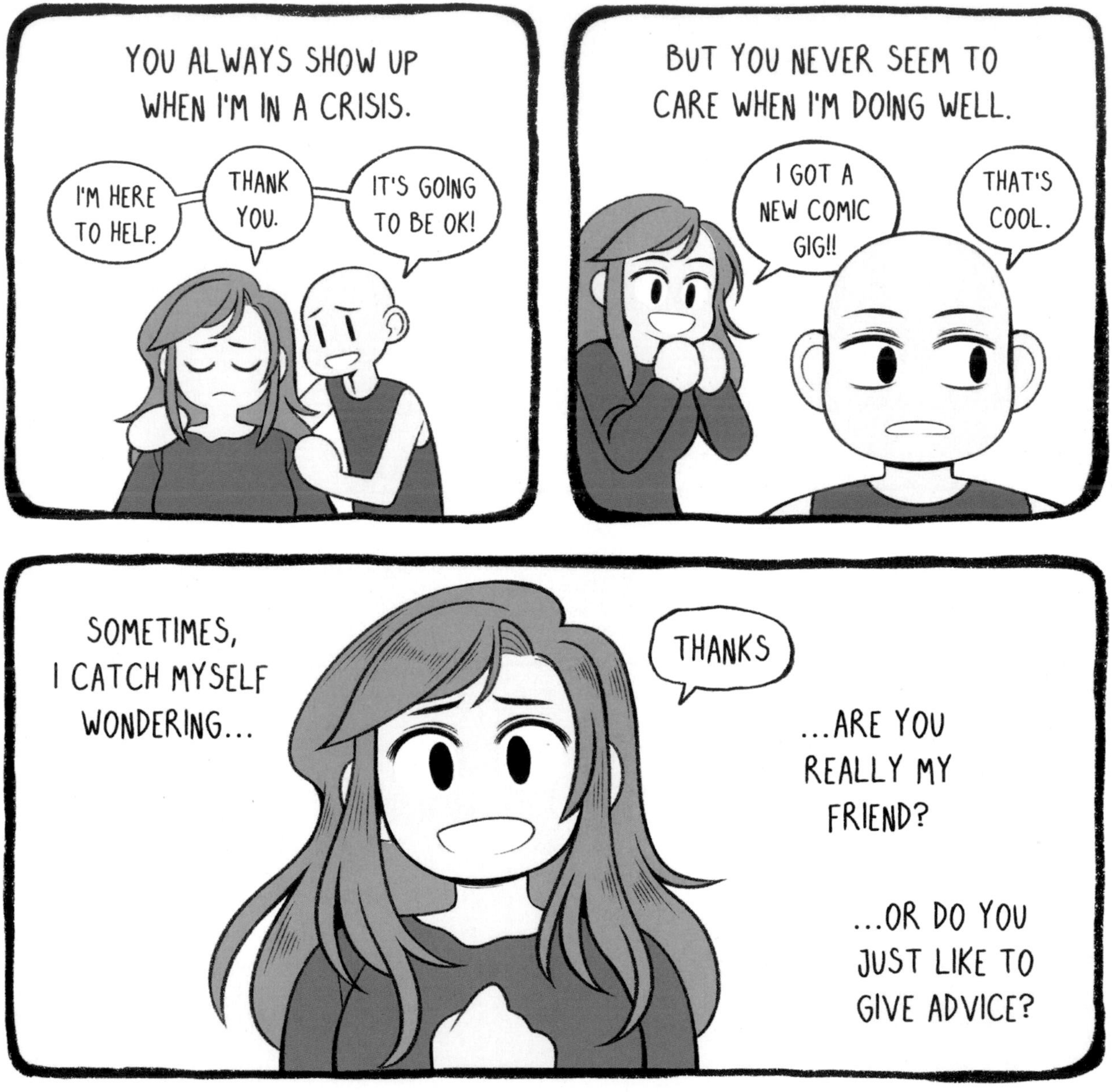
YOU ALWAYS SHOW UP WHEN I'M IN A CRISIS.
I'M HERE TO HELP.
THANK YOU.
IT'S GOING TO BE OK!
BUT YOU NEVER SEEM TO CARE WHEN I'M DOING WELL.
I GOT A NEW COMIC GIG!!
THAT'S COOL.
SOMETIMES, I CATCH MYSELF WONDERING...
THANKS
...ARE YOU REALLY MY FRIEND?
...OR DO YOU JUST LIKE TO GIVE ADVICE?

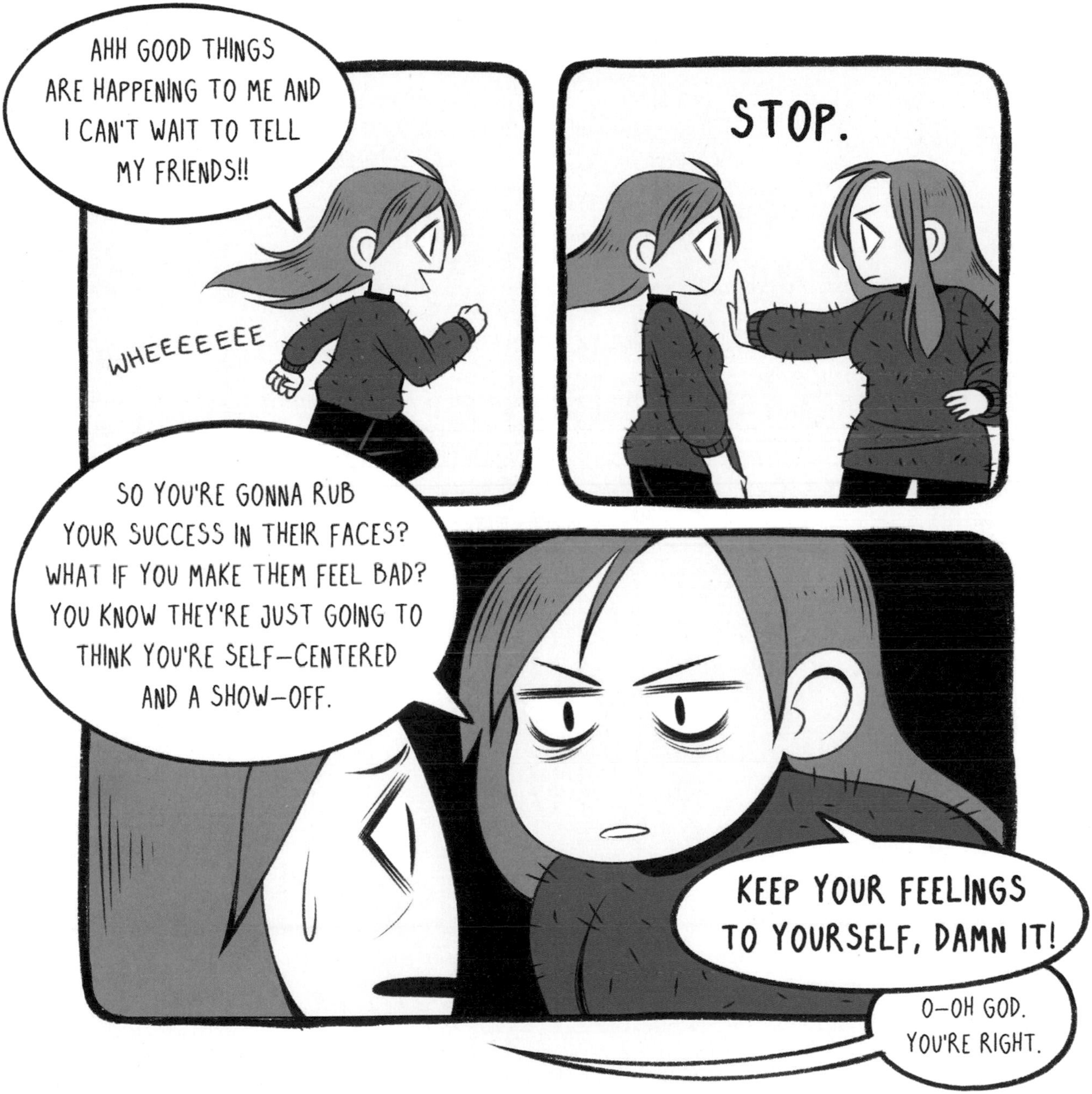
AHH GOOD THINGS ARE HAPPENING TO ME AND I CAN'T WAIT TO TELL MY FRIENDS!!
WHEEEEEEE
STOP.
SO YOU'RE GONNA RUB YOUR SUCCESS IN THEIR FACES? WHAT IF YOU MAKE THEM FEEL BAD? YOU KNOW THEY'RE JUST GOING TO THINK YOU'RE SELF-CENTERED AND A SHOW-OFF.
KEEP YOUR FEELINGS TO YOURSELF, DAMN IT!
O-OH GOD. YOU'RE RIGHT.

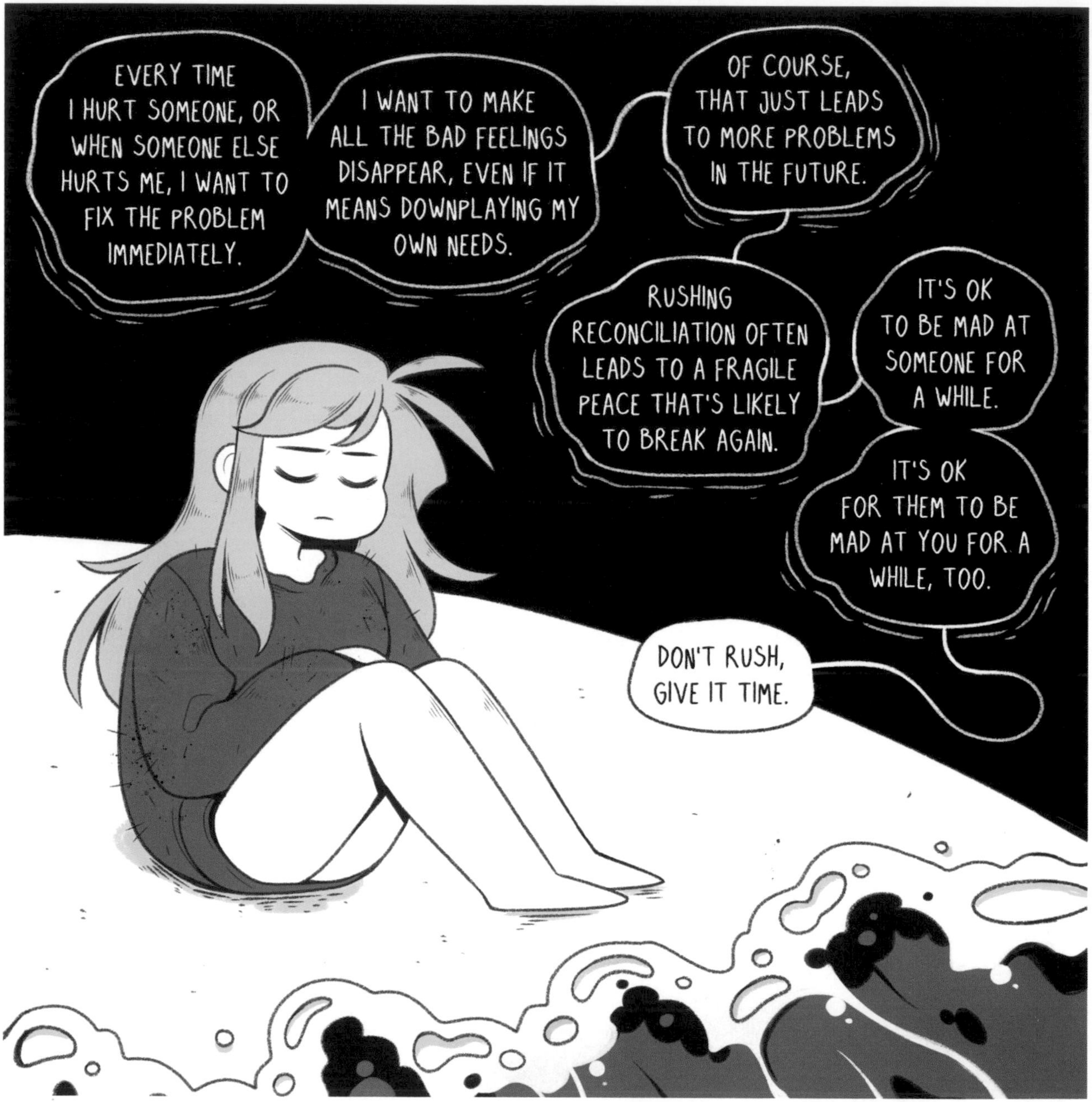
EVERY TIME I HURT SOMEONE, OR WHEN SOMEONE ELSE HURTS ME, I WANT TO FIX THE PROBLEM IMMEDIATELY.
I WANT TO MAKE ALL THE BAD FEELINGS DISAPPEAR, EVEN IF IT MEANS DOWNPLAYING MY OWN NEEDS.
OF COURSE, THAT JUST LEADS TO MORE PROBLEMS IN THE FUTURE.
RUSHING RECONCILIATION OFTEN LEADS TO A FRAGILE PEACE THAT'S LIKELY TO BREAK AGAIN.
IT'S OK TO BE MAD AT SOMEONE FOR A WHILE.
IT'S OK FOR THEM TO BE MAD AT YOU FOR A WHILE, TOO.
DON'T RUSH, GIVE IT TIME.

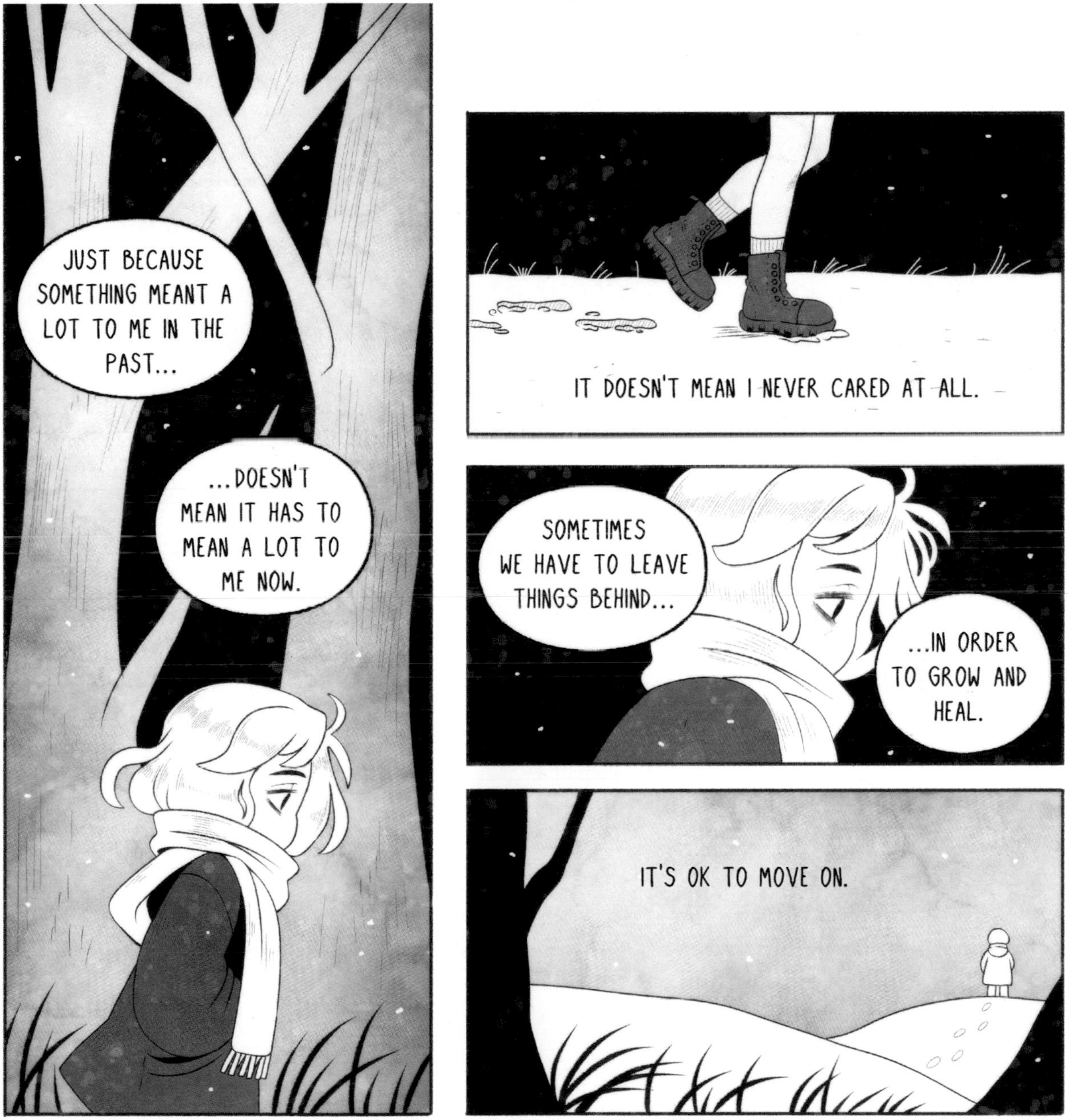
JUST BECAUSE SOMETHING MEANT A LOT TO ME IN THE PAST...
...DOESN'T MEAN IT HAS TO MEAN A LOT TO ME NOW.
IT DOESN'T MEAN I NEVER CARED AT ALL.
SOMETIMES WE HAVE TO LEAVE THINGS BEHIND...
...IN ORDER TO GROW AND HEAL.
IT'S OK TO MOVE ON.

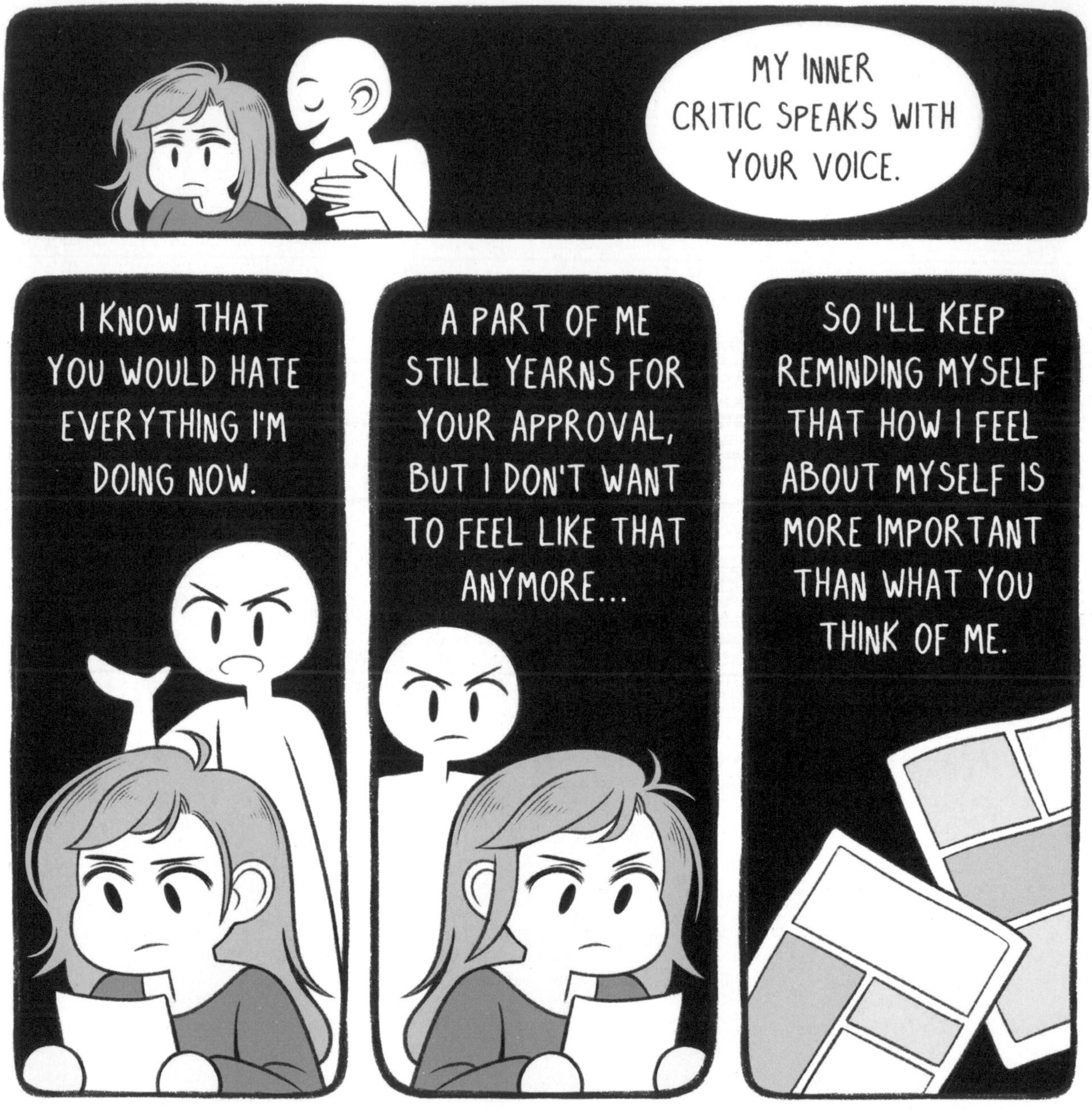
MY INNER CRITIC SPEAKS WITH YOUR VOICE.
I KNOW THAT YOU WOULD HATE EVERYTHING I'M DOING NOW.
A PART OF ME STILL YEARNS FOR YOUR APPROVAL, BUT I DON'T WANT TO FEEL LIKE THAT ANYMORE...
SO I'LL KEEP REMINDING MYSELF THAT HOW I FEEL ABOUT MYSELF IS MORE IMPORTANT THAN WHAT YOU THINK OF ME.

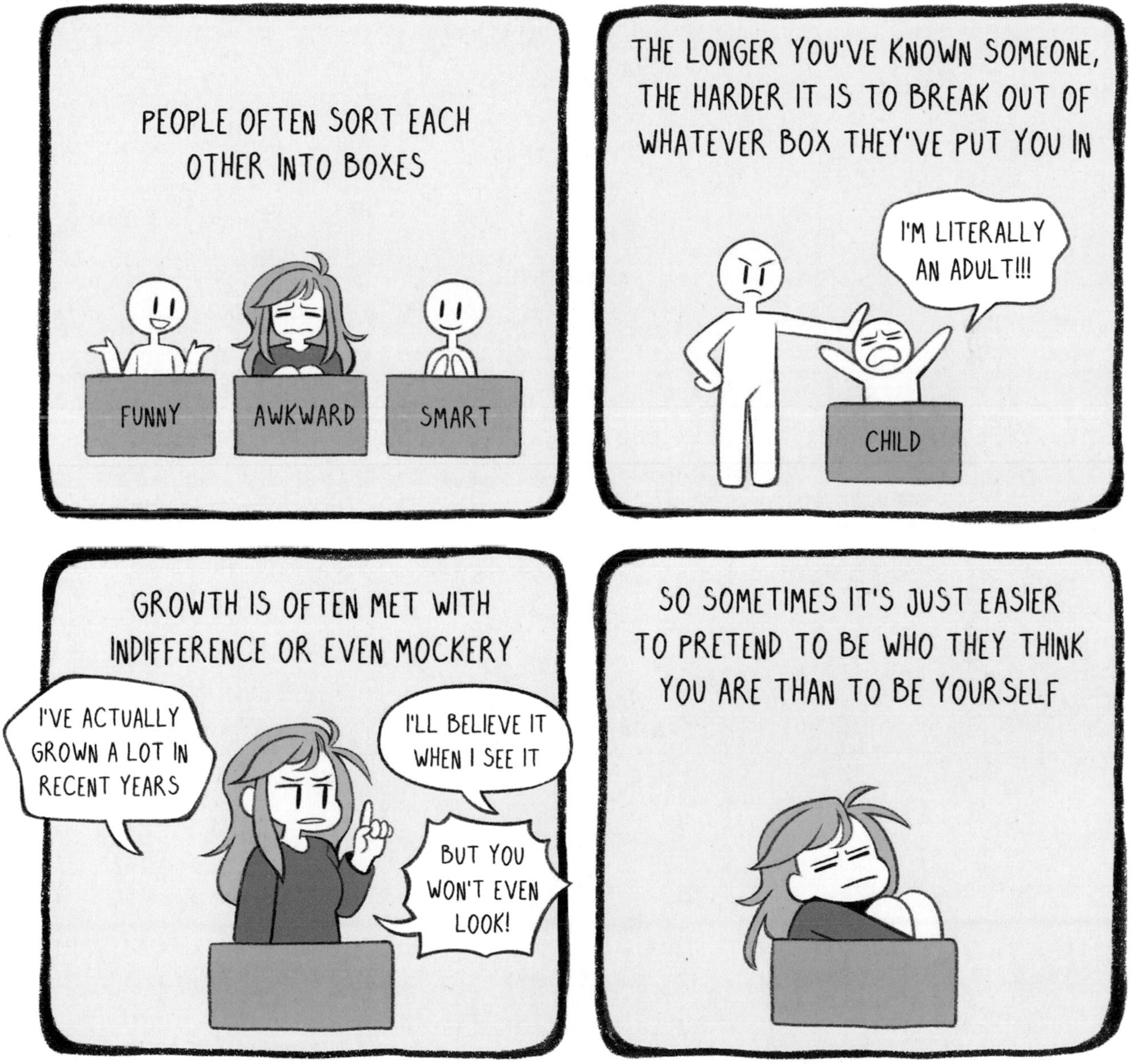
PEOPLE OFTEN SORT EACH OTHER INTO BOXES
FUNNY
AWKWARD
SMART
THE LONGER YOU'VE KNOWN SOMEONE, THE HARDER IT IS TO BREAK OUT OF WHATEVER BOX THEY'VE PUT YOU IN
I'M LITERALLY AN ADULT!!!
CHILD
GROWTH IS OFTEN MET WITH INDIFFERENCE OR EVEN MOCKERY
I'VE ACTUALLY GROWN A LOT IN RECENT YEARS
I'LL BELIEVE IT WHEN I SEE IT
BUT YOU WON'T EVEN LOOK!
SO SOMETIMES IT'S JUST EASIER TO PRETEND TO BE WHO THEY THINK YOU ARE THAN TO BE YOURSELF

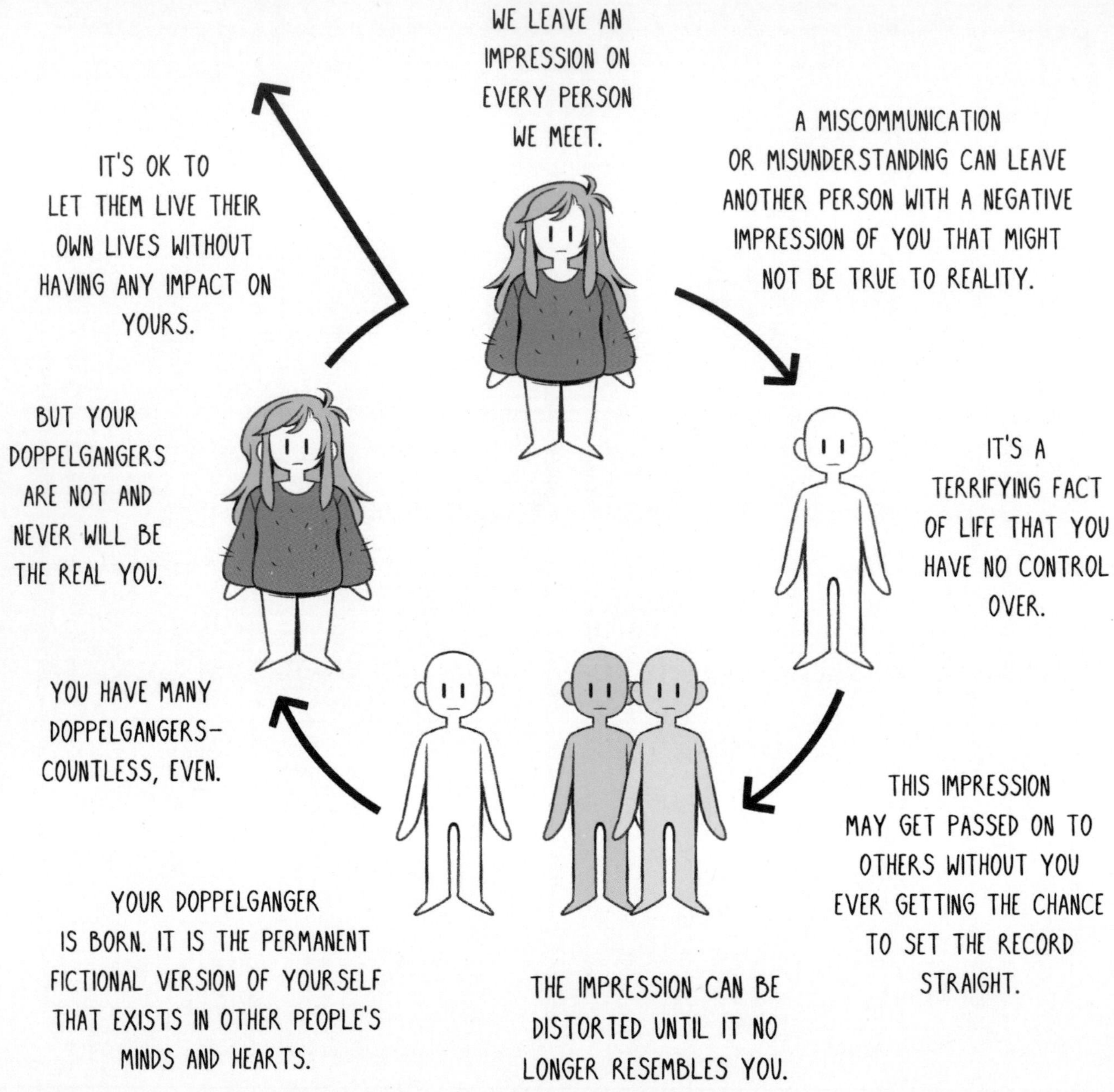
WE LEAVE AN IMPRESSION ON EVERY PERSON WE MEET.
A MISCOMMUNICATION OR MISUNDERSTANDING CAN LEAVE ANOTHER PERSON WITH A NEGATIVE IMPRESSION OF YOU THAT MIGHT NOT BE TRUE TO REALITY.
IT'S A TERRIFYING FACT OF LIFE THAT YOU HAVE NO CONTROL OVER.
THIS IMPRESSION MAY GET PASSED ON TO OTHERS WITHOUT YOU EVER GETTING THE CHANCE TO SET THE RECORD STRAIGHT.
THE IMPRESSION CAN BE DISTORTED UNTIL IT NO LONGER RESEMBLES YOU.
YOUR DOPPELGANGER IS BORN. IT IS THE PERMANENT FICTIONAL VERSION OF YOURSELF THAT EXISTS IN OTHER PEOPLE'S MINDS AND HEARTS.
YOU HAVE MANY DOPPELGANGERS– COUNTLESS, EVEN.
BUT YOUR DOPPELGANGERS ARE NOT AND NEVER WILL BE THE REAL YOU.
IT'S OK TO LET THEM LIVE THEIR OWN LIVES WITHOUT HAVING ANY IMPACT ON YOURS.

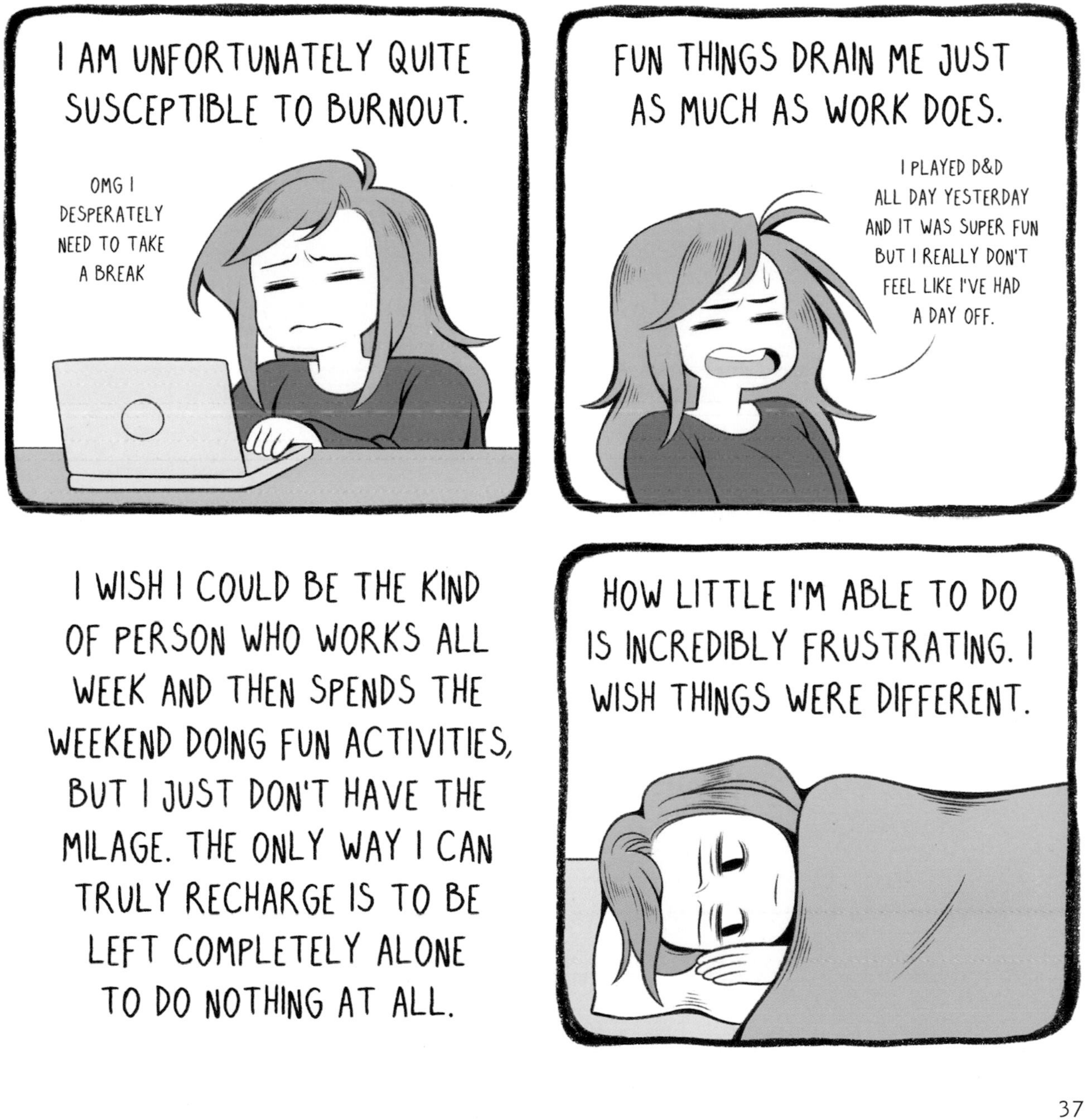
I AM UNFORTUNATELY QUITE SUSCEPTIBLE TO BURNOUT.
OMG I DESPERATELY NEED TO TAKE A BREAK
FUN THINGS DRAIN ME JUST AS MUCH AS WORK DOES.
I PLAYED D&D ALL DAY YESTERDAY AND IT WAS SUPER FUN BUT I REALLY DON'T FEEL LIKE I'VE HAD A DAY OFF.
I WISH I COULD BE THE KIND OF PERSON WHO WORKS ALL WEEK AND THEN SPENDS THE WEEKEND DOING FUN ACTIVITIES, BUT I JUST DON'T HAVE THE MILAGE. THE ONLY WAY I CAN TRULY RECHARGE IS TO BE LEFT COMPLETELY ALONE TO DO NOTHING AT ALL.
HOW LITTLE I'M ABLE TO DO IS INCREDIBLY FRUSTRATING. I WISH THINGS WERE DIFFERENT.

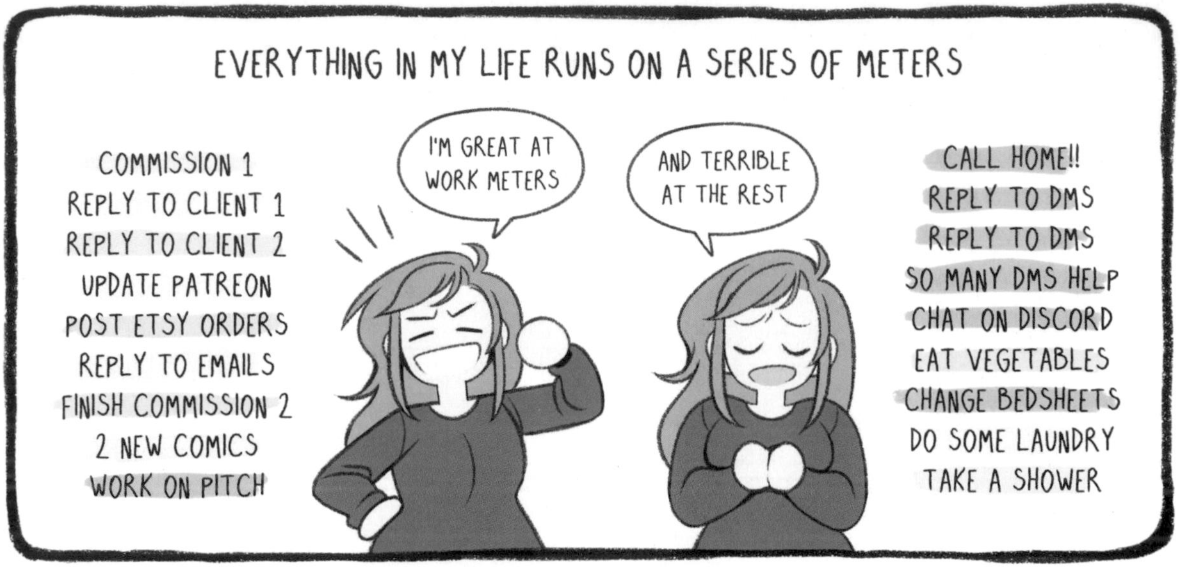
EVERYTHING IN MY LIFE RUNS ON A SERIES OF METERS
COMMISSION 1
REPLY TO CLIENT 1
REPLY TO CLIENT 2
UPDATE PATREON
POST ETSY ORDERS
REPLY TO EMAILS
FINISH COMMISSION 2
2 NEW COMICS
WORK ON PITCH
I'M GREAT AT WORK METERS
AND TERRIBLE AT THE REST
CALL HOME!!
REPLY TO DMS
REPLY TO DMS
SO MANY DMS HELP
CHAT ON DISCORD
EAT VEGETABLES
CHANGE BEDSHEETS
DO SOME LAUNDRY
TAKE A SHOWER

I'M DOING AS MUCH AS I CAN BUT I ALWAYS HAVE METERS IN THE RED. I'M ALWAYS JUST ABOUT MANAGING TO STAY ON TOP OF THINGS, BUT EACH TIME I COMPLETE A TASK, ANOTHER ONE TAKES ITS PLACE IN A NEVER-ENDING CYCLE OF STRESS.

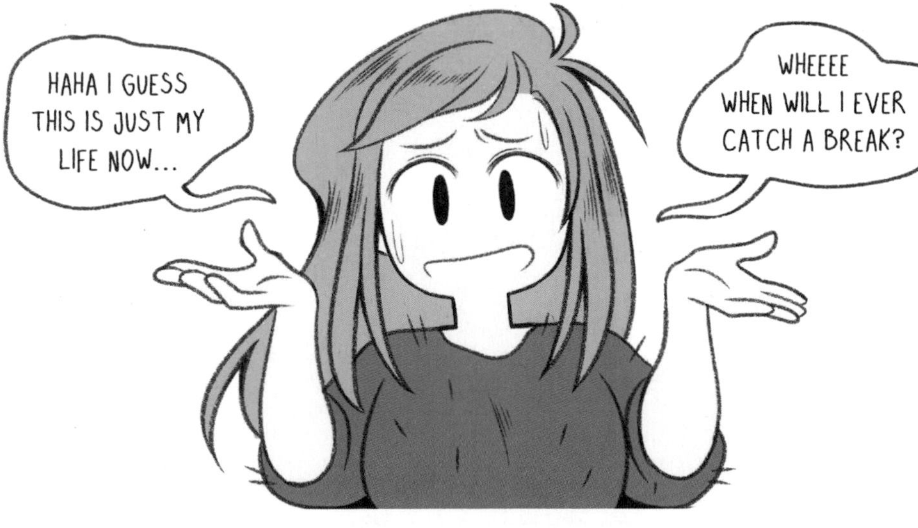
HAHA I GUESS THIS IS JUST MY LIFE NOW...
WHEEEE WHEN WILL I EVER CATCH A BREAK?

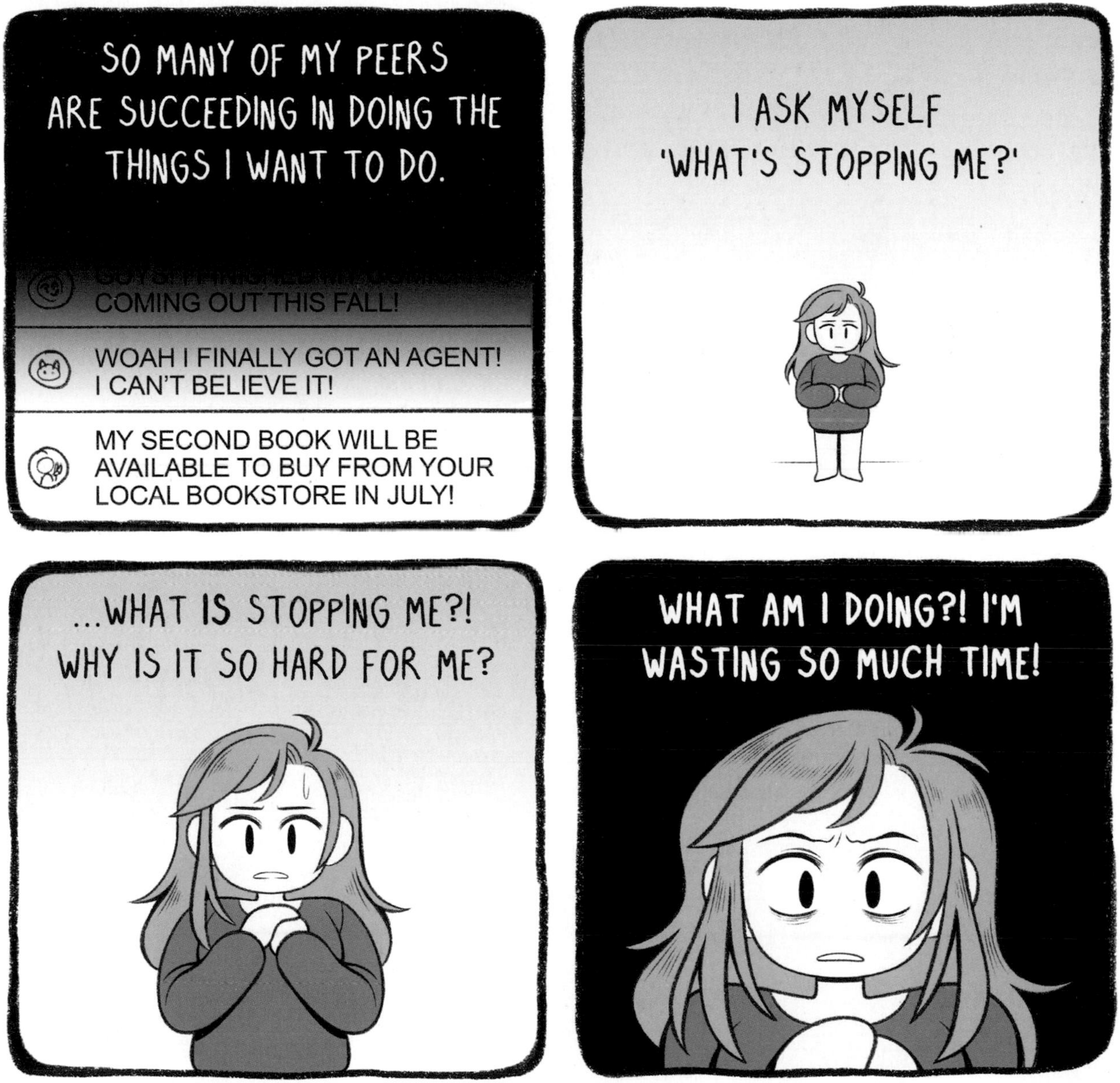
SO MANY OF MY PEERS ARE SUCCEEDING IN DOING THE THINGS I WANT TO DO.
COMING OUT THIS FALL!
WOAH I FINALLY GOT AN AGENT! I CAN'T BELIEVE IT!
MY SECOND BOOK WILL BE AVAILABLE TO BUY FROM YOUR LOCAL BOOKSTORE IN JULY!
I ASK MYSELF 'WHAT'S STOPPING ME?'
...WHAT IS STOPPING ME?! WHY IS IT SO HARD FOR ME?
WHAT AM I DOING?! I'M WASTING SO MUCH TIME!

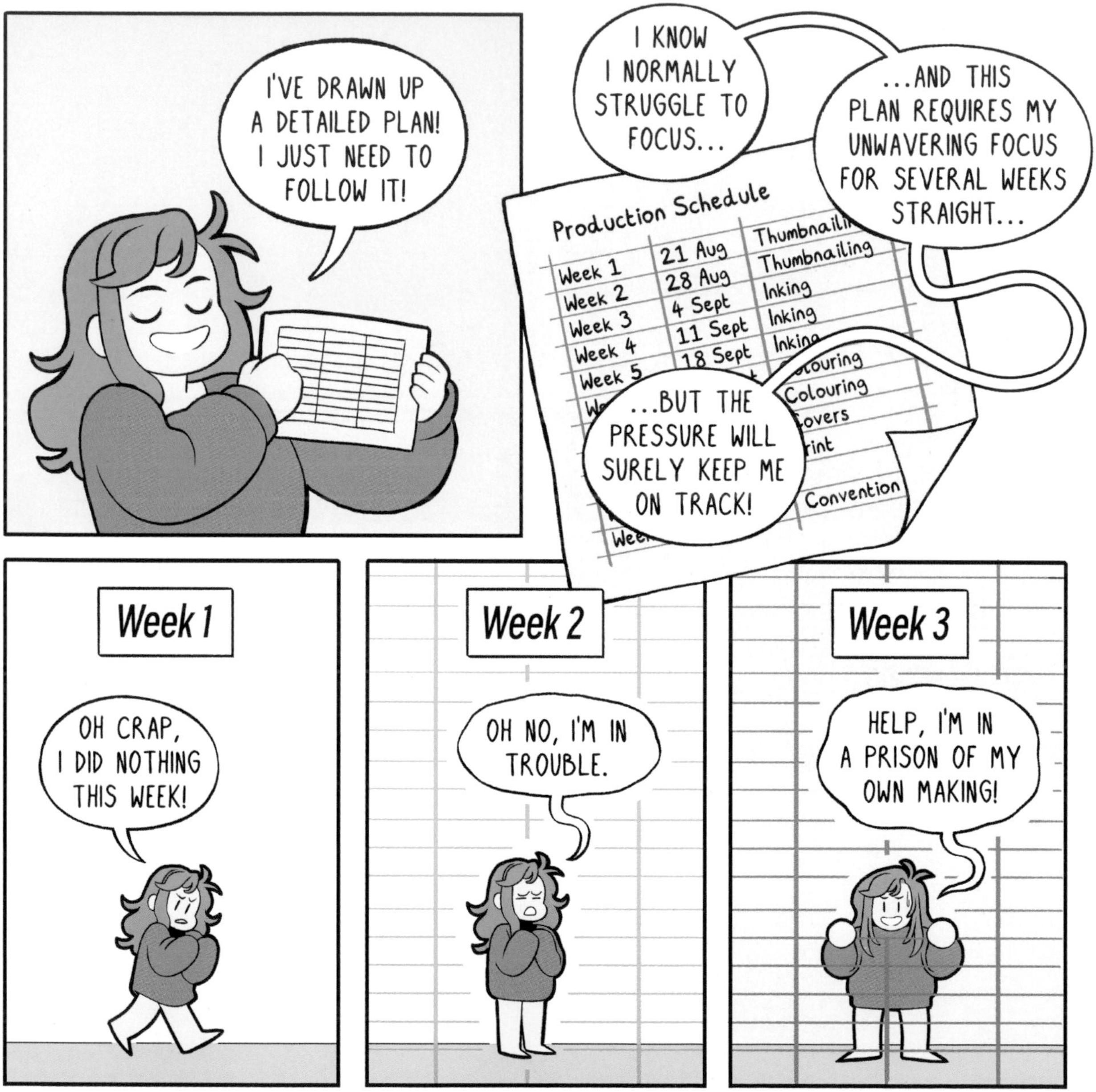
I'VE DRAWN UP A DETAILED PLAN! I JUST NEED TO FOLLOW IT!
I KNOW I NORMALLY STRUGGLE TO FOCUS...
...AND THIS PLAN REQUIRES MY UNWAVERING FOCUS FOR SEVERAL WEEKS STRAIGHT...
...BUT THE PRESSURE WILL SURELY KEEP ME ON TRACK!
Production Schedule
Week 1
Week 2
Week 3
Week 4
Week 5
21 Aug
28 Aug
4 Sept
11 Sept
18 Sept
Thumbnailing
Inking
Inking
Colouring
Convention
Week 1
OH CRAP, I DID NOTHING THIS WEEK!
Week 2
OH NO, I'M IN TROUBLE.
Week 3
HELP, I'M IN A PRISON OF MY OWN MAKING!

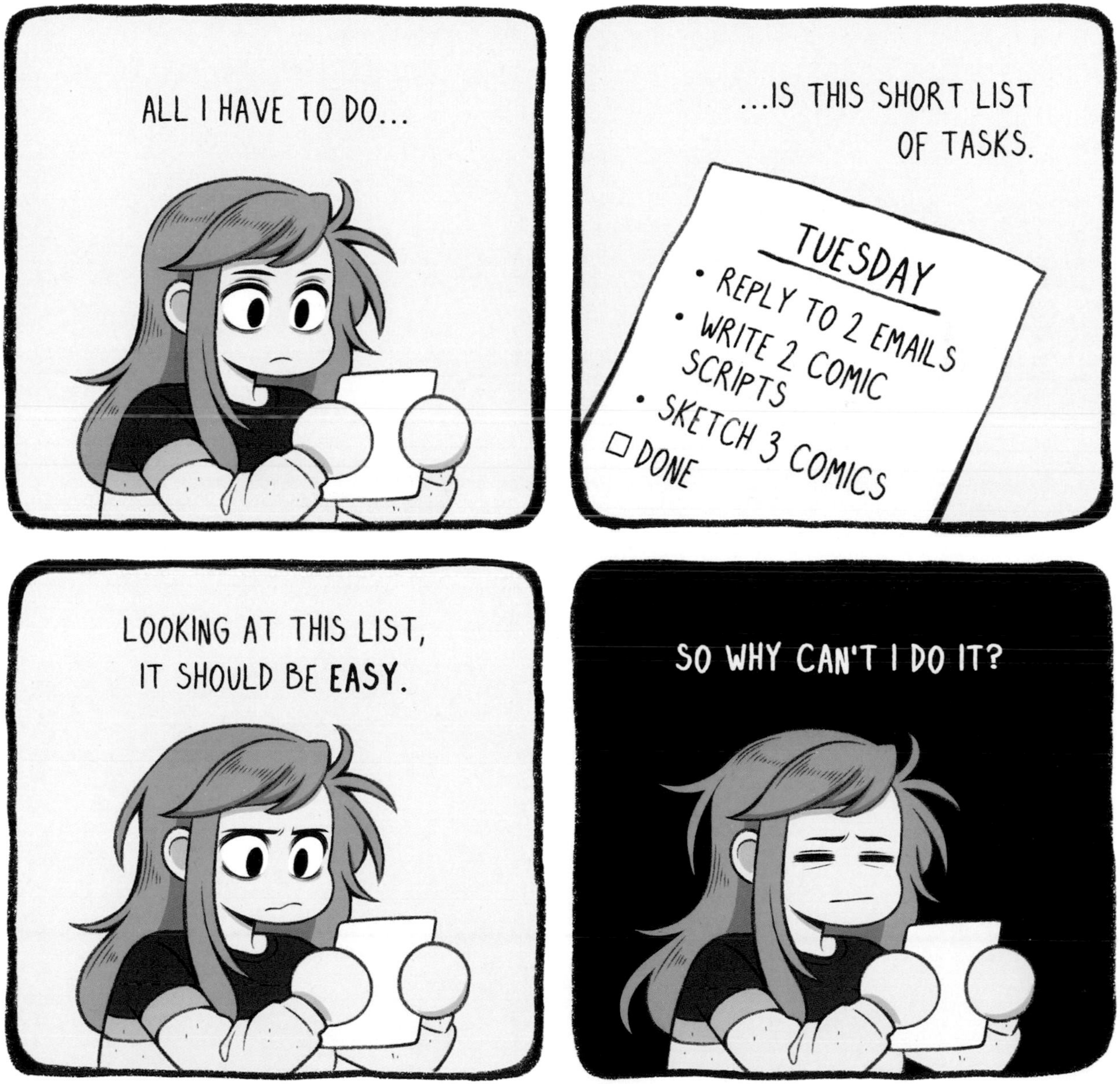
ALL I HAVE TO DO...
...IS THIS SHORT LIST OF TASKS.
TUESDAY
• REPLY TO 2 EMAILS
• WRITE 2 COMIC SCRIPTS
• SKETCH 3 COMICS
☐ DONE
LOOKING AT THIS LIST, IT SHOULD BE EASY.
SO WHY CAN'T I DO IT?

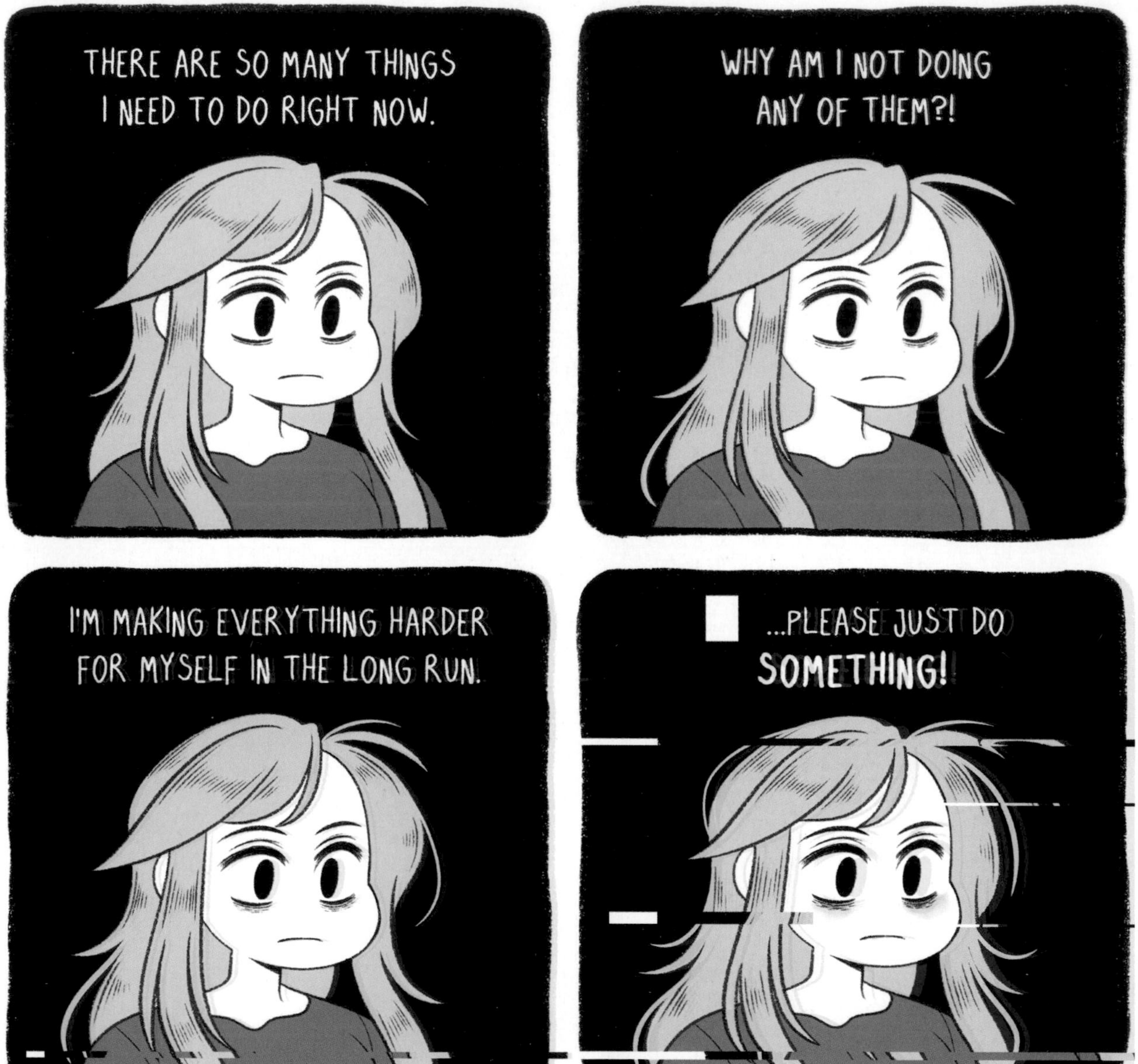
THERE ARE SO MANY THINGS I NEED TO DO RIGHT NOW.
WHY AM I NOT DOING ANY OF THEM?!
I'M MAKING EVERYTHING HARDER FOR MYSELF IN THE LONG RUN.
...PLEASE JUST DO SOMETHING!

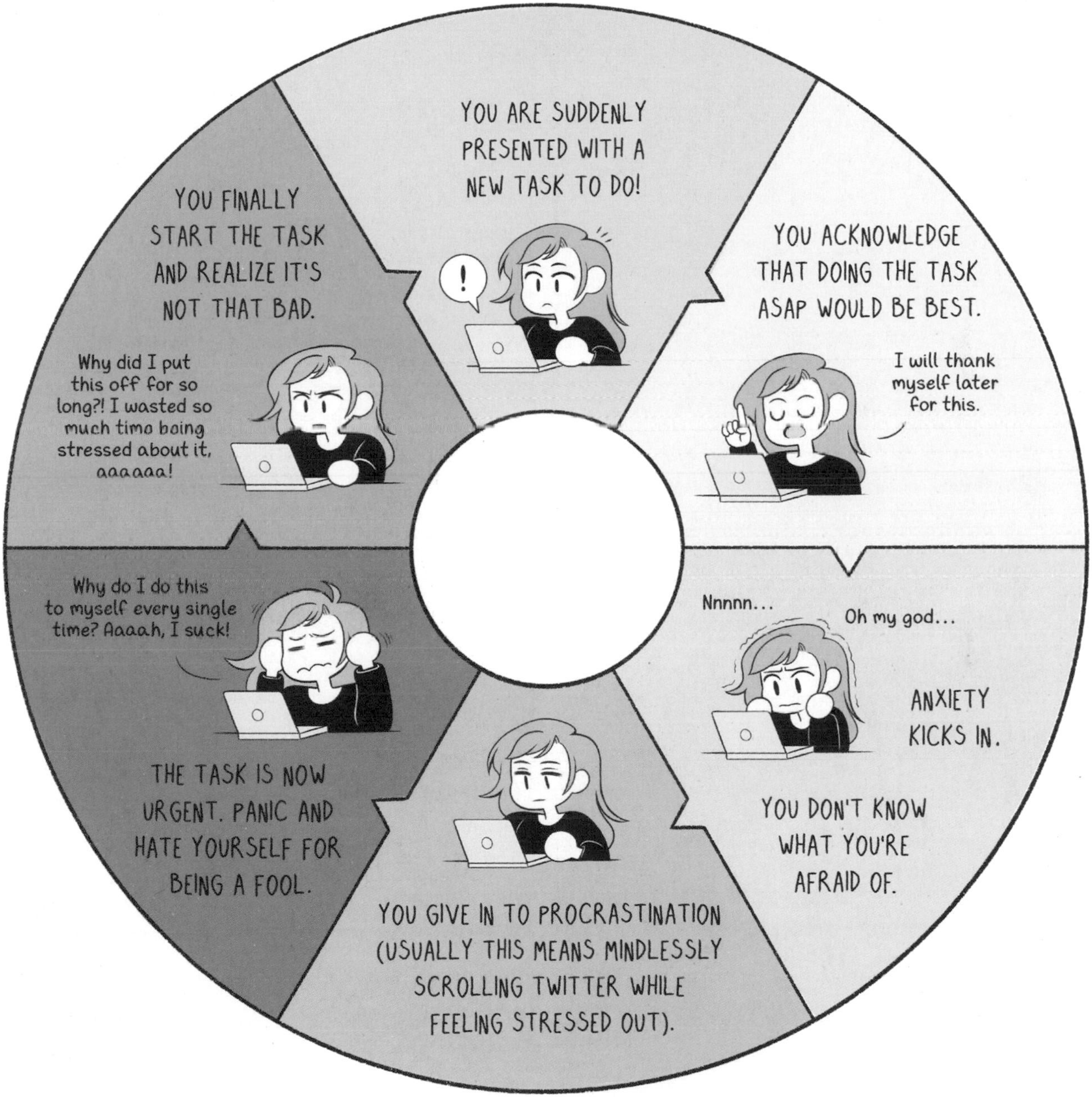
YOU ARE SUDDENLY PRESENTED WITH A NEW TASK TO DO!
!
YOU ACKNOWLEDGE THAT DOING THE TASK ASAP WOULD BE BEST.
I will thank myself later for this.
Nnnnn...
Oh my god...
ANXIETY KICKS IN.
YOU DON'T KNOW WHAT YOU'RE AFRAID OF.
YOU GIVE IN TO PROCRASTINATION (USUALLY THIS MEANS MINDLESSLY SCROLLING TWITTER WHILE FEELING STRESSED OUT).
Why do I do this to myself every single time? Aaaah, I suck!
THE TASK IS NOW URGENT. PANIC AND HATE YOURSELF FOR BEING A FOOL.
YOU FINALLY START THE TASK AND REALIZE IT'S NOT THAT BAD.
Why did I put this off for so long?! I wasted so much time being stressed about it, aaaaaa!

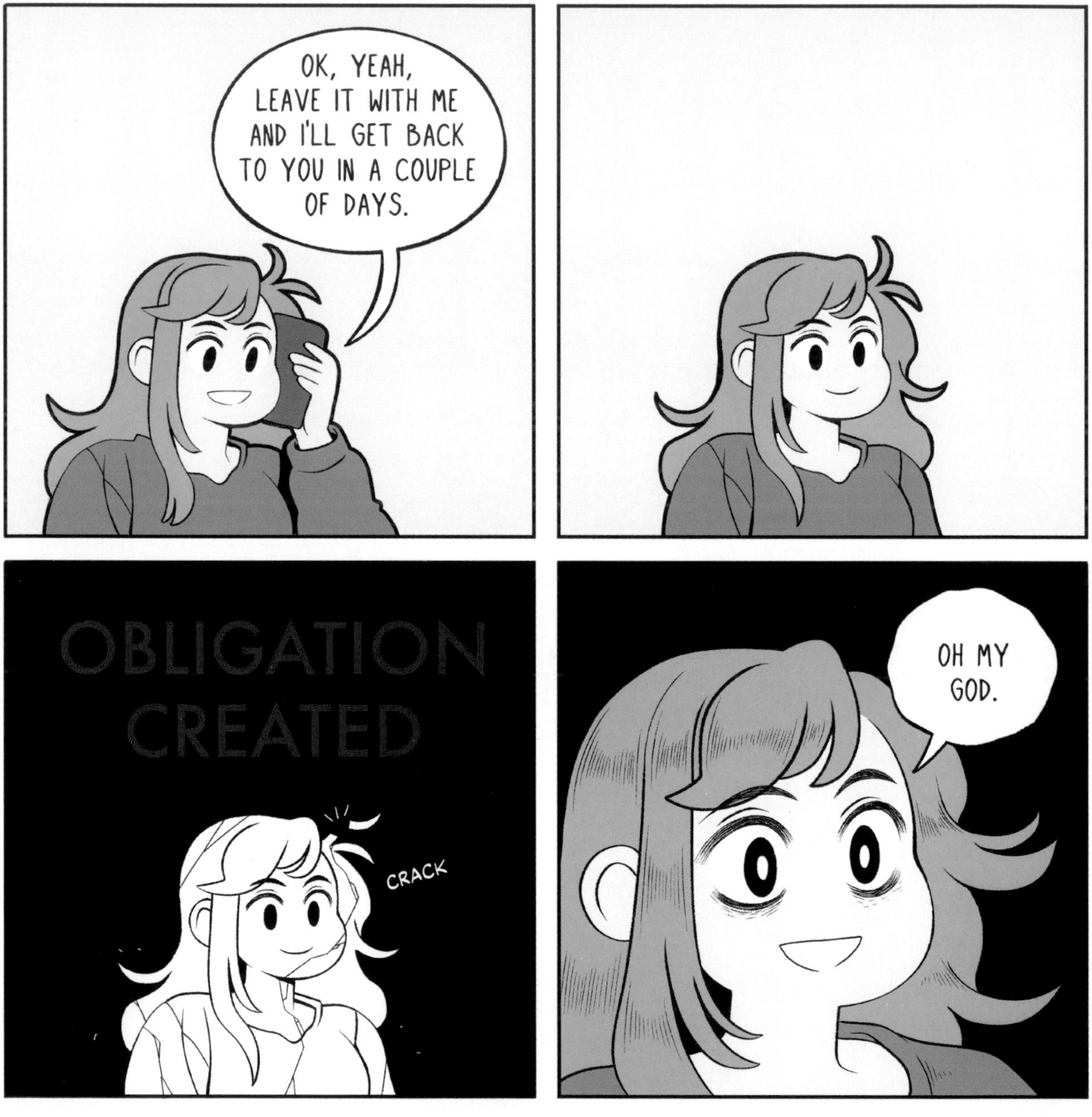
OK, YEAH, LEAVE IT WITH ME AND I'LL GET BACK TO YOU IN A COUPLE OF DAYS.
OBLIGATION CREATED
CRACK
OH MY GOD.

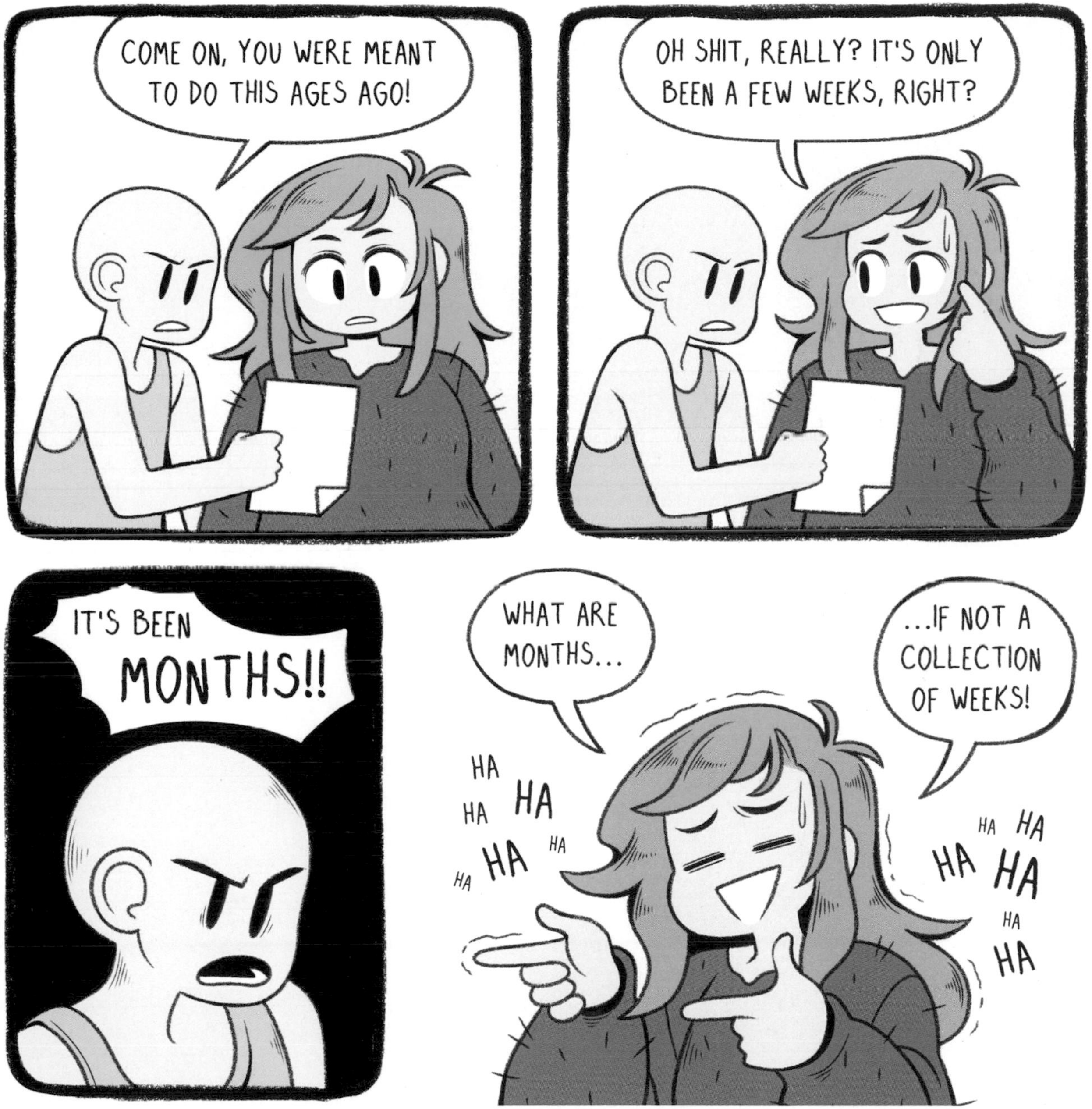
COME ON, YOU WERE MEANT TO DO THIS AGES AGO!
OH SHIT, REALLY? IT'S ONLY BEEN A FEW WEEKS, RIGHT?
IT'S BEEN MONTHS!!
WHAT ARE MONTHS...
...IF NOT A COLLECTION OF WEEKS!
HA HA HA HA HA HA HA
HA HA HA HA HA HA

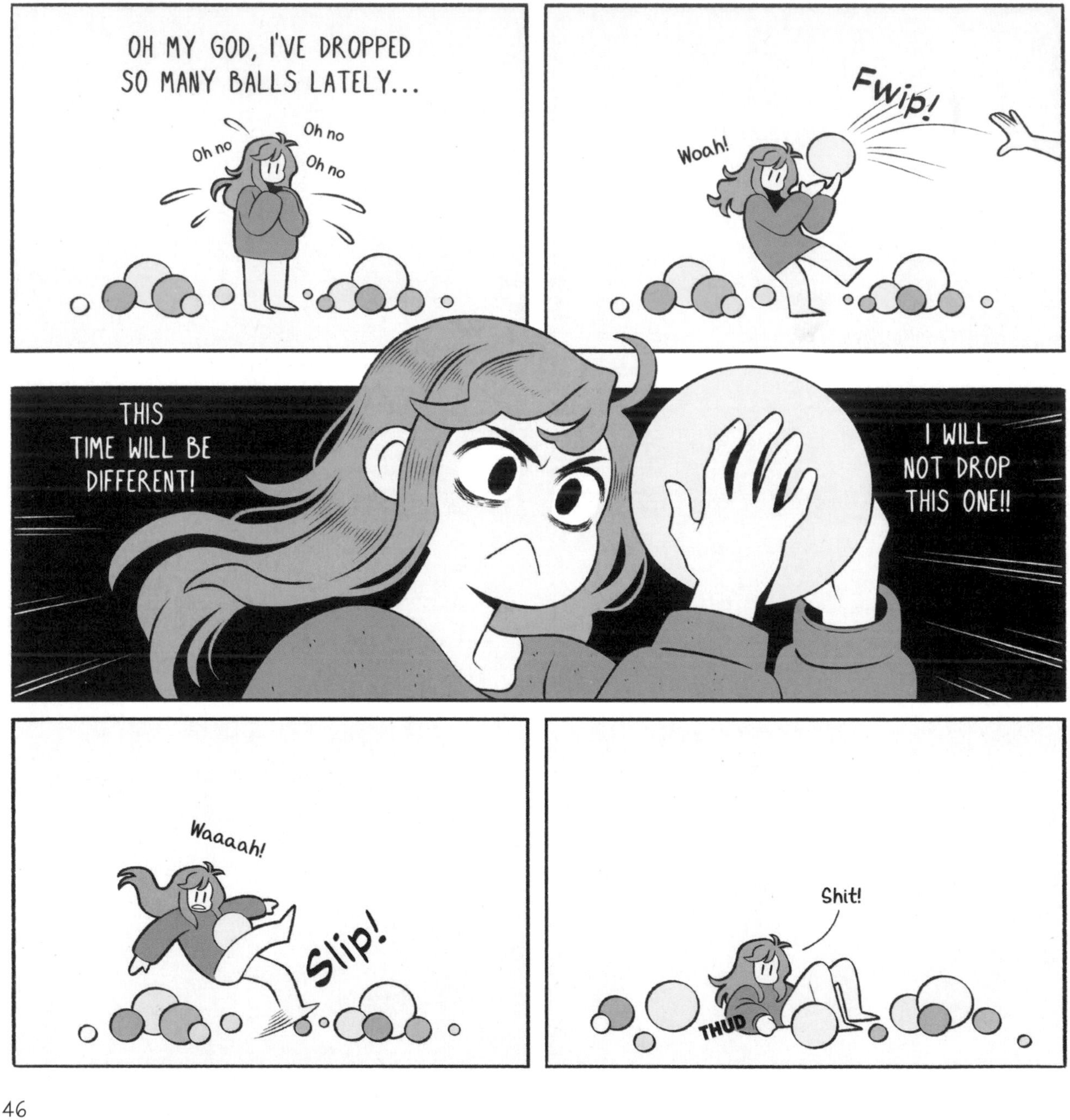
OH MY GOD, I'VE DROPPED SO MANY BALLS LATELY...
Oh no
Oh no
Oh no
Woah!
Fwip!
THIS TIME WILL BE DIFFERENT!
I WILL NOT DROP THIS ONE!!
Waaaah!
Slip!
Shit!
THUD

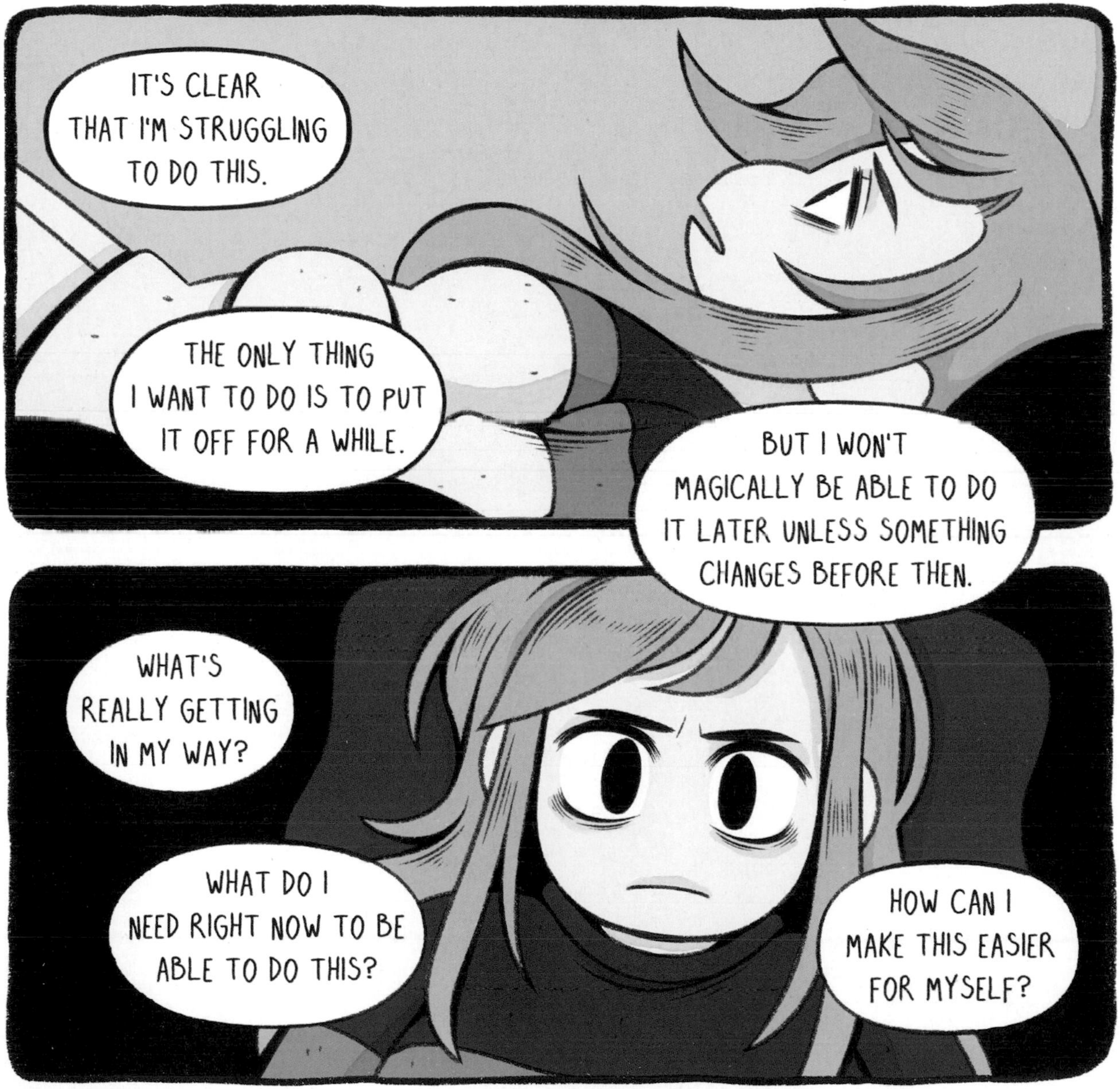
IT'S CLEAR THAT I'M STRUGGLING TO DO THIS.
THE ONLY THING I WANT TO DO IS TO PUT IT OFF FOR A WHILE.
BUT I WON'T MAGICALLY BE ABLE TO DO IT LATER UNLESS SOMETHING CHANGES BEFORE THEN.
WHAT'S REALLY GETTING IN MY WAY?
WHAT DO I NEED RIGHT NOW TO BE ABLE TO DO THIS?
HOW CAN I MAKE THIS EASIER FOR MYSELF?

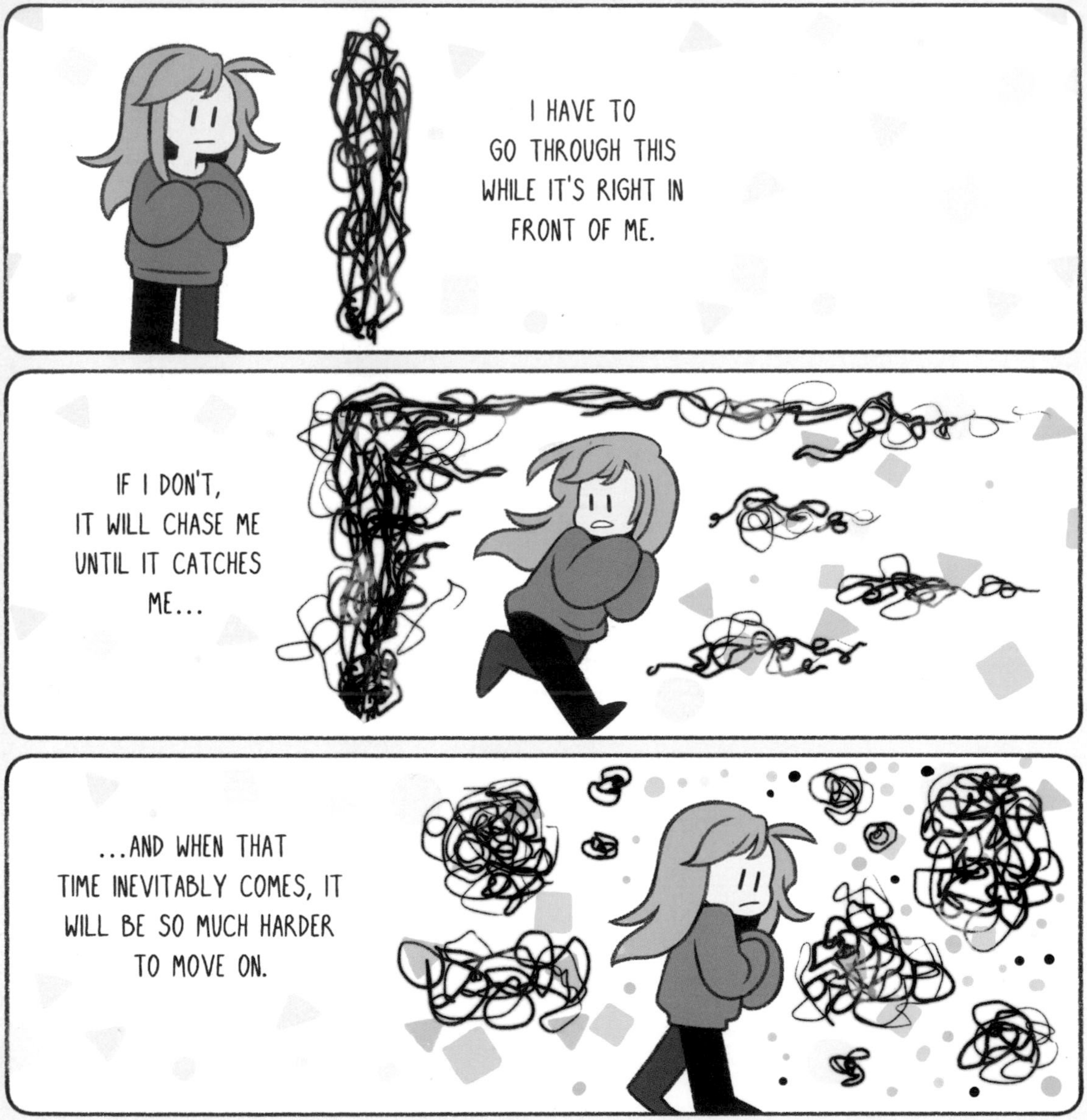
I HAVE TO GO THROUGH THIS WHILE IT'S RIGHT IN FRONT OF ME.
IF I DON'T, IT WILL CHASE ME UNTIL IT CATCHES ME...
...AND WHEN THAT TIME INEVITABLY COMES, IT WILL BE SO MUCH HARDER TO MOVE ON.

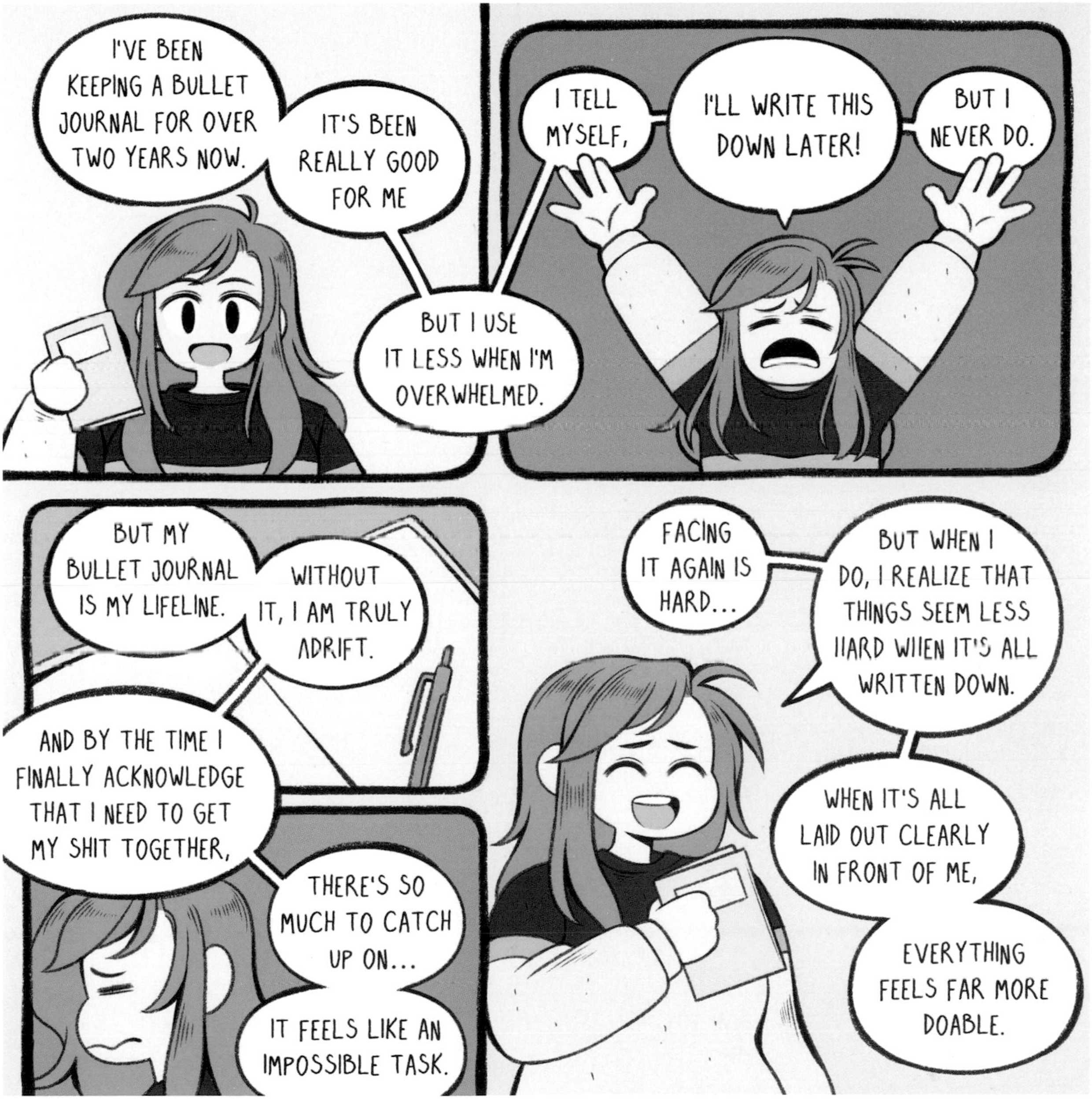
I'VE BEEN KEEPING A BULLET JOURNAL FOR OVER TWO YEARS NOW.
IT'S BEEN REALLY GOOD FOR ME
BUT I USE IT LESS WHEN I'M OVERWHELMED.
I TELL MYSELF,
I'LL WRITE THIS DOWN LATER!
BUT I NEVER DO.
BUT MY BULLET JOURNAL IS MY LIFELINE.
WITHOUT IT, I AM TRULY ADRIFT.
AND BY THE TIME I FINALLY ACKNOWLEDGE THAT I NEED TO GET MY SHIT TOGETHER,
THERE'S SO MUCH TO CATCH UP ON...
IT FEELS LIKE AN IMPOSSIBLE TASK.
FACING IT AGAIN IS HARD...
BUT WHEN I DO, I REALIZE THAT THINGS SEEM LESS HARD WHEN IT'S ALL WRITTEN DOWN.
WHEN IT'S ALL LAID OUT CLEARLY IN FRONT OF ME,
EVERYTHING FEELS FAR MORE DOABLE.

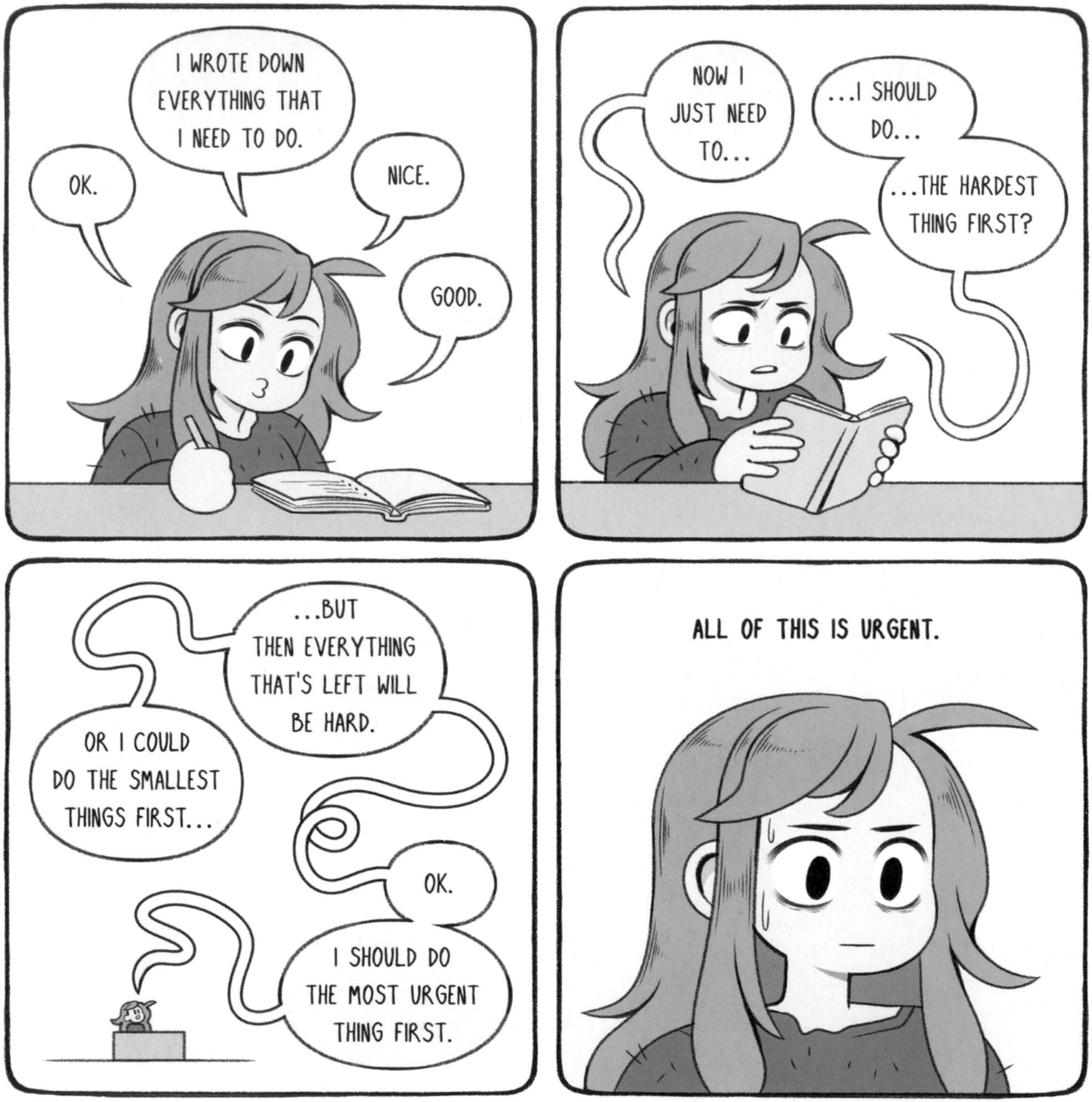
I WROTE DOWN EVERYTHING THAT I NEED TO DO.
OK.
NICE.
GOOD.
NOW I JUST NEED TO...
...I SHOULD DO...
...THE HARDEST THING FIRST?
...BUT THEN EVERYTHING THAT'S LEFT WILL BE HARD.
OR I COULD DO THE SMALLEST THINGS FIRST...
OK.
I SHOULD DO THE MOST URGENT THING FIRST.
ALL OF THIS IS URGENT.

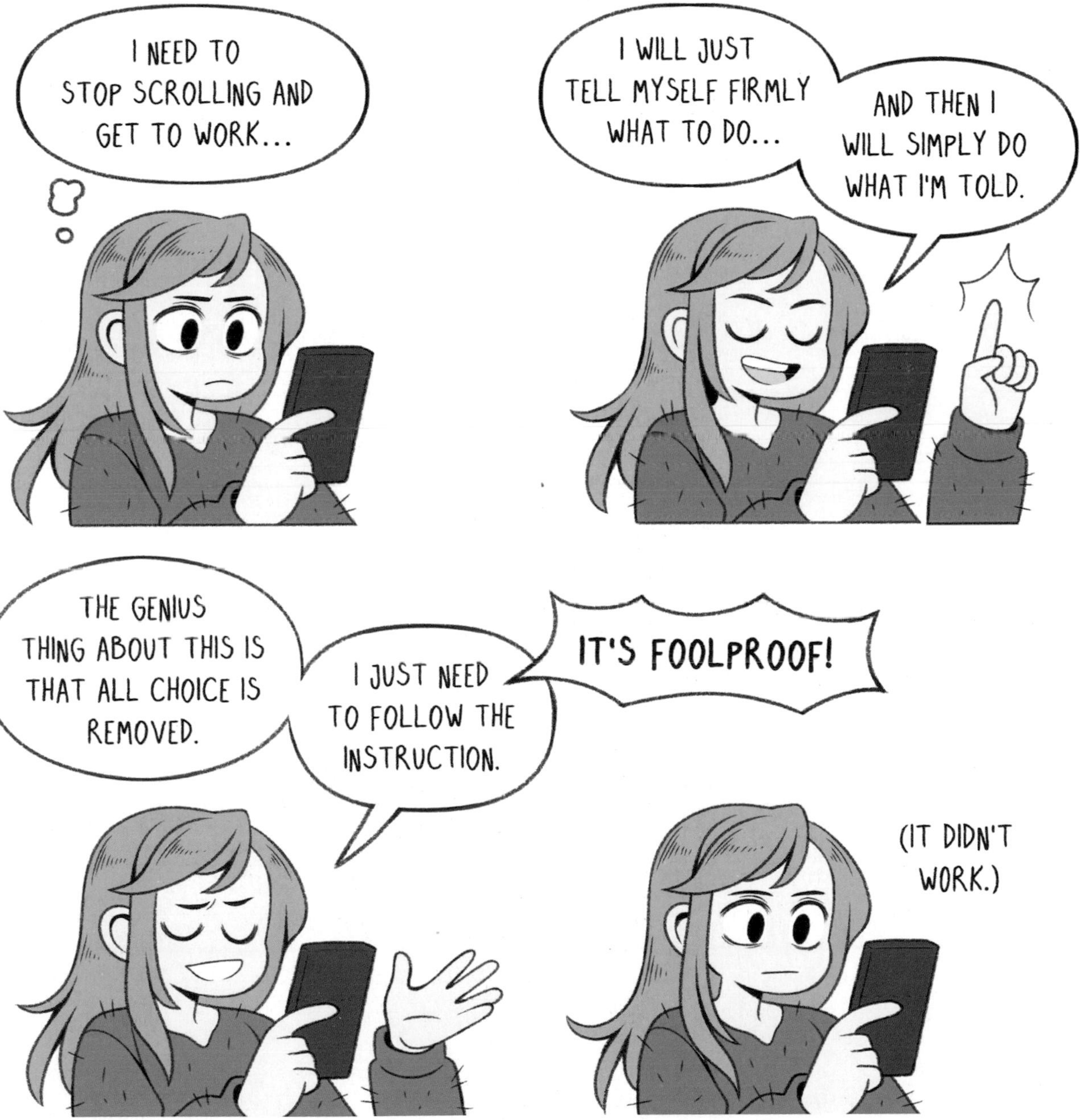
I NEED TO STOP SCROLLING AND GET TO WORK...
I WILL JUST TELL MYSELF FIRMLY WHAT TO DO...
AND THEN I WILL SIMPLY DO WHAT I'M TOLD.
THE GENIUS THING ABOUT THIS IS THAT ALL CHOICE IS REMOVED.
I JUST NEED TO FOLLOW THE INSTRUCTION.
IT'S FOOLPROOF!
(IT DIDN'T WORK.)

# REPLYING TO AN EMAIL I'VE BEEN PUTTING OFF FOR ~~WEEKS:~~ MONTHS

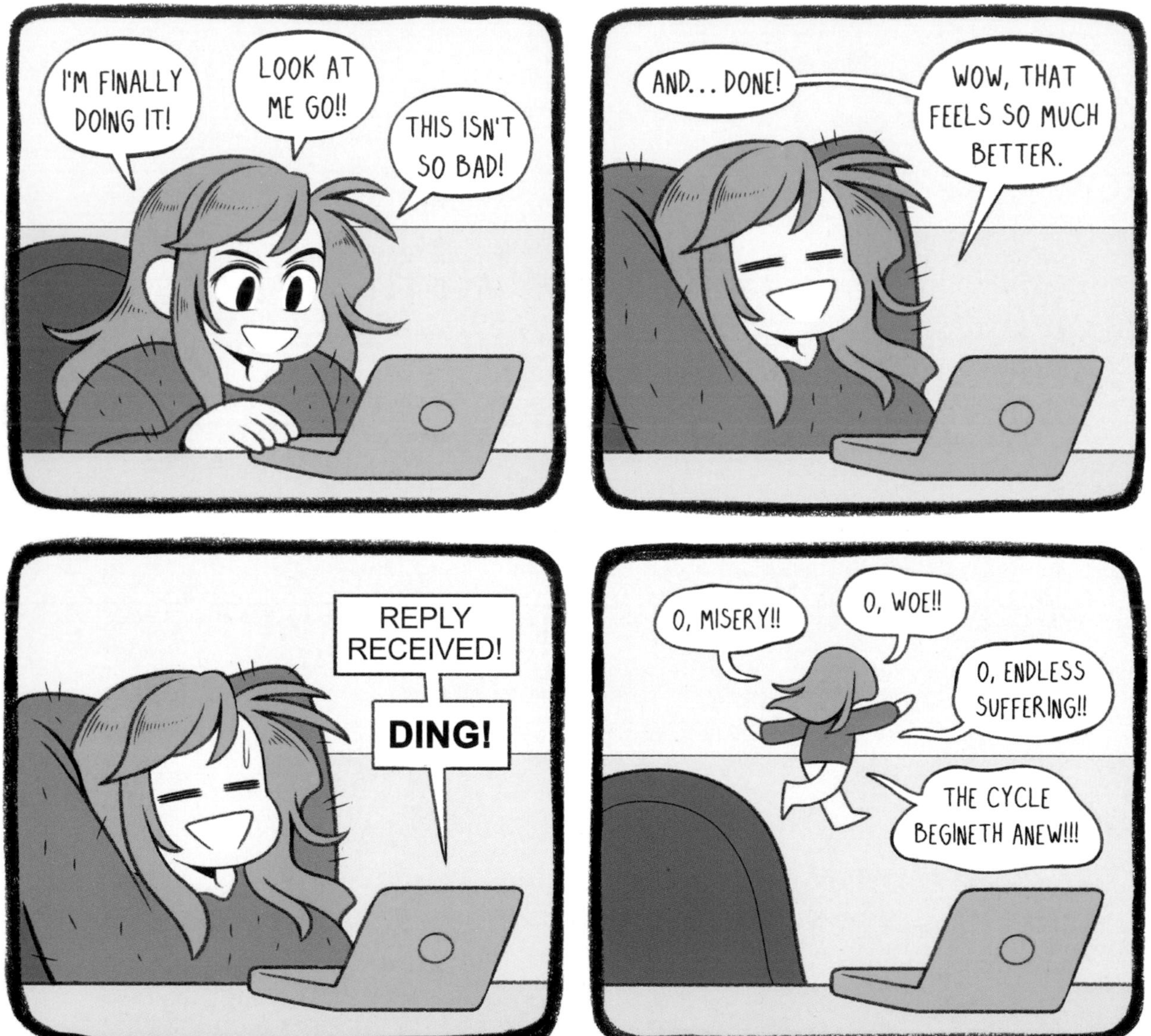
I'M FINALLY DOING IT!
LOOK AT ME GO!!
THIS ISN'T SO BAD!
AND... DONE!
WOW, THAT FEELS SO MUCH BETTER.
REPLY RECEIVED!
DING!
O, MISERY!!
O, WOE!!
O, ENDLESS SUFFERING!!
THE CYCLE BEGINETH ANEW!!!

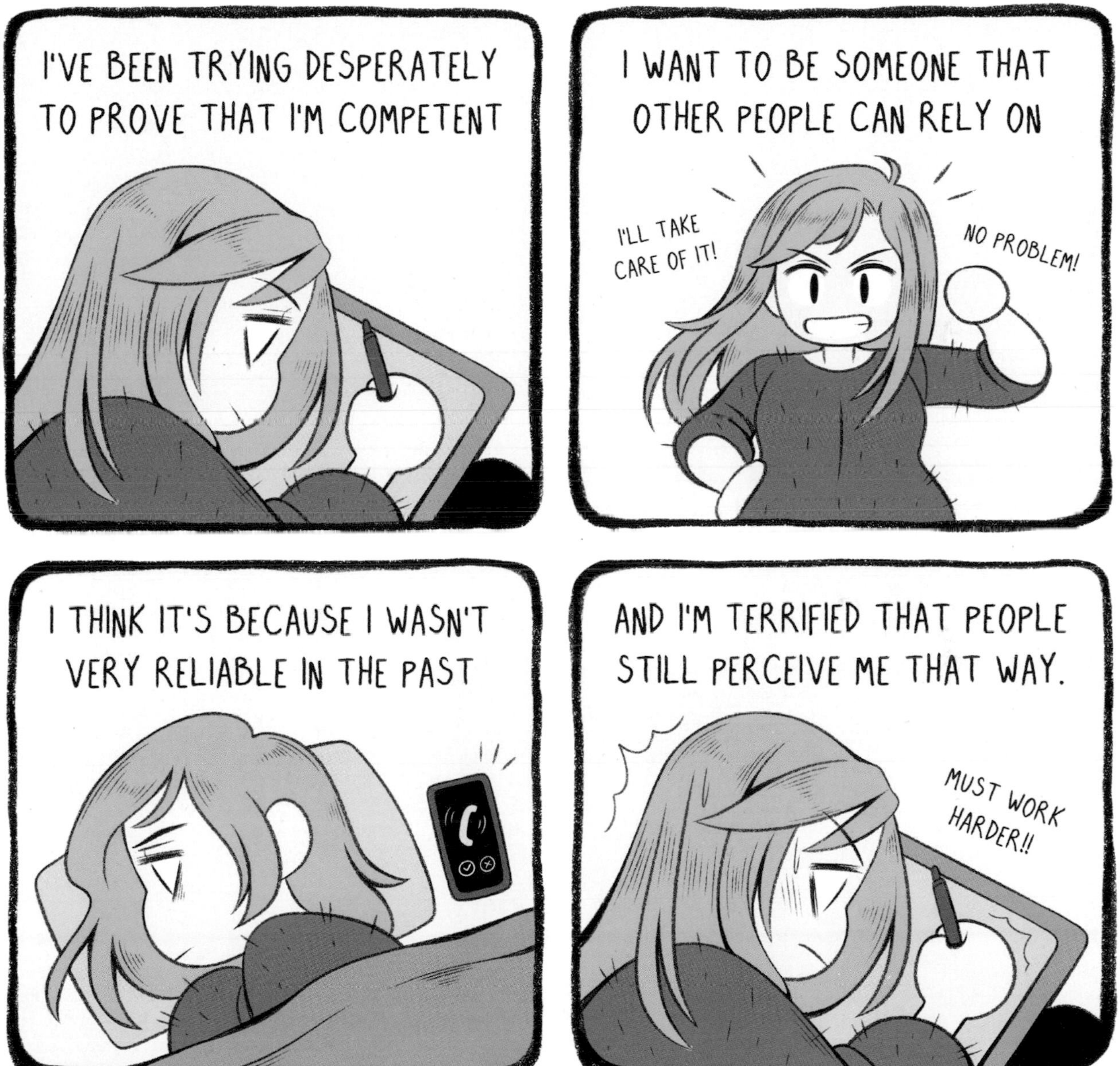
I'VE BEEN TRYING DESPERATELY TO PROVE THAT I'M COMPETENT
I WANT TO BE SOMEONE THAT OTHER PEOPLE CAN RELY ON
I'LL TAKE CARE OF IT!
NO PROBLEM!
I THINK IT'S BECAUSE I WASN'T VERY RELIABLE IN THE PAST
AND I'M TERRIFIED THAT PEOPLE STILL PERCEIVE ME THAT WAY.
MUST WORK HARDER!!

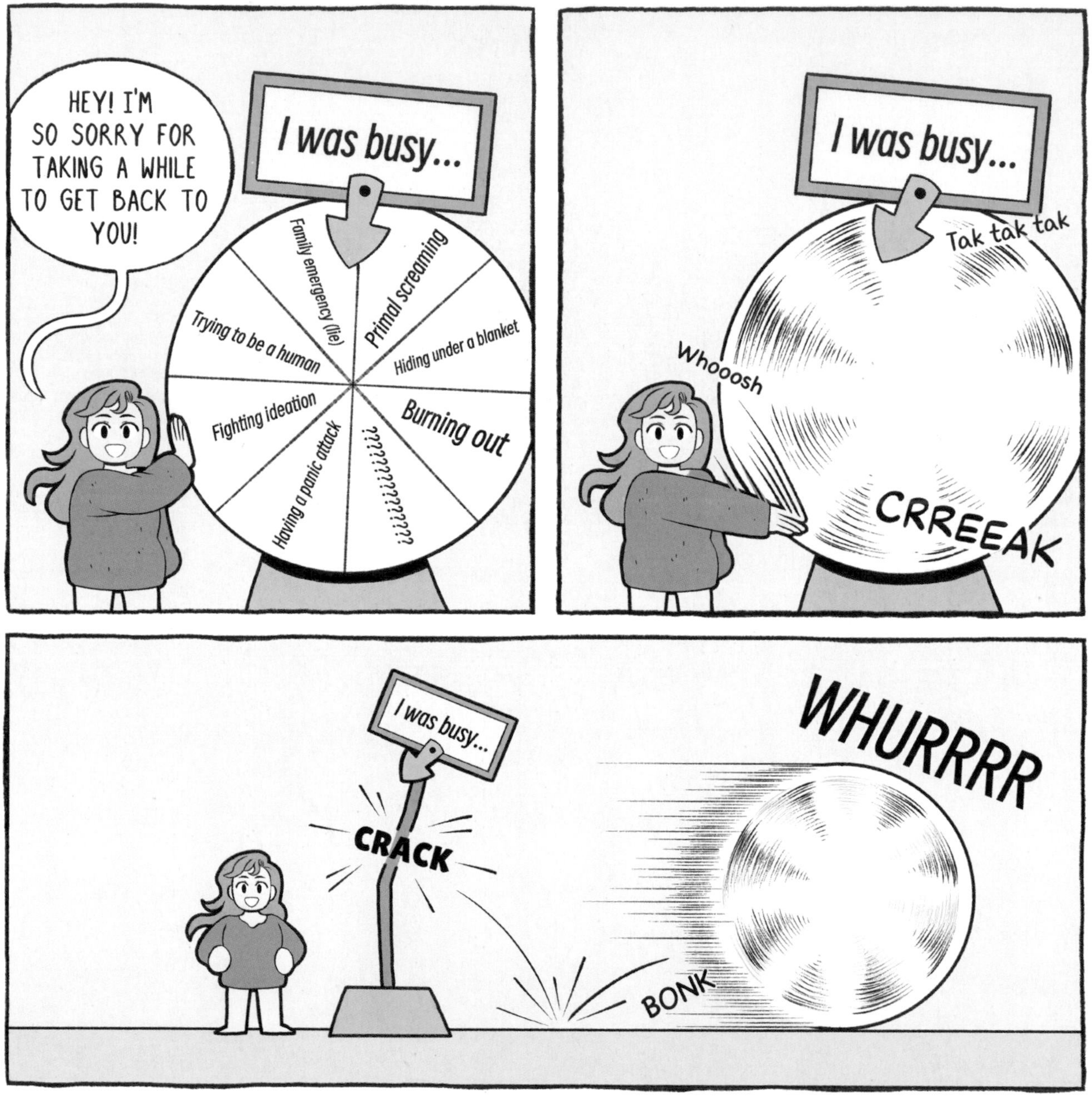
HEY! I'M SO SORRY FOR TAKING A WHILE TO GET BACK TO YOU!
I was busy...
Family emergency (lie)
Primal screaming
Hiding under a blanket
Burning out
??????????????
Having a panic attack
Fighting ideation
Trying to be a human
I was busy...
Tak tak tak
Whooosh
CRREEAK
I was busy...
WHURRRR
CRACK
BONK

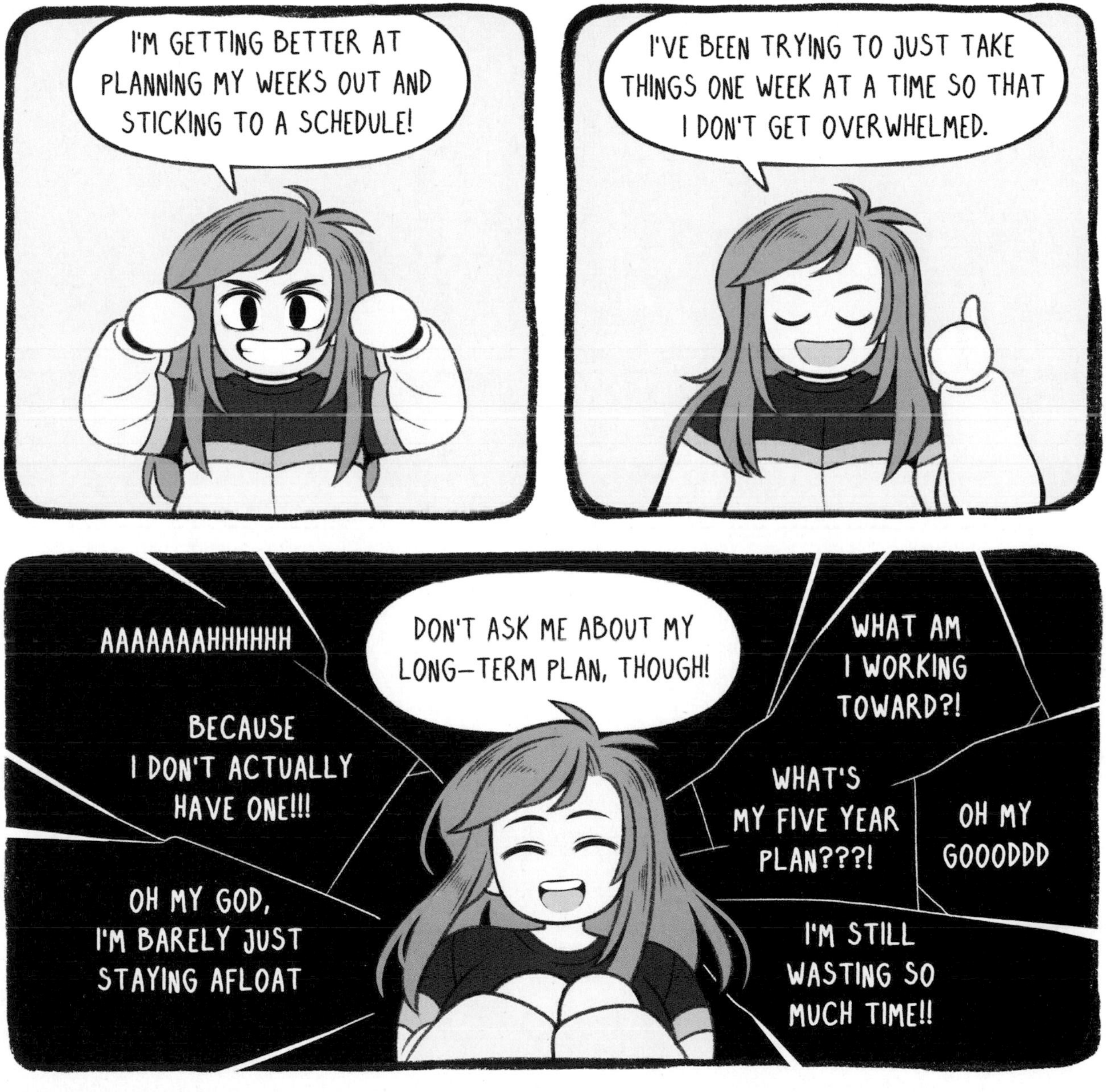
I'M GETTING BETTER AT PLANNING MY WEEKS OUT AND STICKING TO A SCHEDULE!
I'VE BEEN TRYING TO JUST TAKE THINGS ONE WEEK AT A TIME SO THAT I DON'T GET OVERWHELMED.
DON'T ASK ME ABOUT MY LONG-TERM PLAN, THOUGH!
AAAAAAAHHHHHH
BECAUSE I DON'T ACTUALLY HAVE ONE!!!
OH MY GOD, I'M BARELY JUST STAYING AFLOAT
WHAT AM I WORKING TOWARD?!
WHAT'S MY FIVE YEAR PLAN???!
OH MY GOOODDD
I'M STILL WASTING SO MUCH TIME!!

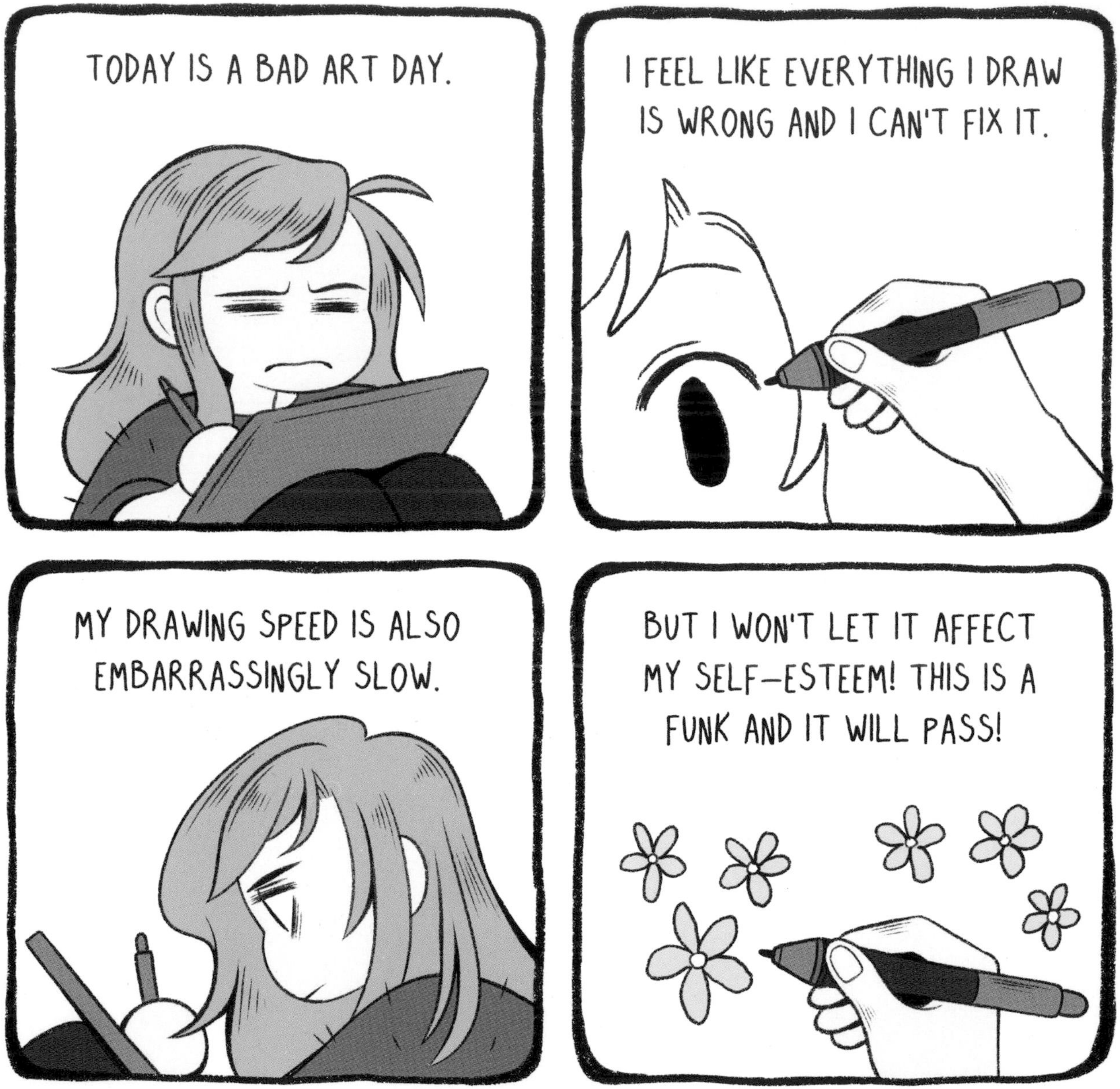
TODAY IS A BAD ART DAY.
I FEEL LIKE EVERYTHING I DRAW IS WRONG AND I CAN'T FIX IT.
MY DRAWING SPEED IS ALSO EMBARRASSINGLY SLOW.
BUT I WON'T LET IT AFFECT MY SELF-ESTEEM! THIS IS A FUNK AND IT WILL PASS!

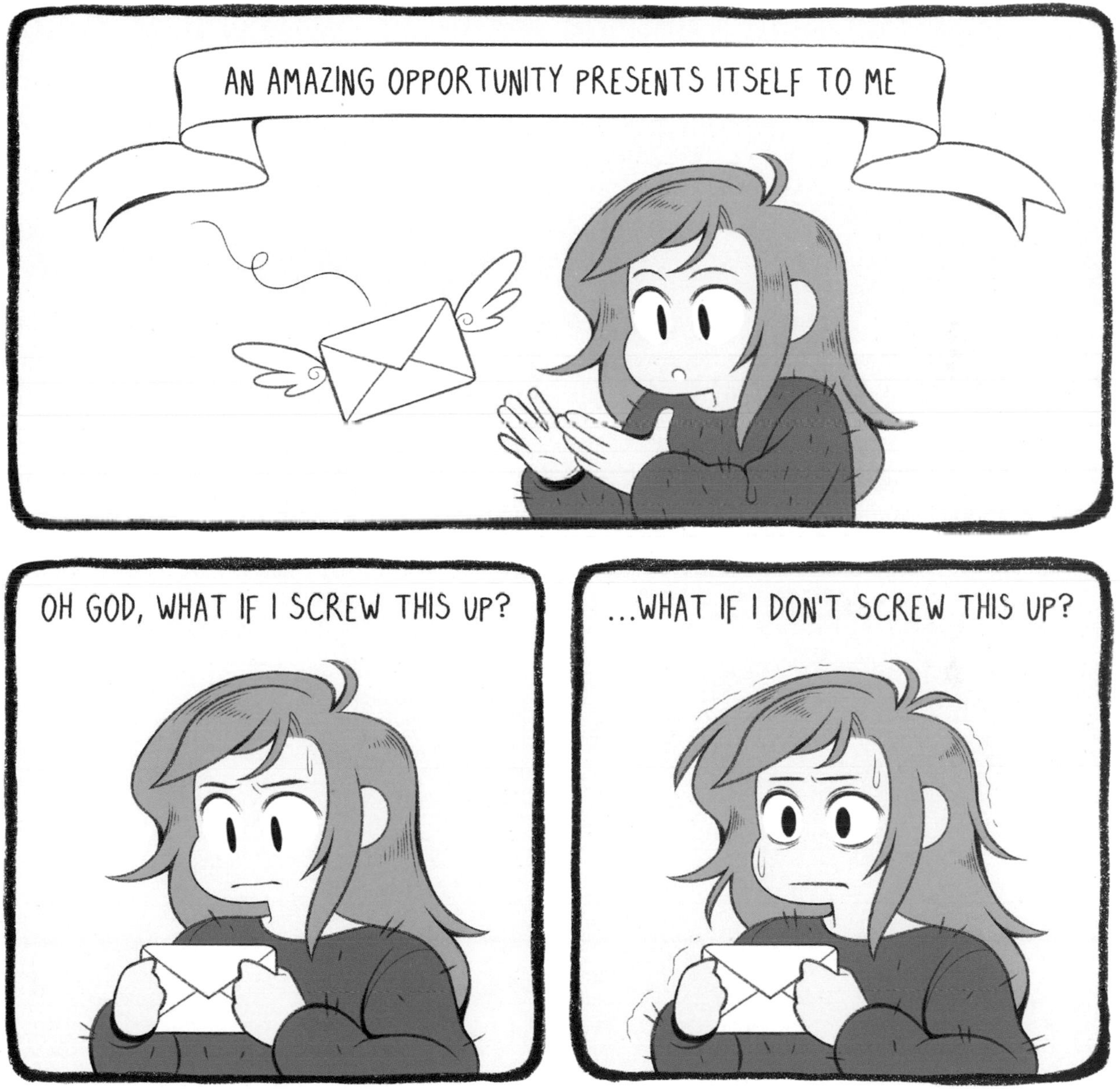
AN AMAZING OPPORTUNITY PRESENTS ITSELF TO ME
OH GOD, WHAT IF I SCREW THIS UP?
...WHAT IF I DON'T SCREW THIS UP?

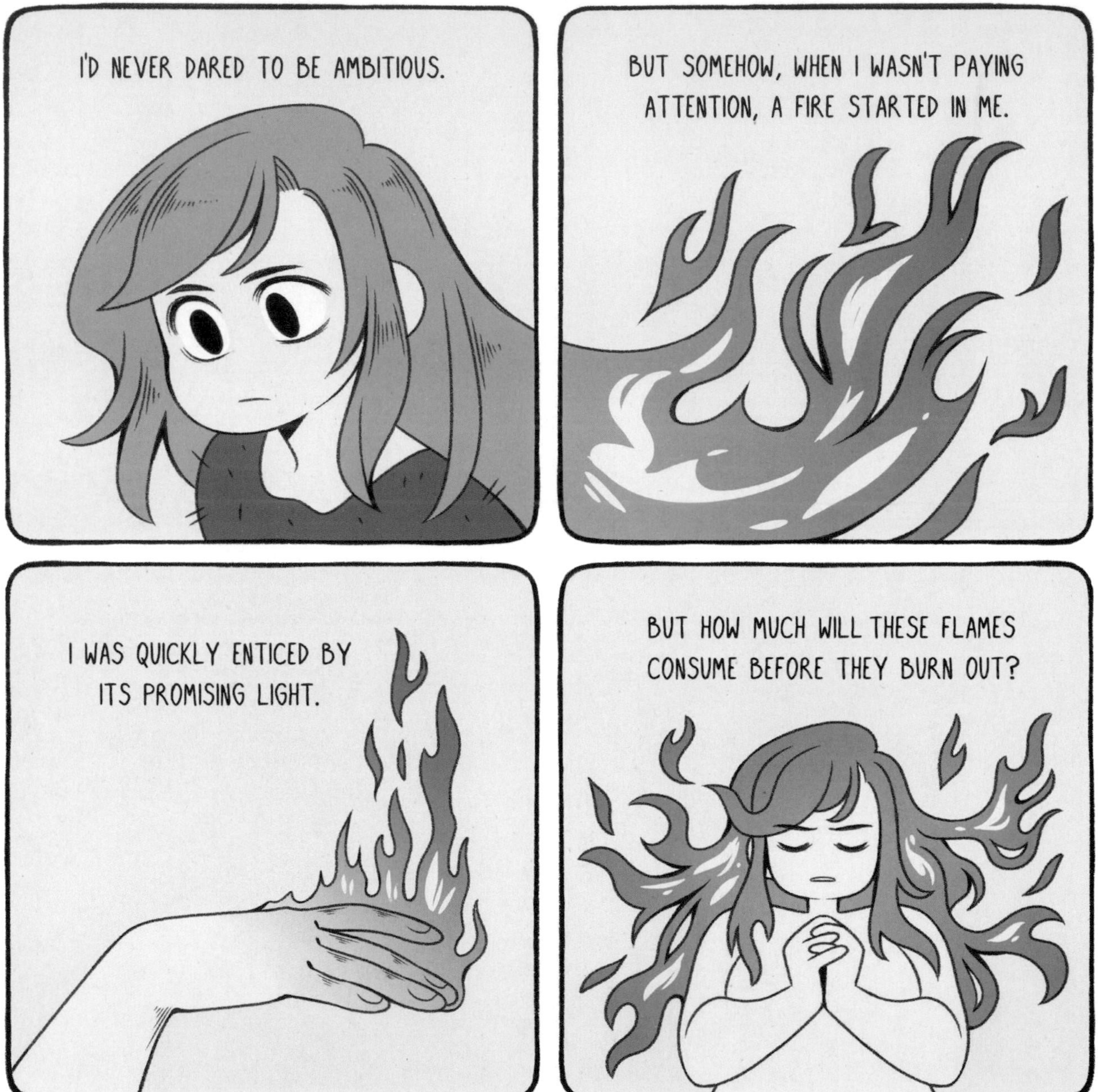
I'D NEVER DARED TO BE AMBITIOUS.
BUT SOMEHOW, WHEN I WASN'T PAYING ATTENTION, A FIRE STARTED IN ME.
I WAS QUICKLY ENTICED BY ITS PROMISING LIGHT.
BUT HOW MUCH WILL THESE FLAMES CONSUME BEFORE THEY BURN OUT?

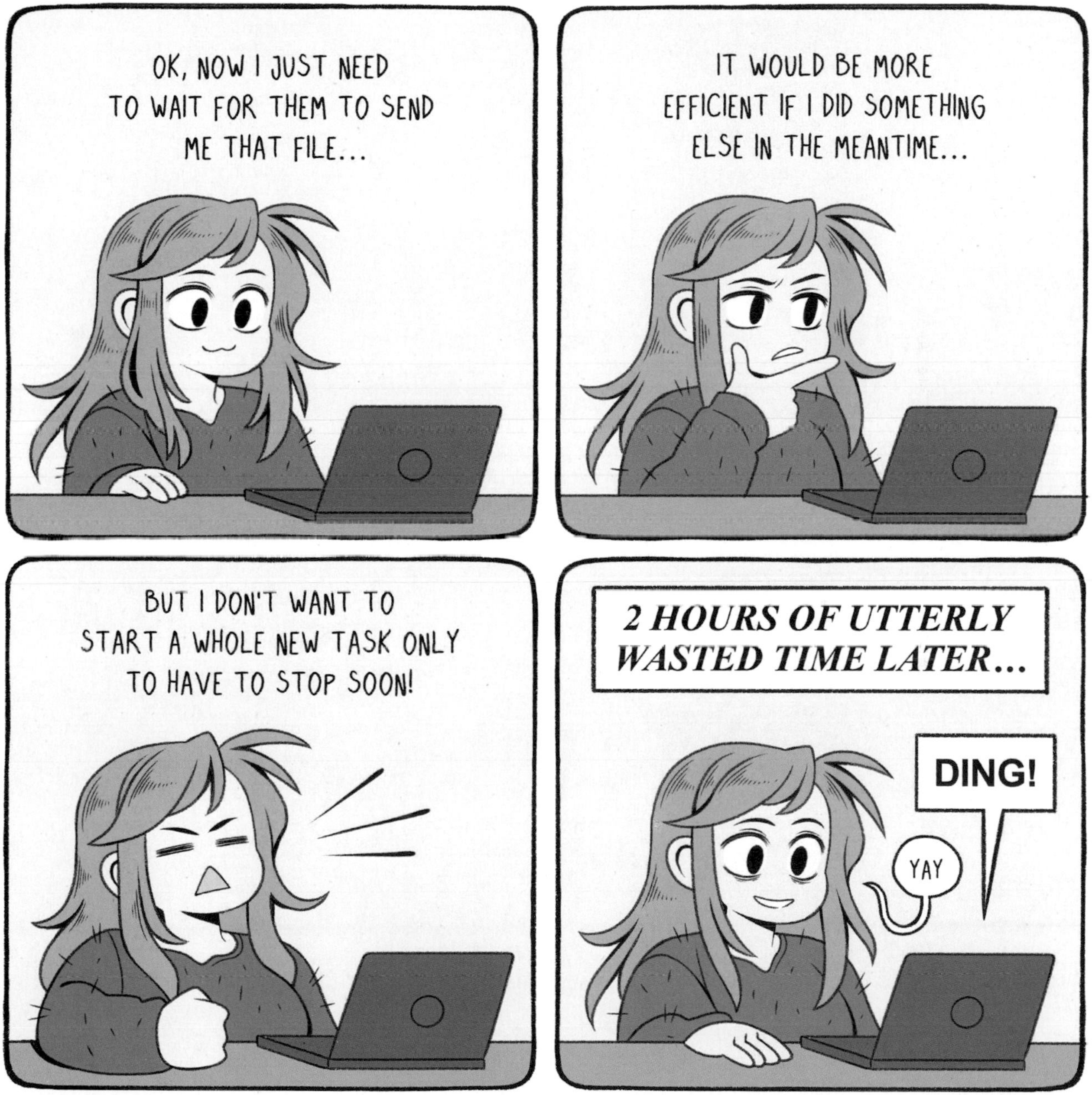
OK, NOW I JUST NEED TO WAIT FOR THEM TO SEND ME THAT FILE...
IT WOULD BE MORE EFFICIENT IF I DID SOMETHING ELSE IN THE MEANTIME...
BUT I DON'T WANT TO START A WHOLE NEW TASK ONLY TO HAVE TO STOP SOON!
2 HOURS OF UTTERLY WASTED TIME LATER...
DING!
YAY

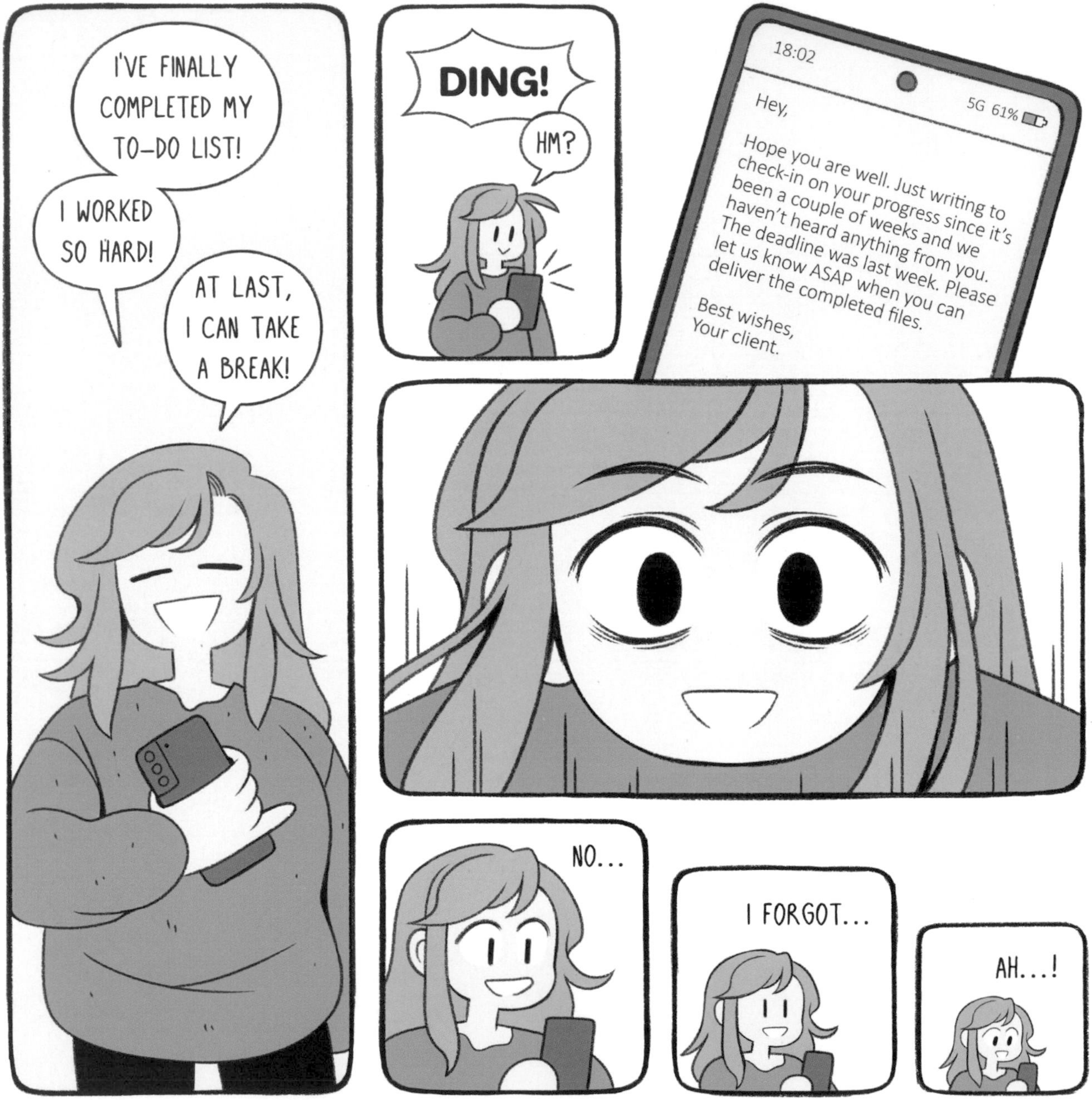
I'VE FINALLY COMPLETED MY TO-DO LIST!
I WORKED SO HARD!
AT LAST, I CAN TAKE A BREAK!
DING!
HM?
18:02
5G 61%
Hey,
Hope you are well. Just writing to check-in on your progress since it's been a couple of weeks and we haven't heard anything from you. The deadline was last week. Please let us know ASAP when you can deliver the completed files.
Best wishes,
Your client.
NO...
I FORGOT...
AH...!

I FEEL LIKE I'M ALWAYS TAKING THREE STEPS FORWARD

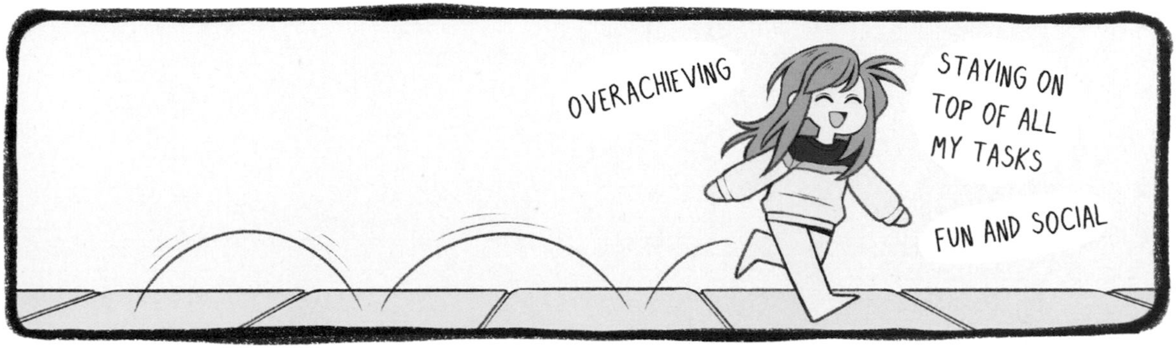
OVERACHIEVING
STAYING ON TOP OF ALL MY TASKS
FUN AND SOCIAL

...AND TWO STEPS BACK.

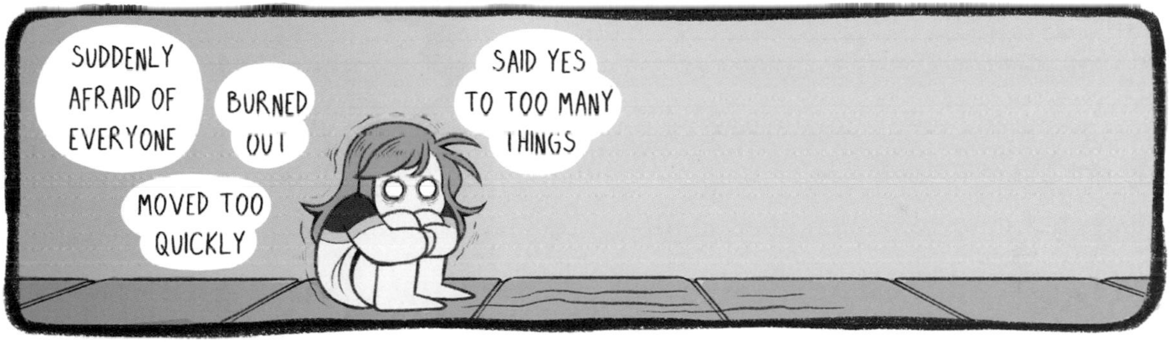
SUDDENLY AFRAID OF EVERYONE
BURNED OUT
SAID YES TO TOO MANY THINGS
MOVED TOO QUICKLY

IT'S VERY INEFFICIENT, BUT IT'S ALL I CAN DO RIGHT NOW.

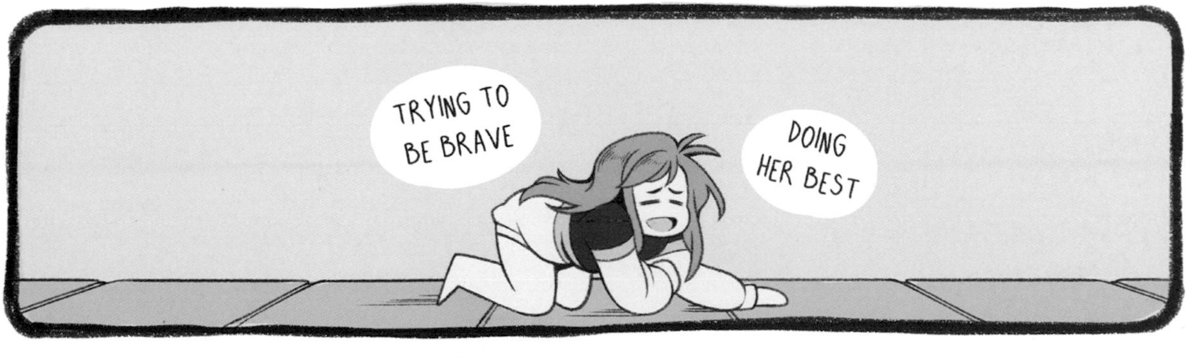
TRYING TO BE BRAVE
DOING HER BEST

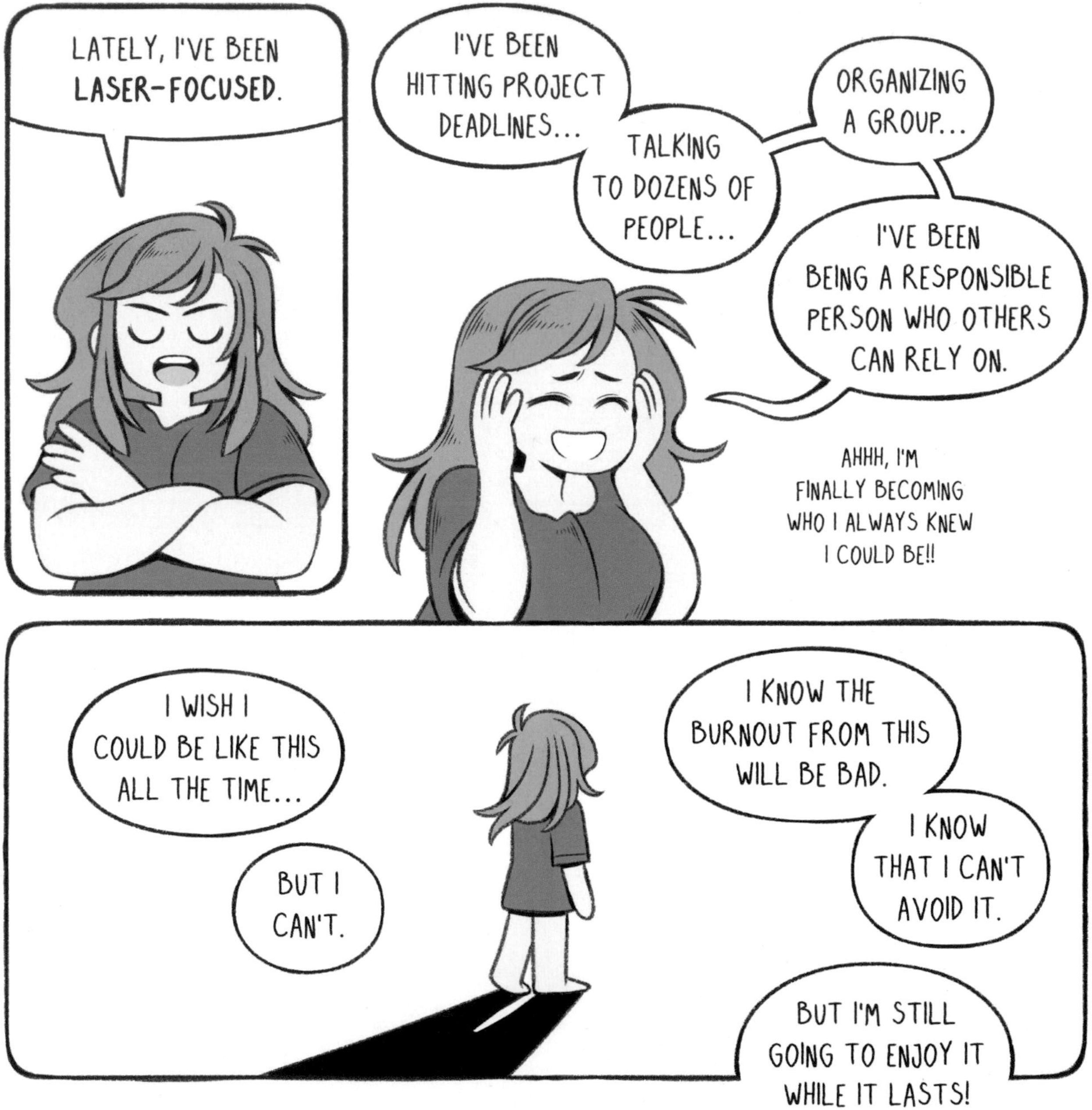

LATELY, I'VE BEEN LASER-FOCUSED.
I'VE BEEN HITTING PROJECT DEADLINES...
TALKING TO DOZENS OF PEOPLE...
ORGANIZING A GROUP...
I'VE BEEN BEING A RESPONSIBLE PERSON WHO OTHERS CAN RELY ON.
AHHH, I'M FINALLY BECOMING WHO I ALWAYS KNEW I COULD BE!!
I WISH I COULD BE LIKE THIS ALL THE TIME...
BUT I CAN'T.
I KNOW THE BURNOUT FROM THIS WILL BE BAD.
I KNOW THAT I CAN'T AVOID IT.
BUT I'M STILL GOING TO ENJOY IT WHILE IT LASTS!

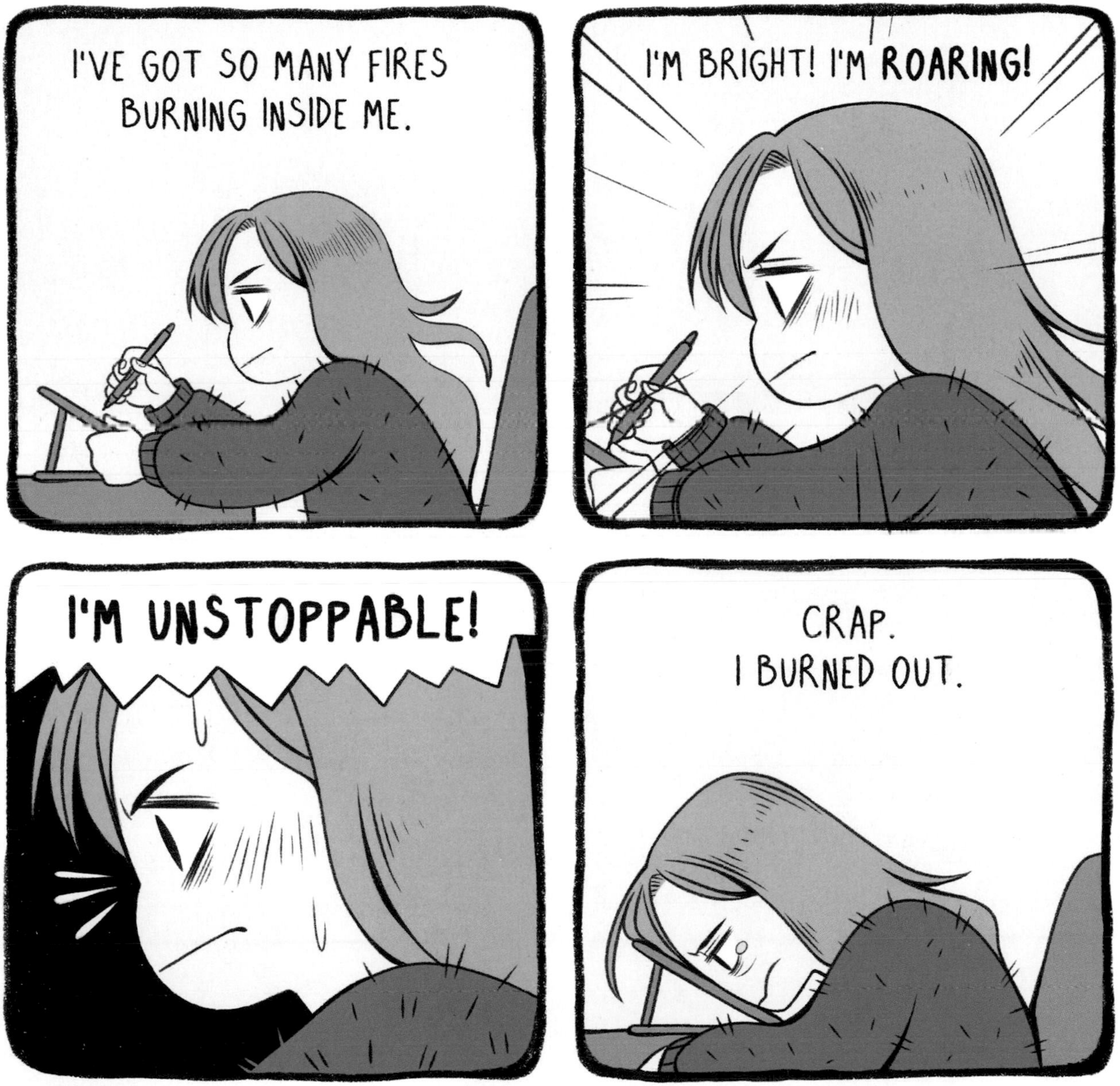
I'VE GOT SO MANY FIRES BURNING INSIDE ME.
I'M BRIGHT! I'M ROARING!
I'M UNSTOPPABLE!
CRAP.
I BURNED OUT.

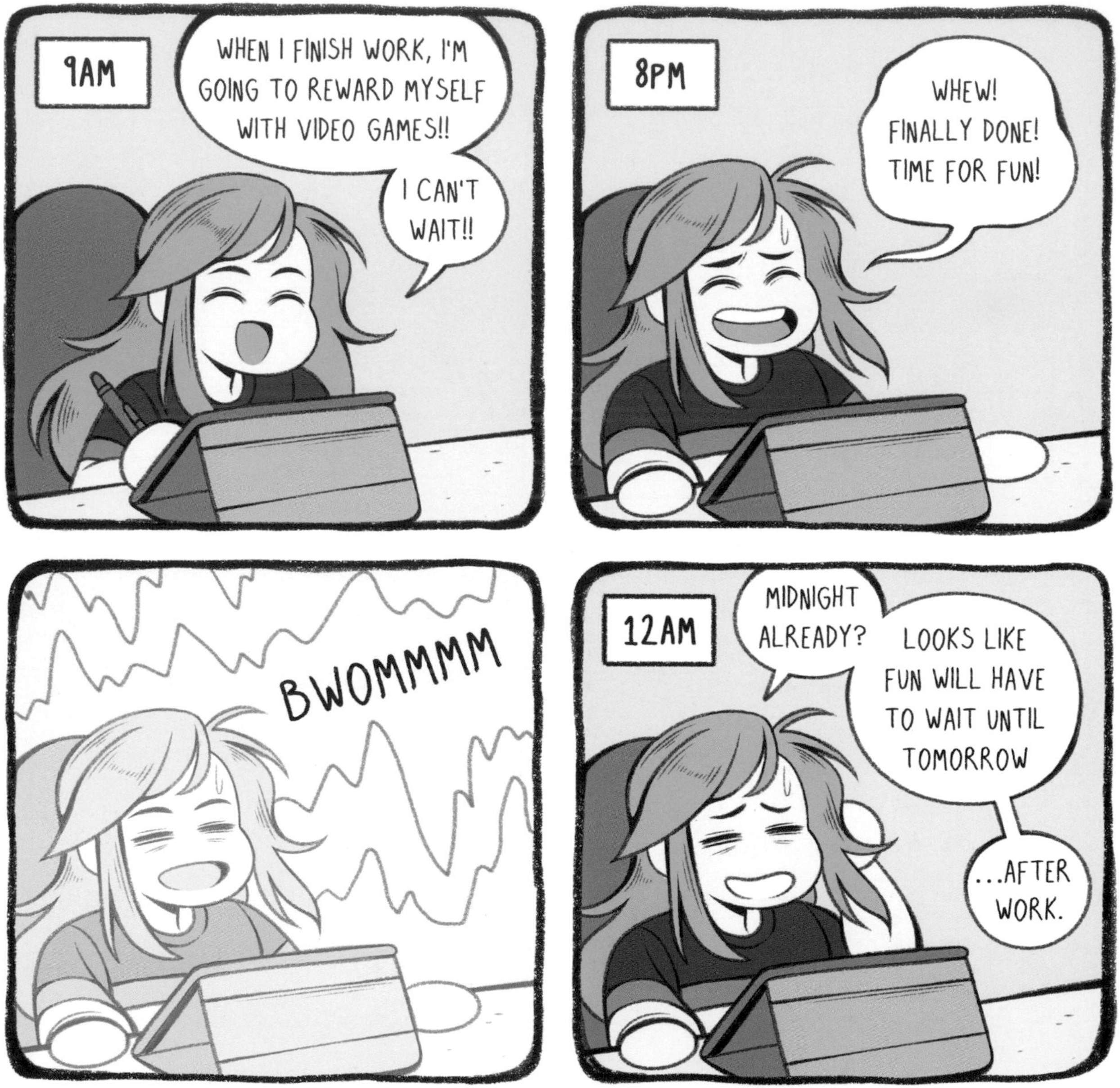
9AM
WHEN I FINISH WORK, I'M GOING TO REWARD MYSELF WITH VIDEO GAMES!!
I CAN'T WAIT!!
8PM
WHEW! FINALLY DONE! TIME FOR FUN!
BWOMMMM
12AM
MIDNIGHT ALREADY?
LOOKS LIKE FUN WILL HAVE TO WAIT UNTIL TOMORROW
...AFTER WORK.

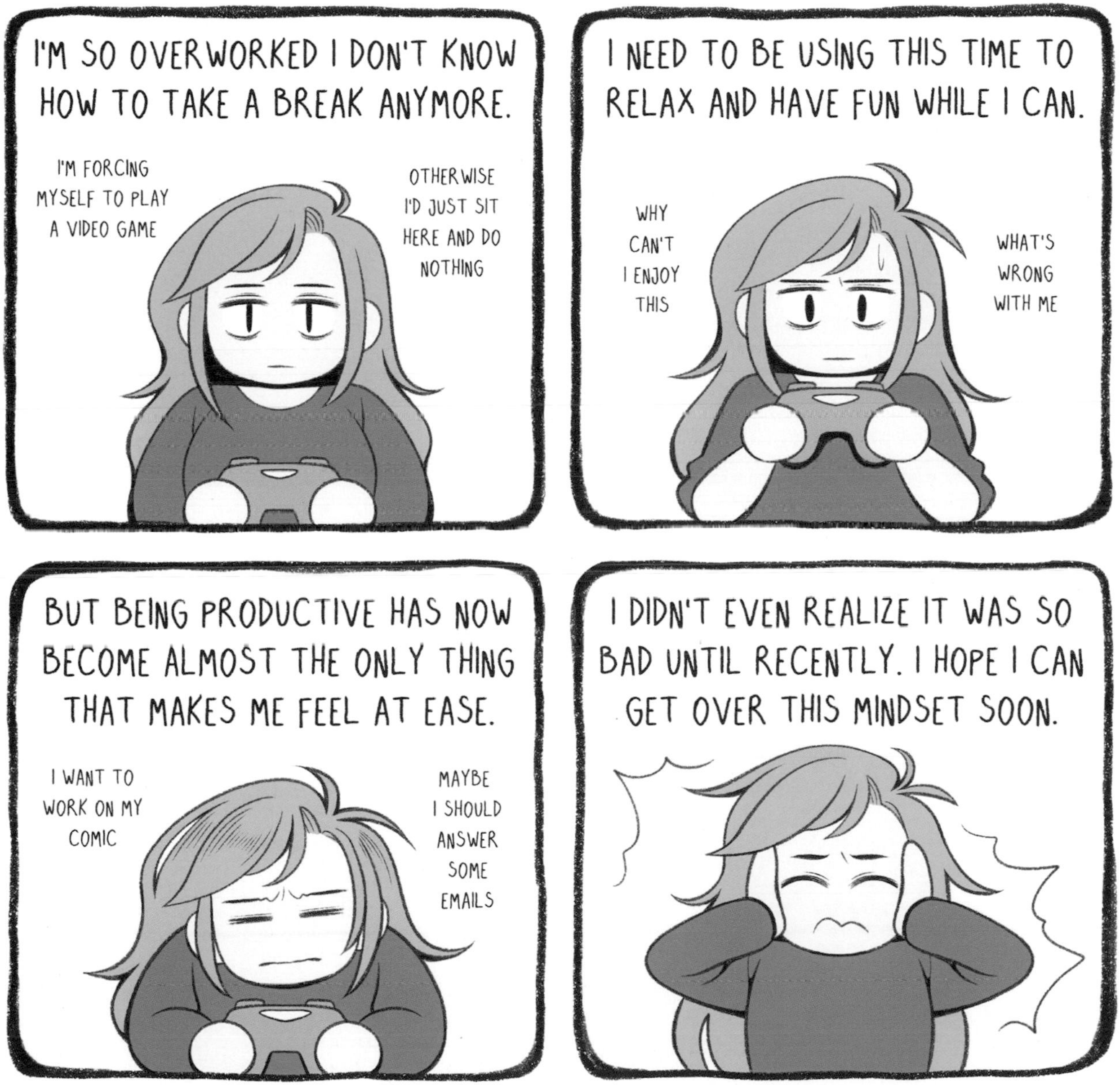

I'M SO OVERWORKED I DON'T KNOW HOW TO TAKE A BREAK ANYMORE.
I'M FORCING MYSELF TO PLAY A VIDEO GAME
OTHERWISE I'D JUST SIT HERE AND DO NOTHING
I NEED TO BE USING THIS TIME TO RELAX AND HAVE FUN WHILE I CAN.
WHY CAN'T I ENJOY THIS
WHAT'S WRONG WITH ME
BUT BEING PRODUCTIVE HAS NOW BECOME ALMOST THE ONLY THING THAT MAKES ME FEEL AT EASE.
I WANT TO WORK ON MY COMIC
MAYBE I SHOULD ANSWER SOME EMAILS
I DIDN'T EVEN REALIZE IT WAS SO BAD UNTIL RECENTLY. I HOPE I CAN GET OVER THIS MINDSET SOON.

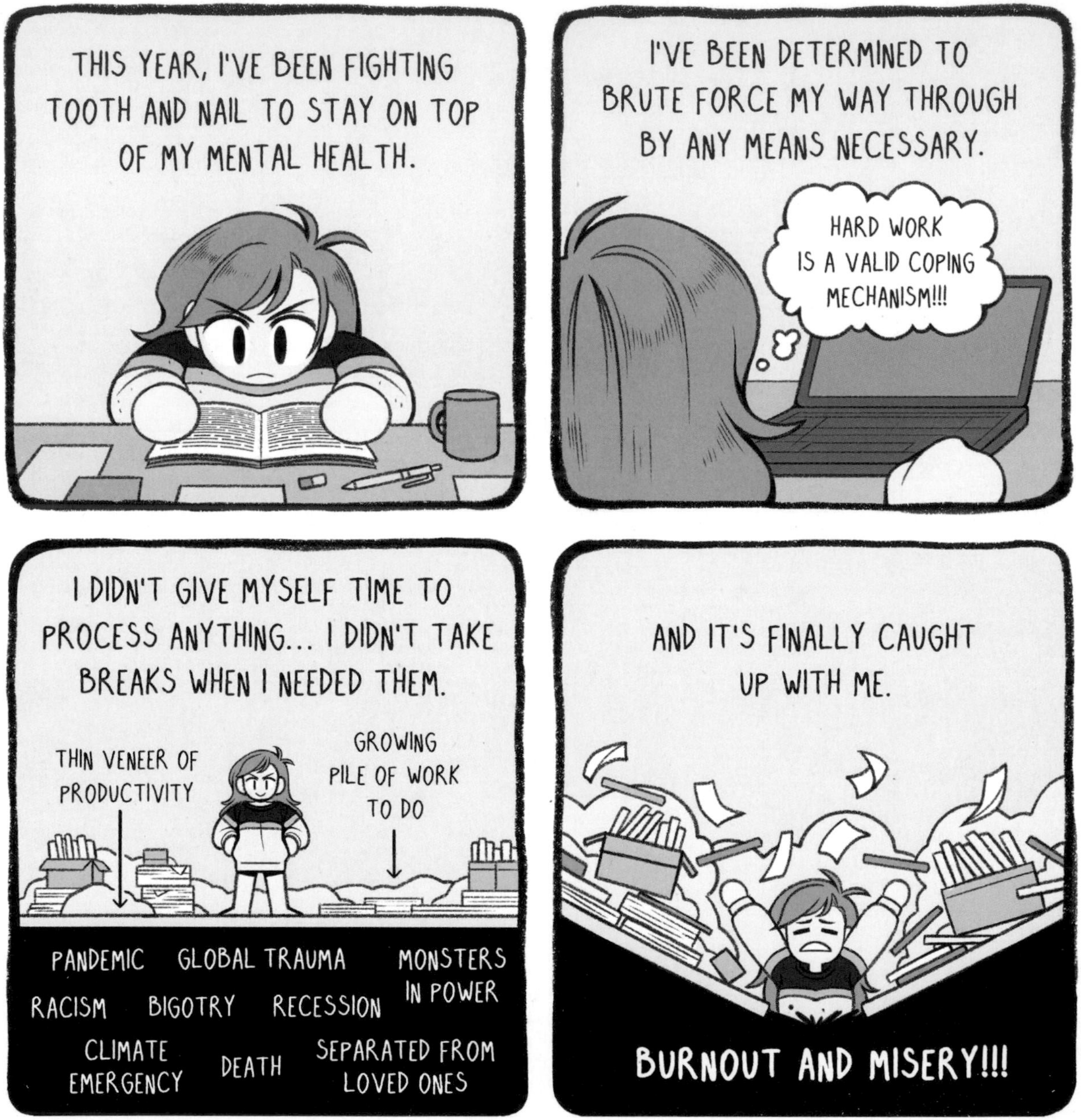
THIS YEAR, I'VE BEEN FIGHTING TOOTH AND NAIL TO STAY ON TOP OF MY MENTAL HEALTH.
I'VE BEEN DETERMINED TO BRUTE FORCE MY WAY THROUGH BY ANY MEANS NECESSARY.
HARD WORK IS A VALID COPING MECHANISM!!!
I DIDN'T GIVE MYSELF TIME TO PROCESS ANYTHING... I DIDN'T TAKE BREAKS WHEN I NEEDED THEM.
THIN VENEER OF PRODUCTIVITY
GROWING PILE OF WORK TO DO
PANDEMIC
GLOBAL TRAUMA
MONSTERS IN POWER
RACISM
BIGOTRY
RECESSION
CLIMATE EMERGENCY
DEATH
SEPARATED FROM LOVED ONES
AND IT'S FINALLY CAUGHT UP WITH ME.
BURNOUT AND MISERY!!!

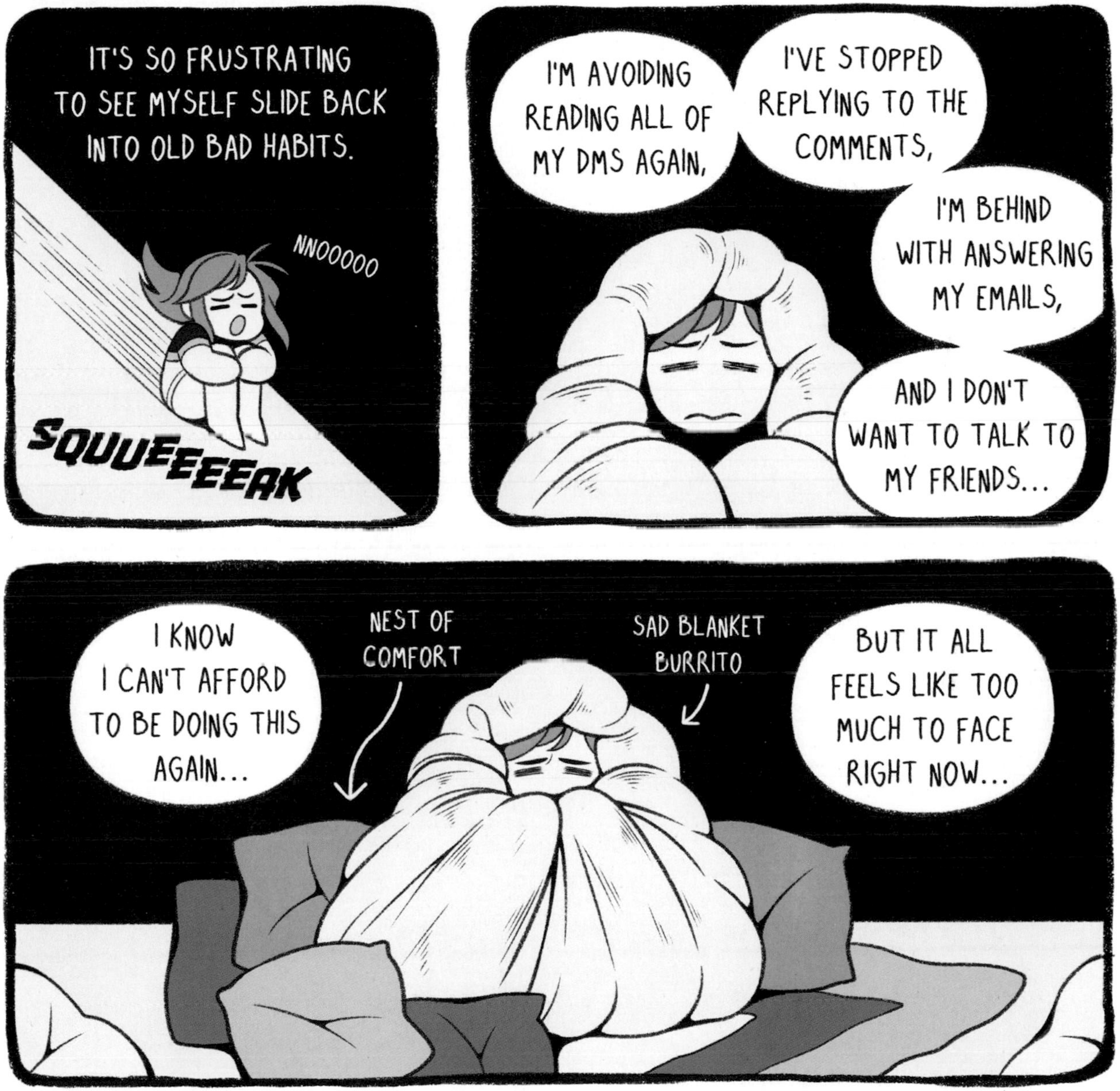
IT'S SO FRUSTRATING TO SEE MYSELF SLIDE BACK INTO OLD BAD HABITS.
NNOOOOO
SQUUEEEEEAK
I'M AVOIDING READING ALL OF MY DMS AGAIN,
I'VE STOPPED REPLYING TO THE COMMENTS,
I'M BEHIND WITH ANSWERING MY EMAILS,
AND I DON'T WANT TO TALK TO MY FRIENDS...
I KNOW I CAN'T AFFORD TO BE DOING THIS AGAIN...
NEST OF COMFORT
SAD BLANKET BURRITO
BUT IT ALL FEELS LIKE TOO MUCH TO FACE RIGHT NOW...

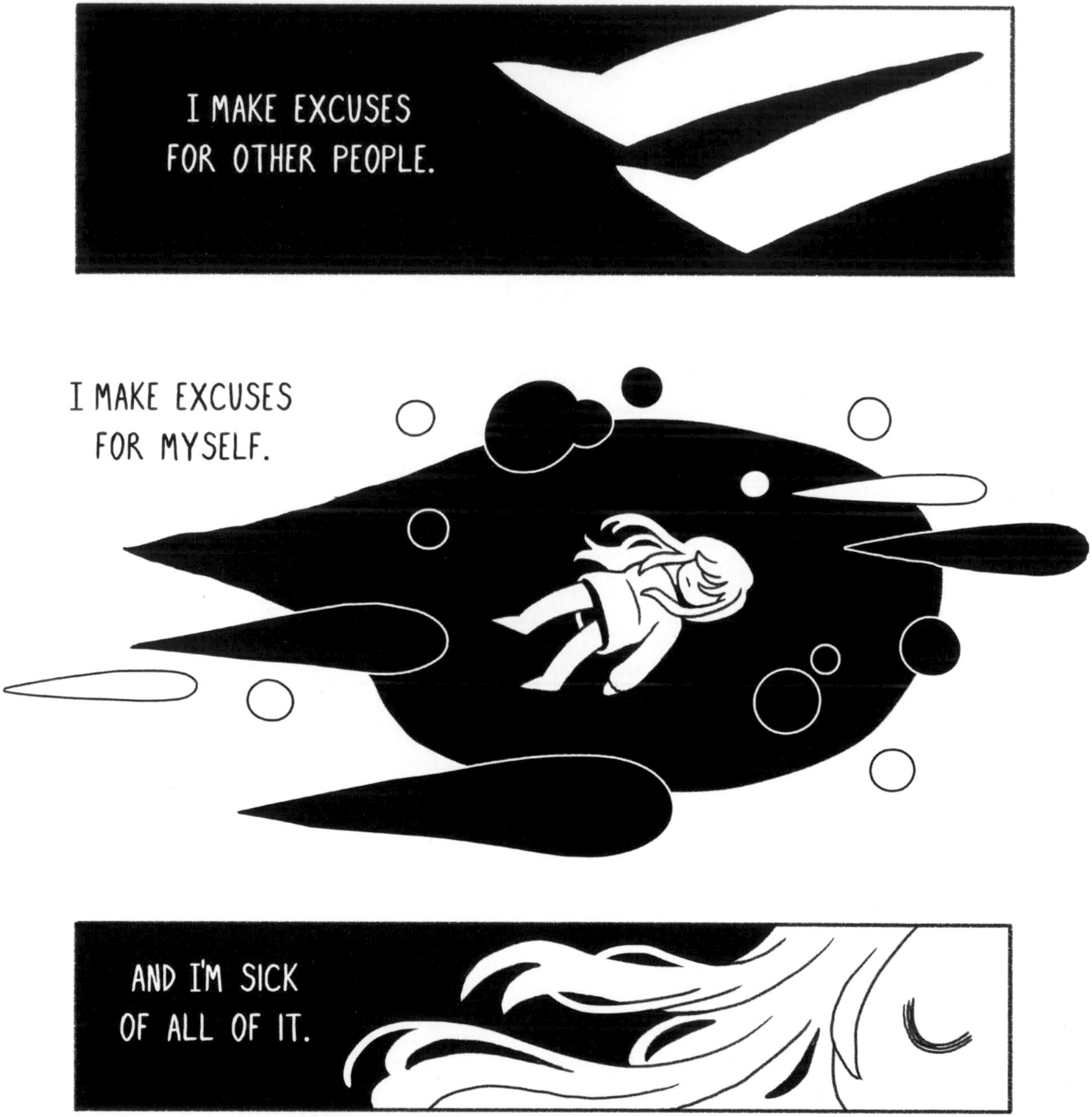
I MAKE EXCUSES
FOR OTHER PEOPLE.
I MAKE EXCUSES
FOR MYSELF.
AND I'M SICK
OF ALL OF IT.

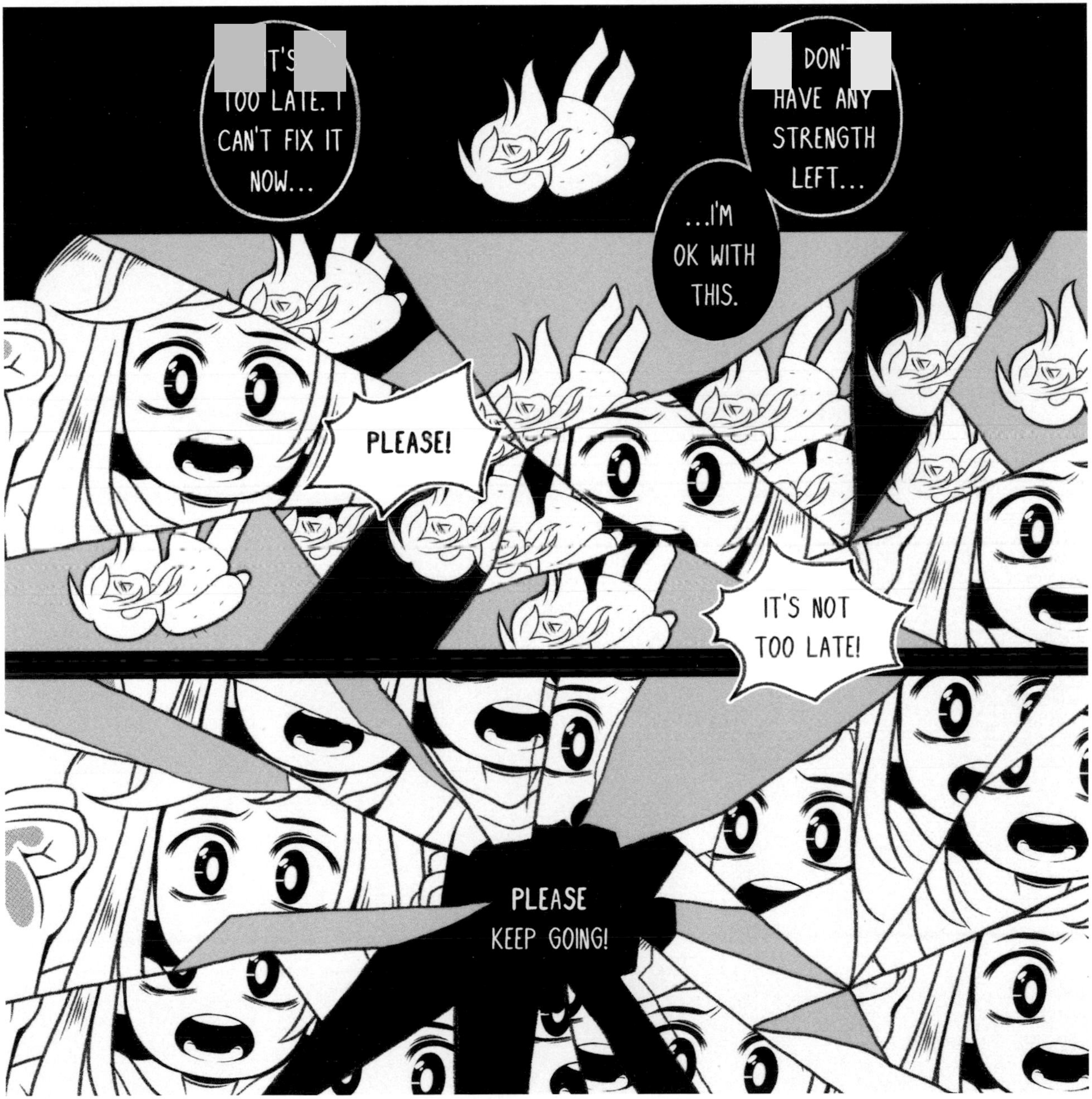
IT'S TOO LATE. I CAN'T FIX IT NOW...
DON'T HAVE ANY STRENGTH LEFT...
...I'M OK WITH THIS.
PLEASE!
IT'S NOT TOO LATE!
PLEASE KEEP GOING!

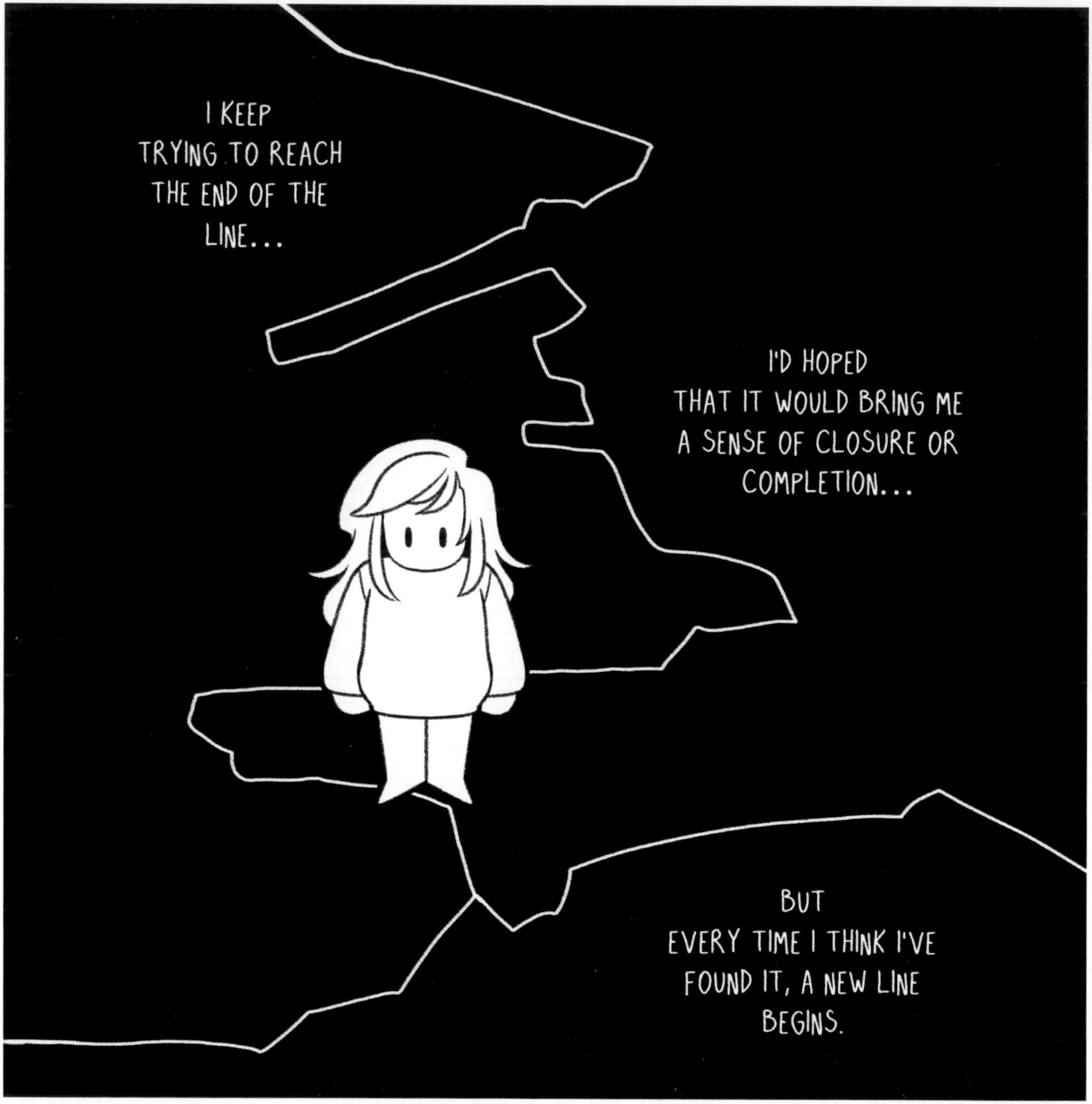
I KEEP TRYING TO REACH THE END OF THE LINE...
I'D HOPED THAT IT WOULD BRING ME A SENSE OF CLOSURE OR COMPLETION...
BUT EVERY TIME I THINK I'VE FOUND IT, A NEW LINE BEGINS.

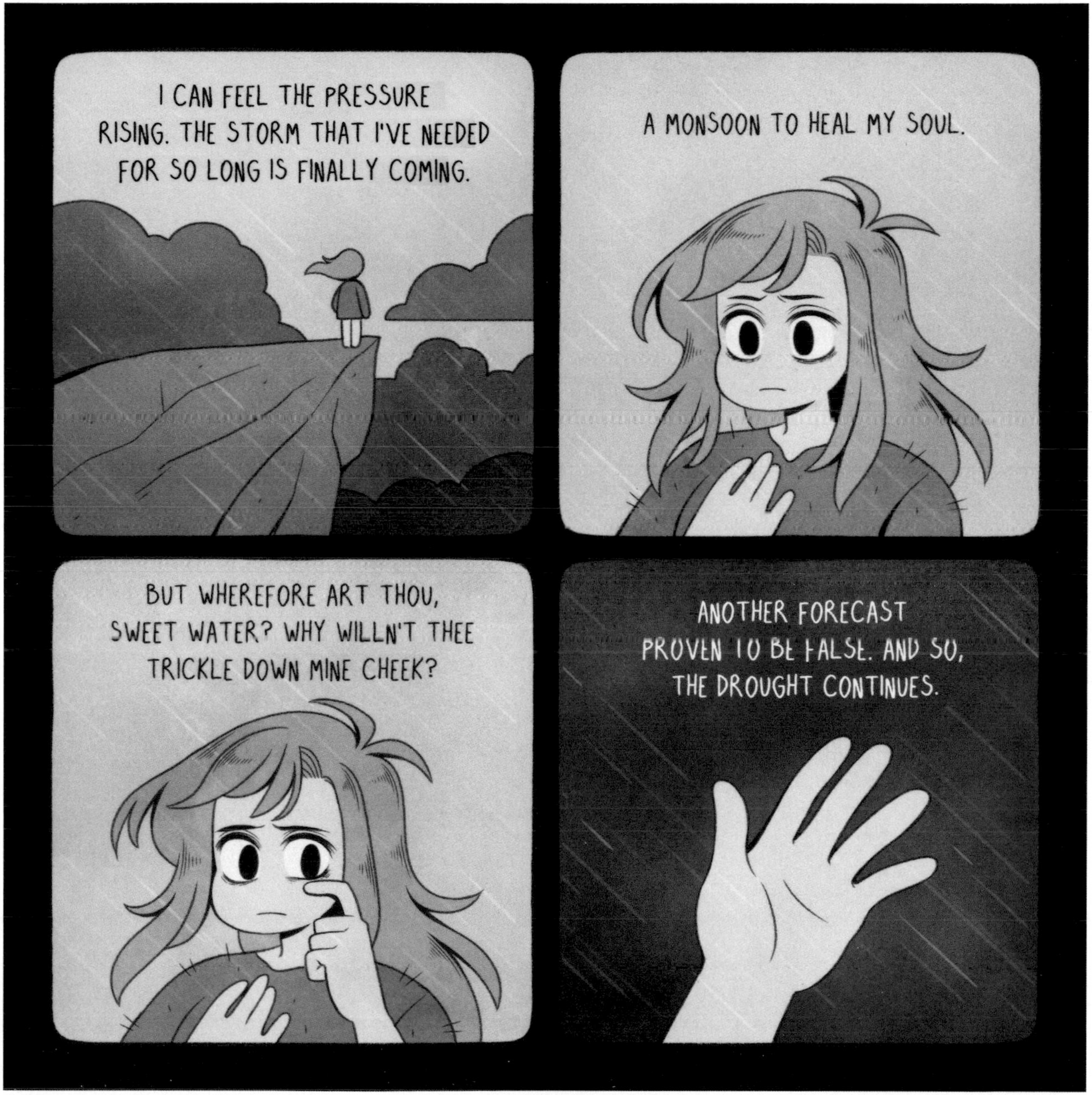
I CAN FEEL THE PRESSURE RISING. THE STORM THAT I'VE NEEDED FOR SO LONG IS FINALLY COMING.
A MONSOON TO HEAL MY SOUL.
BUT WHEREFORE ART THOU, SWEET WATER? WHY WILLN'T THEE TRICKLE DOWN MINE CHEEK?
ANOTHER FORECAST PROVEN TO BE FALSE. AND SO, THE DROUGHT CONTINUES.

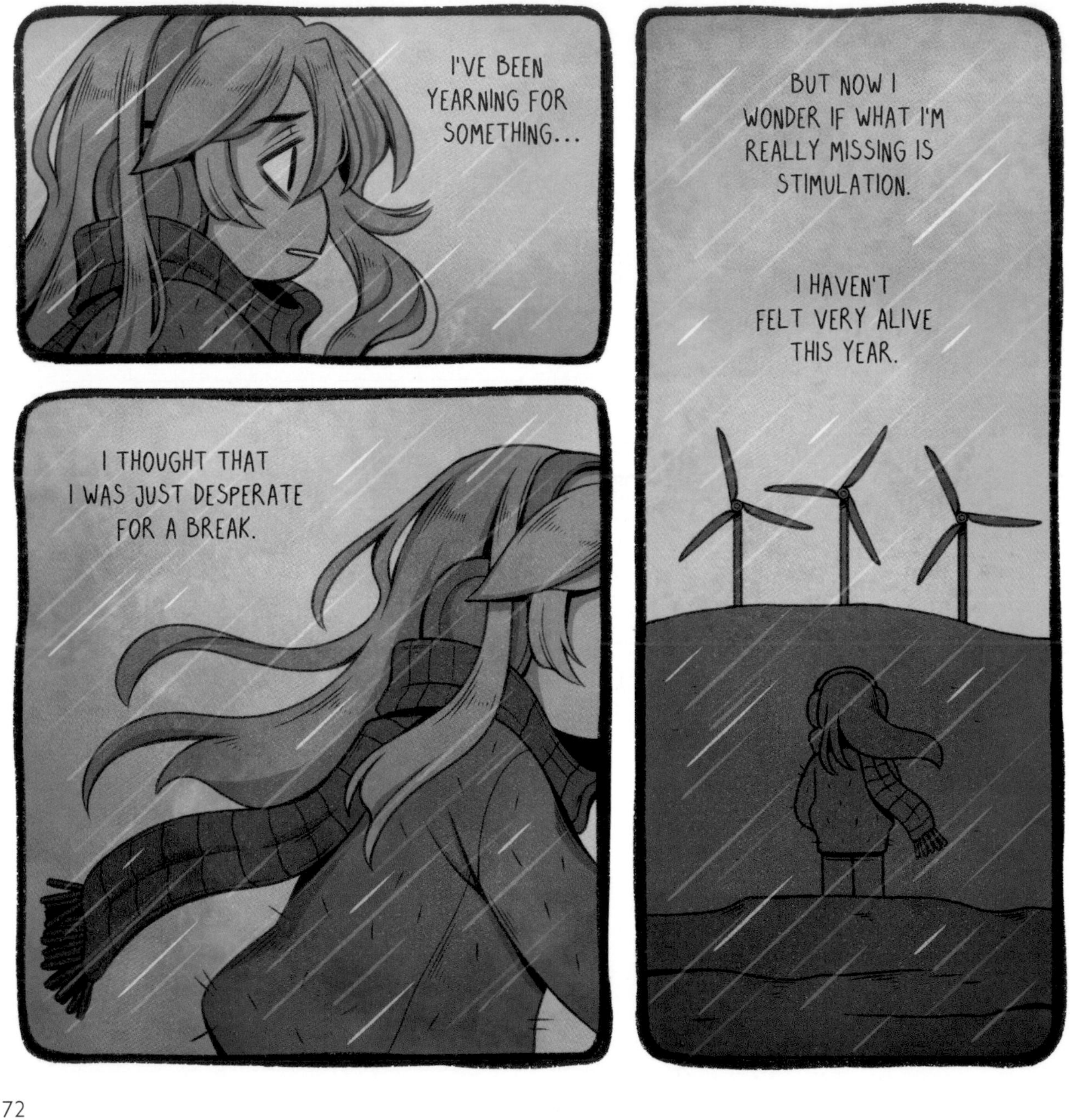
I'VE BEEN YEARNING FOR SOMETHING...
I THOUGHT THAT I WAS JUST DESPERATE FOR A BREAK.
BUT NOW I WONDER IF WHAT I'M REALLY MISSING IS STIMULATION.
I HAVEN'T FELT VERY ALIVE THIS YEAR.

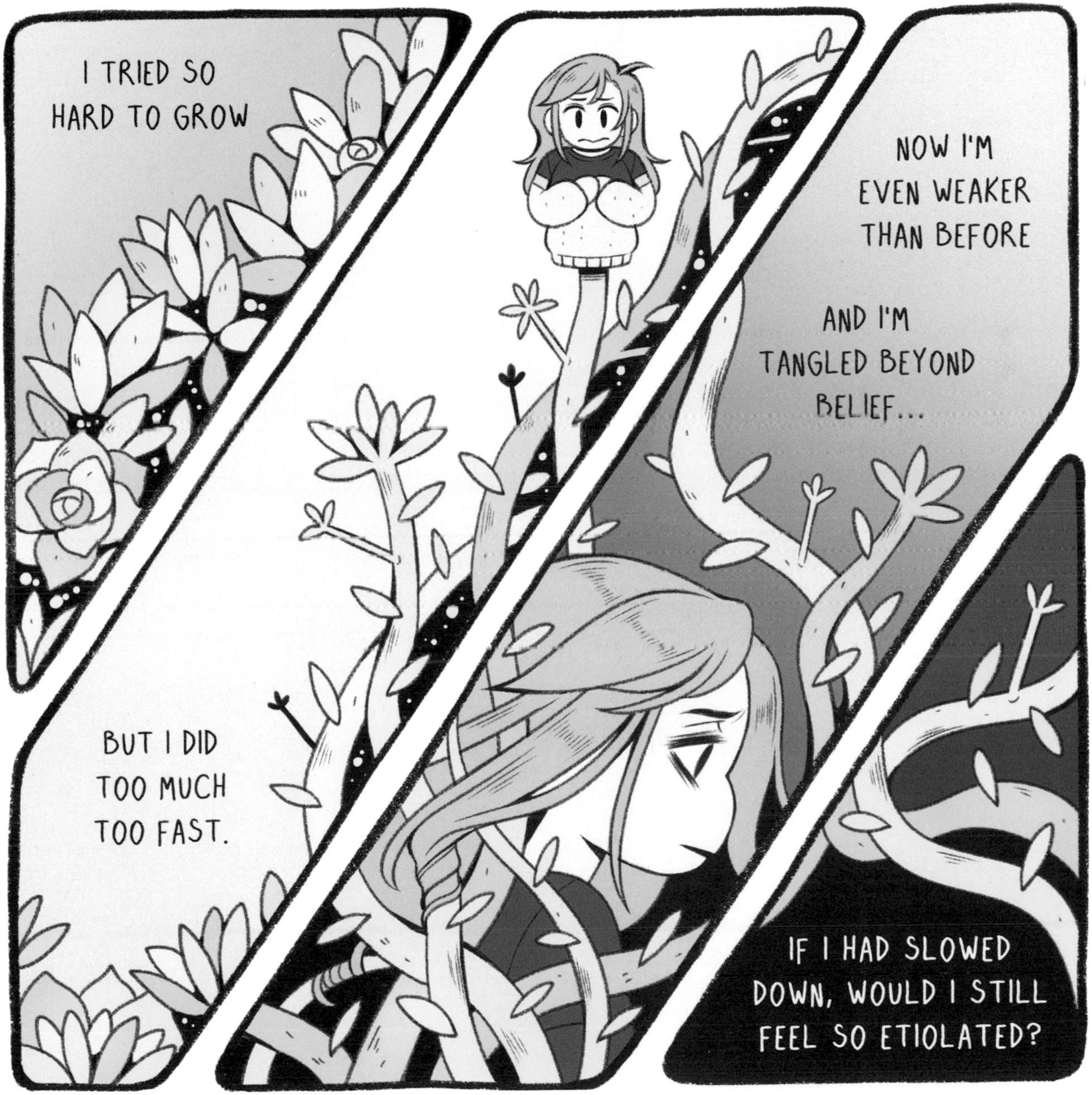
I TRIED SO HARD TO GROW
BUT I DID TOO MUCH TOO FAST.
NOW I'M EVEN WEAKER THAN BEFORE
AND I'M TANGLED BEYOND BELIEF...
IF I HAD SLOWED DOWN, WOULD I STILL FEEL SO ETIOLATED?

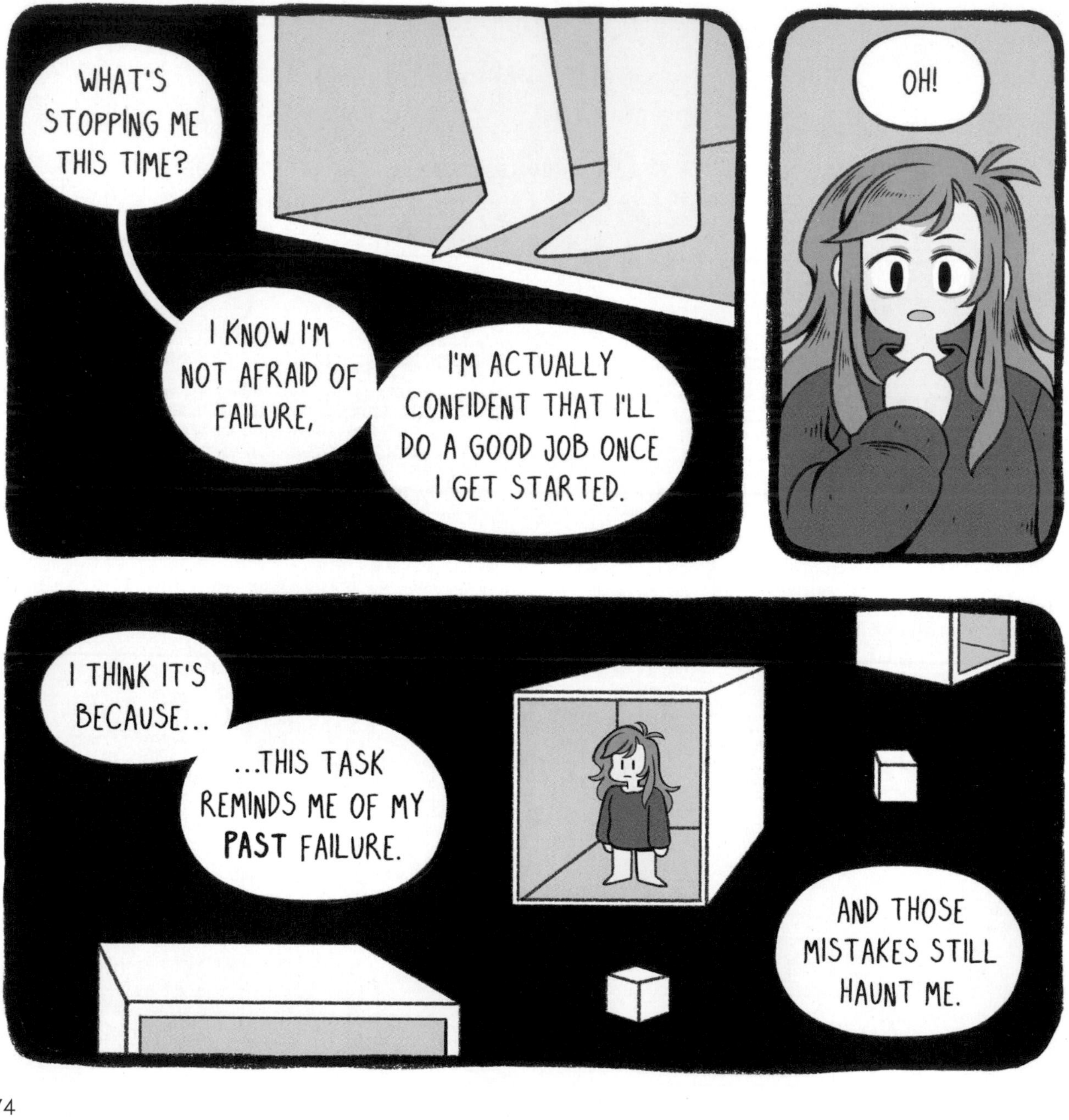
WHAT'S STOPPING ME THIS TIME?
I KNOW I'M NOT AFRAID OF FAILURE,
I'M ACTUALLY CONFIDENT THAT I'LL DO A GOOD JOB ONCE I GET STARTED.
OH!
I THINK IT'S BECAUSE...
...THIS TASK REMINDS ME OF MY PAST FAILURE.
AND THOSE MISTAKES STILL HAUNT ME.

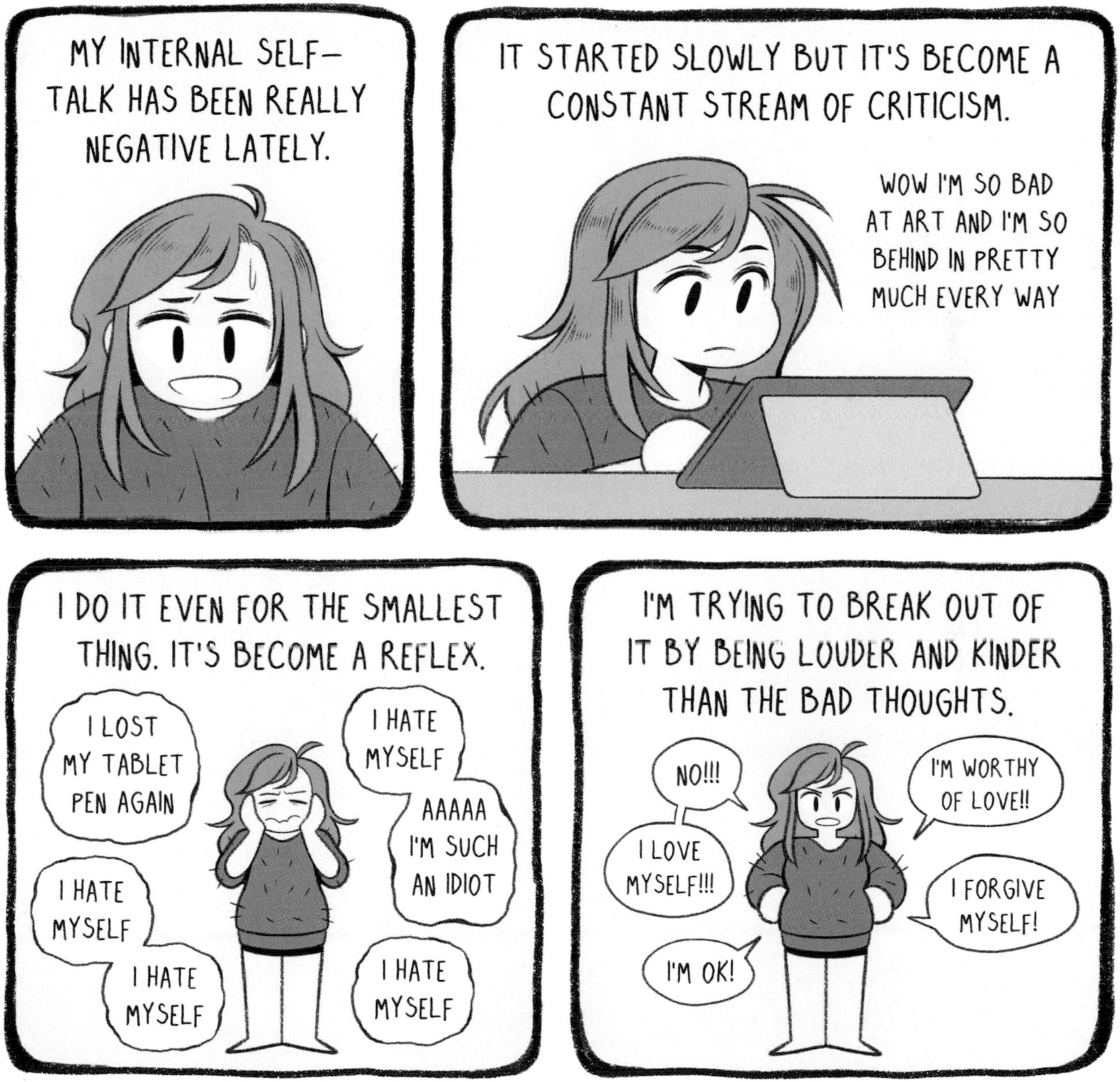

MY INTERNAL SELF-TALK HAS BEEN REALLY NEGATIVE LATELY.
IT STARTED SLOWLY BUT IT'S BECOME A CONSTANT STREAM OF CRITICISM.
WOW I'M SO BAD AT ART AND I'M SO BEHIND IN PRETTY MUCH EVERY WAY
I DO IT EVEN FOR THE SMALLEST THING. IT'S BECOME A REFLEX.
I LOST MY TABLET PEN AGAIN
I HATE MYSELF
AAAAA I'M SUCH AN IDIOT
I HATE MYSELF
I HATE MYSELF
I HATE MYSELF
I'M TRYING TO BREAK OUT OF IT BY BEING LOUDER AND KINDER THAN THE BAD THOUGHTS.
NO!!!
I LOVE MYSELF!!!
I'M WORTHY OF LOVE!!
I FORGIVE MYSELF!
I'M OK!

# THE ONLY 2 MOODS:

WOW I AM ABSOLUTE FUCKING GARBAGE

I AM SO FUCKING POWERFUL LITERALLY NO ONE CAN STOP ME

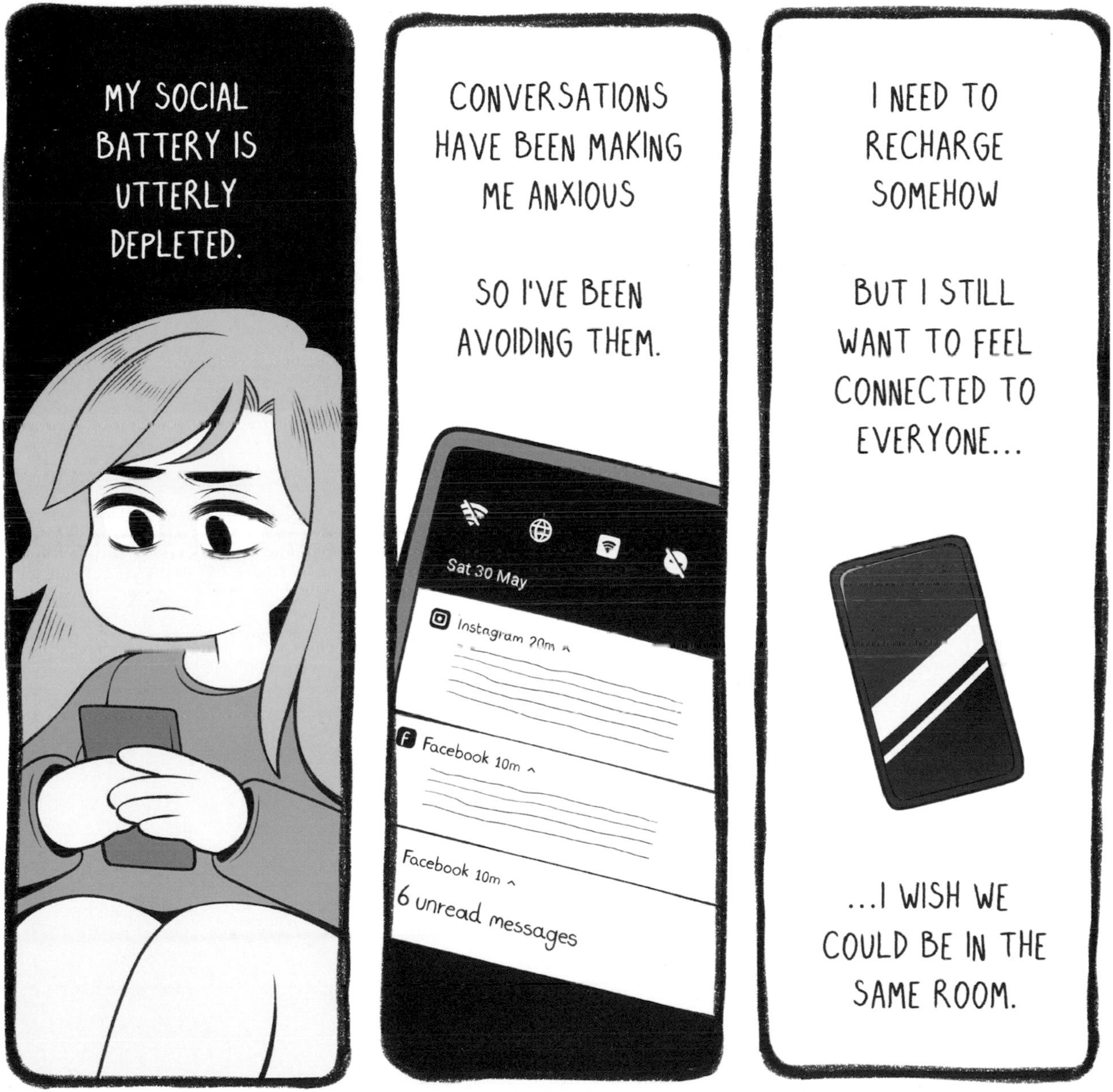
MY SOCIAL BATTERY IS UTTERLY DEPLETED.
CONVERSATIONS HAVE BEEN MAKING ME ANXIOUS
SO I'VE BEEN AVOIDING THEM.
Sat 30 May
Instagram 20m
Facebook 10m
Facebook 10m
6 unread messages
I NEED TO RECHARGE SOMEHOW
BUT I STILL WANT TO FEEL CONNECTED TO EVERYONE...
...I WISH WE COULD BE IN THE SAME ROOM.

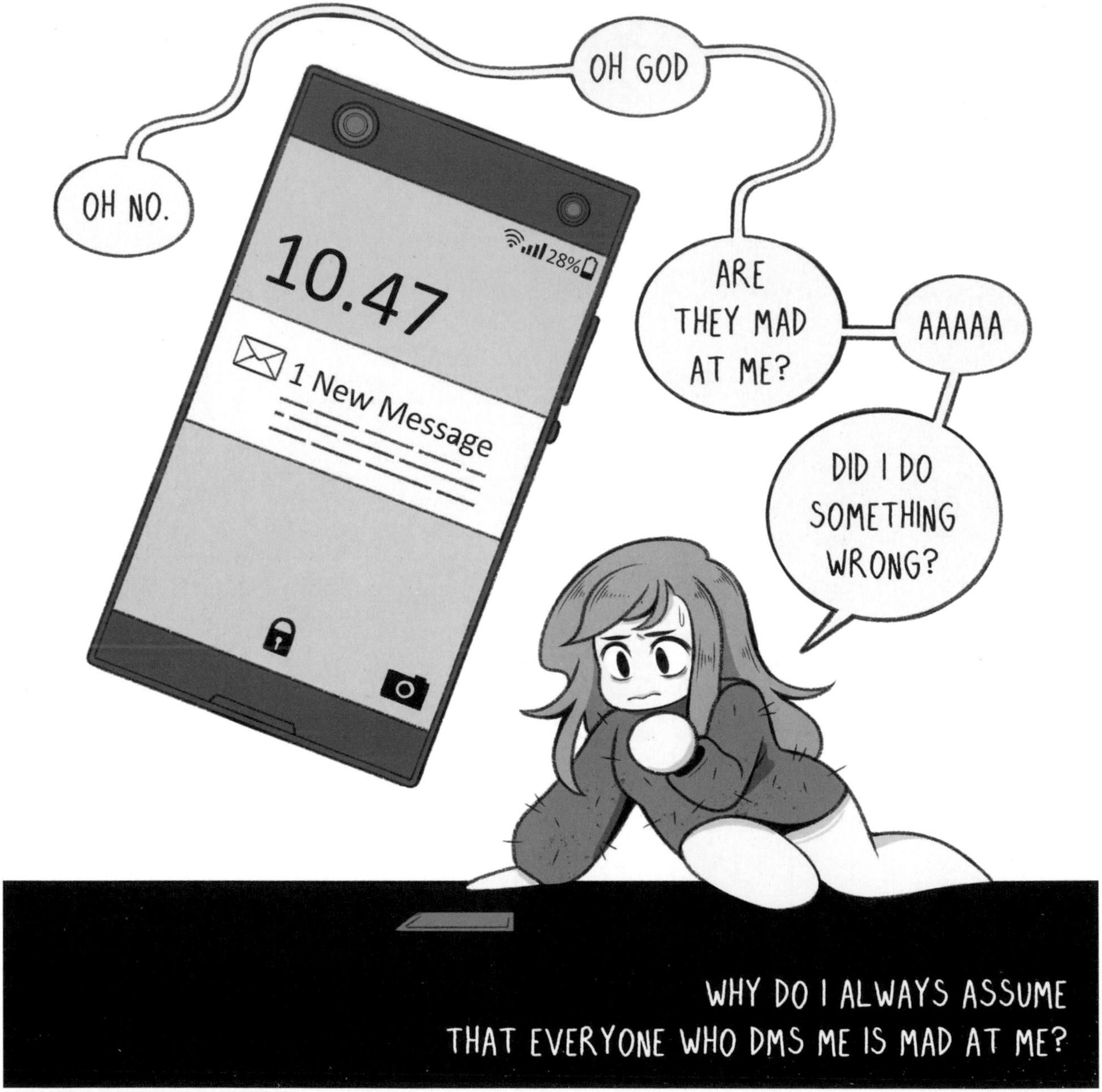
OH NO.
OH GOD
ARE THEY MAD AT ME?
AAAAA
DID I DO SOMETHING WRONG?
10.47
28%
1 New Message
WHY DO I ALWAYS ASSUME
THAT EVERYONE WHO DMS ME IS MAD AT ME?

I DON'T WANT
TO BE CONSTANTLY
AVAILABLE.

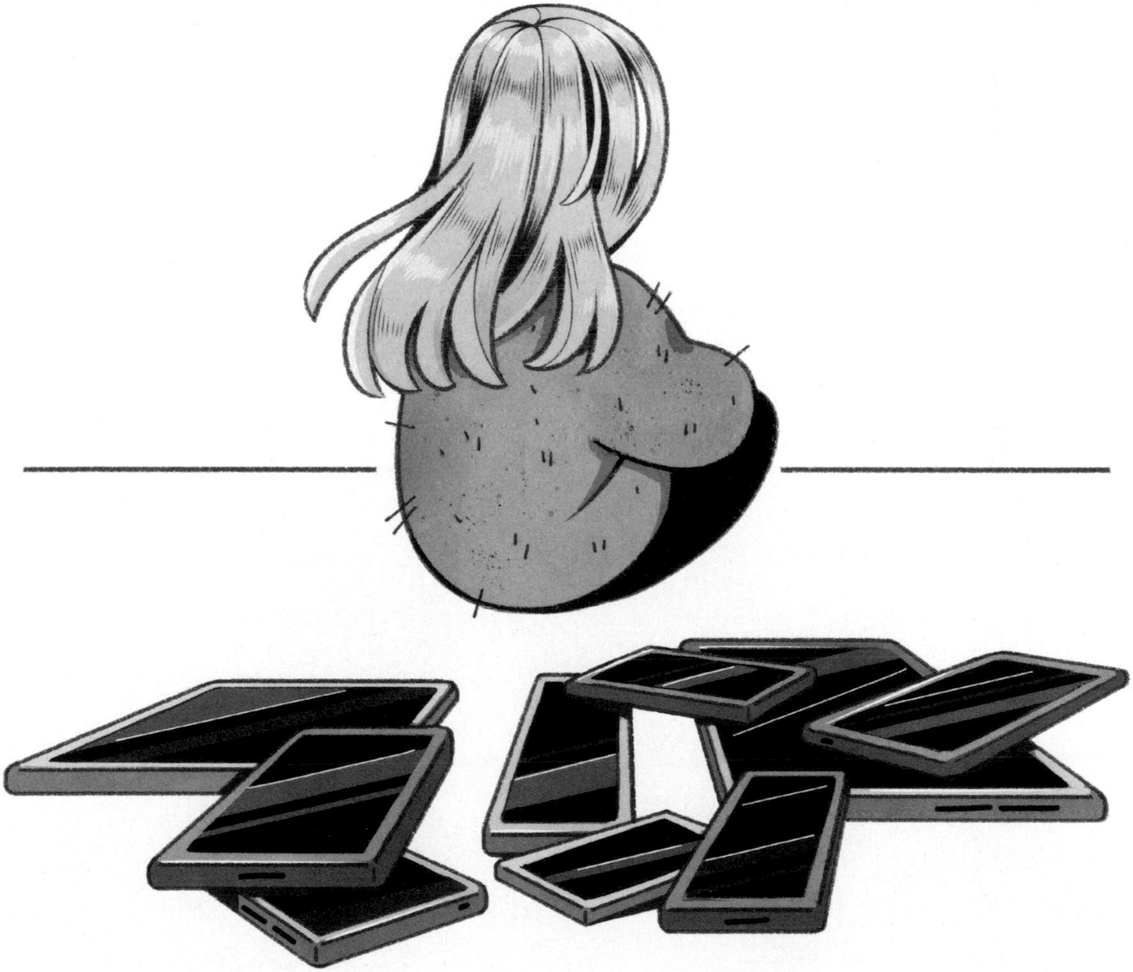

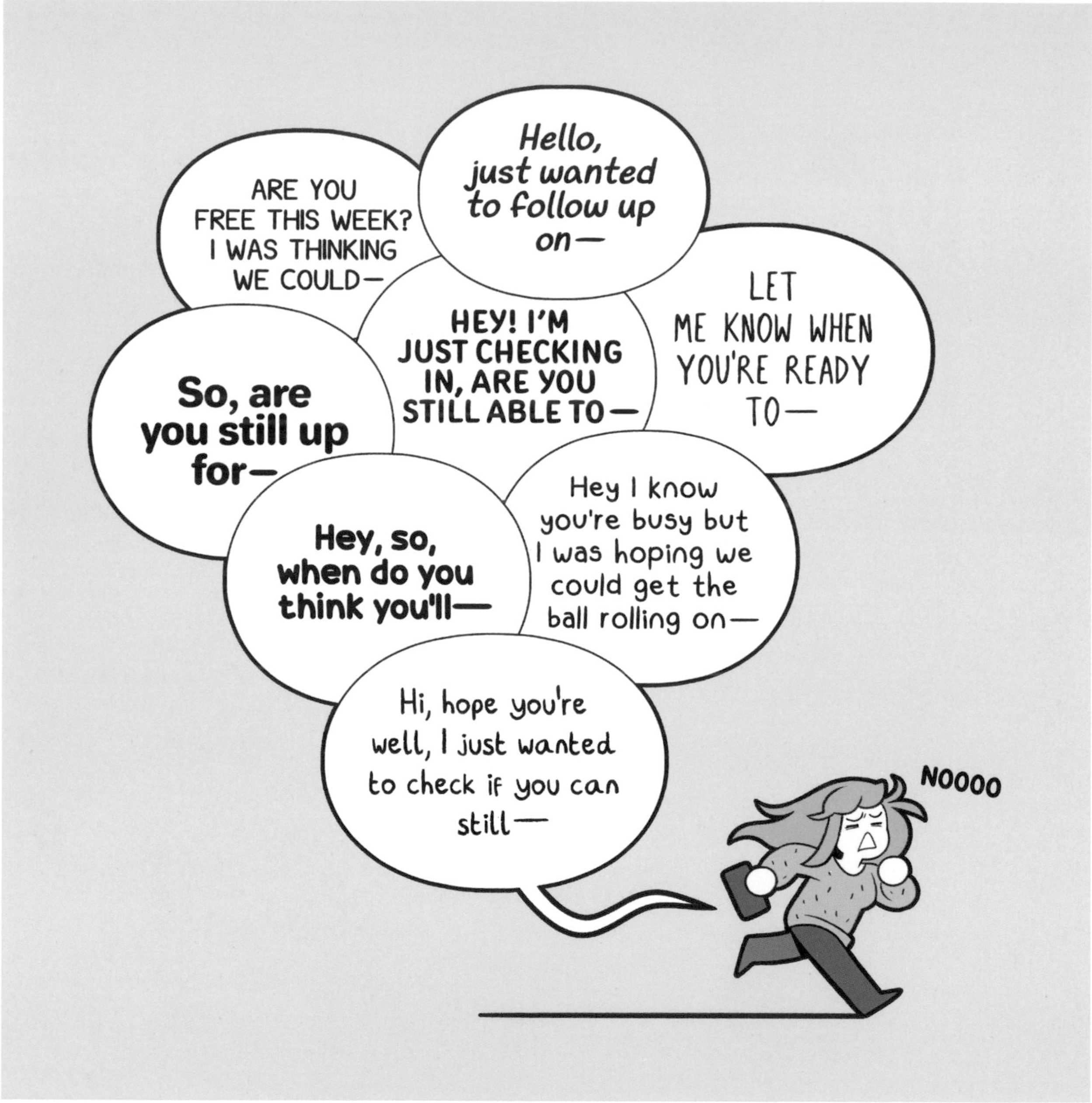
ARE YOU FREE THIS WEEK? I WAS THINKING WE COULD—
Hello, just wanted to follow up on—
LET ME KNOW WHEN YOU'RE READY TO—
HEY! I'M JUST CHECKING IN, ARE YOU STILL ABLE TO—
So, are you still up for—
Hey I know you're busy but I was hoping we could get the ball rolling on—
Hey, so, when do you think you'll—
Hi, hope you're well, I just wanted to check if you can still—
NOOOO

MAKING A PHONECALL

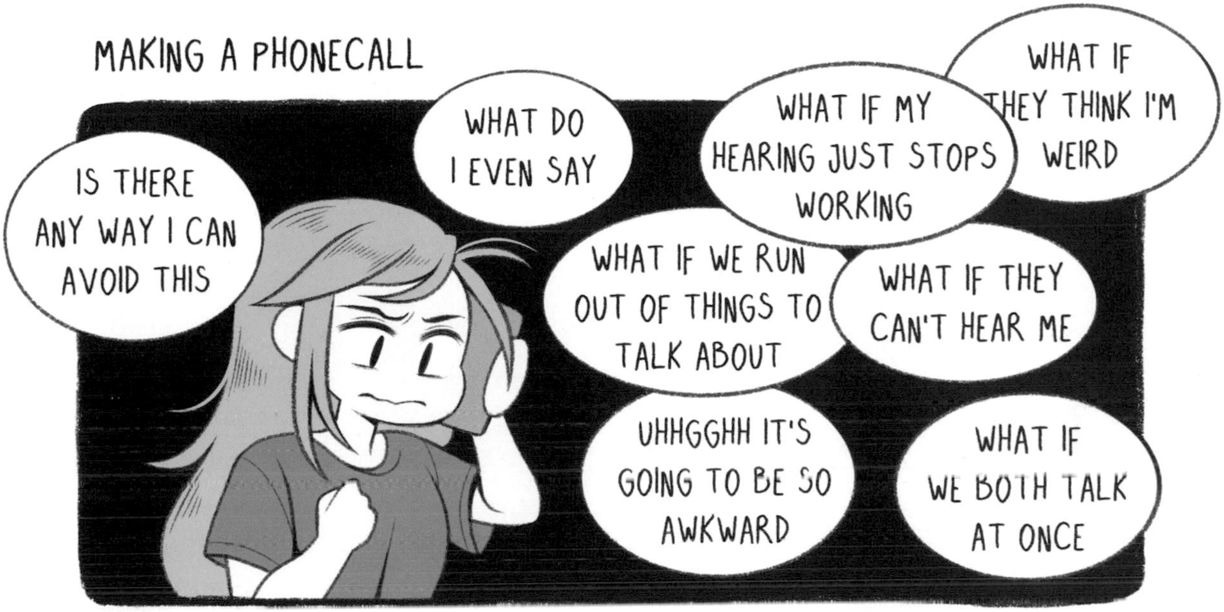
IS THERE ANY WAY I CAN AVOID THIS
WHAT DO I EVEN SAY
WHAT IF MY HEARING JUST STOPS WORKING
WHAT IF THEY THINK I'M WEIRD
WHAT IF WE RUN OUT OF THINGS TO TALK ABOUT
WHAT IF THEY CAN'T HEAR ME
UHHGGHH IT'S GOING TO BE SO AWKWARD
WHAT IF WE BOTH TALK AT ONCE

RECEIVING A PHONECALL

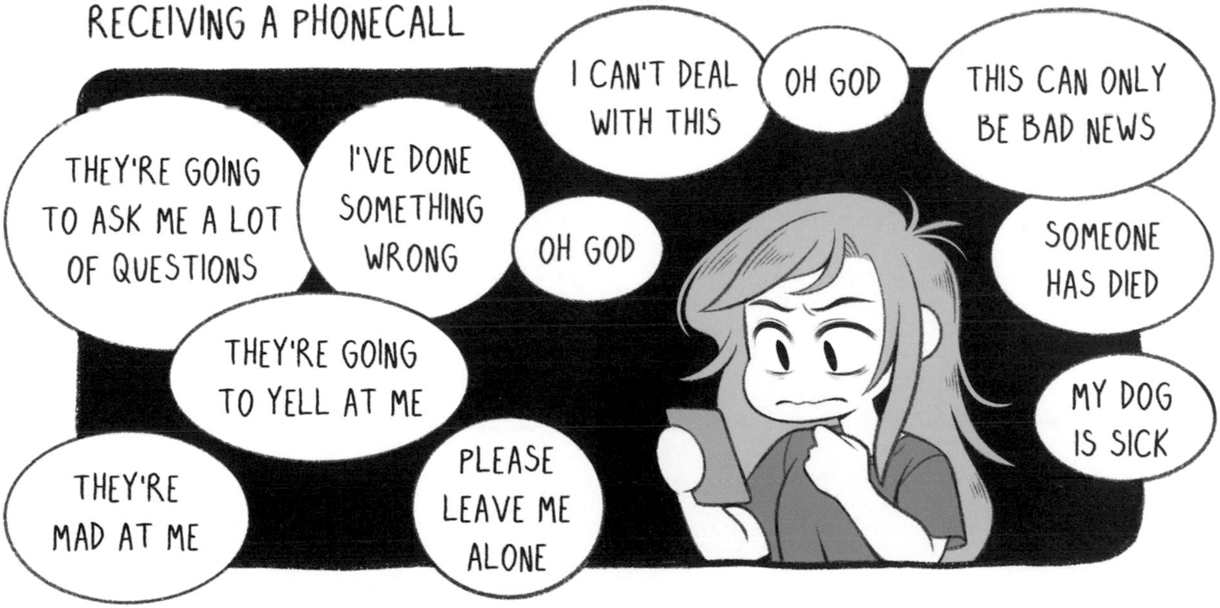
I CAN'T DEAL WITH THIS
OH GOD
THIS CAN ONLY BE BAD NEWS
THEY'RE GOING TO ASK ME A LOT OF QUESTIONS
I'VE DONE SOMETHING WRONG
OH GOD
SOMEONE HAS DIED
THEY'RE GOING TO YELL AT ME
MY DOG IS SICK
THEY'RE MAD AT ME
PLEASE LEAVE ME ALONE

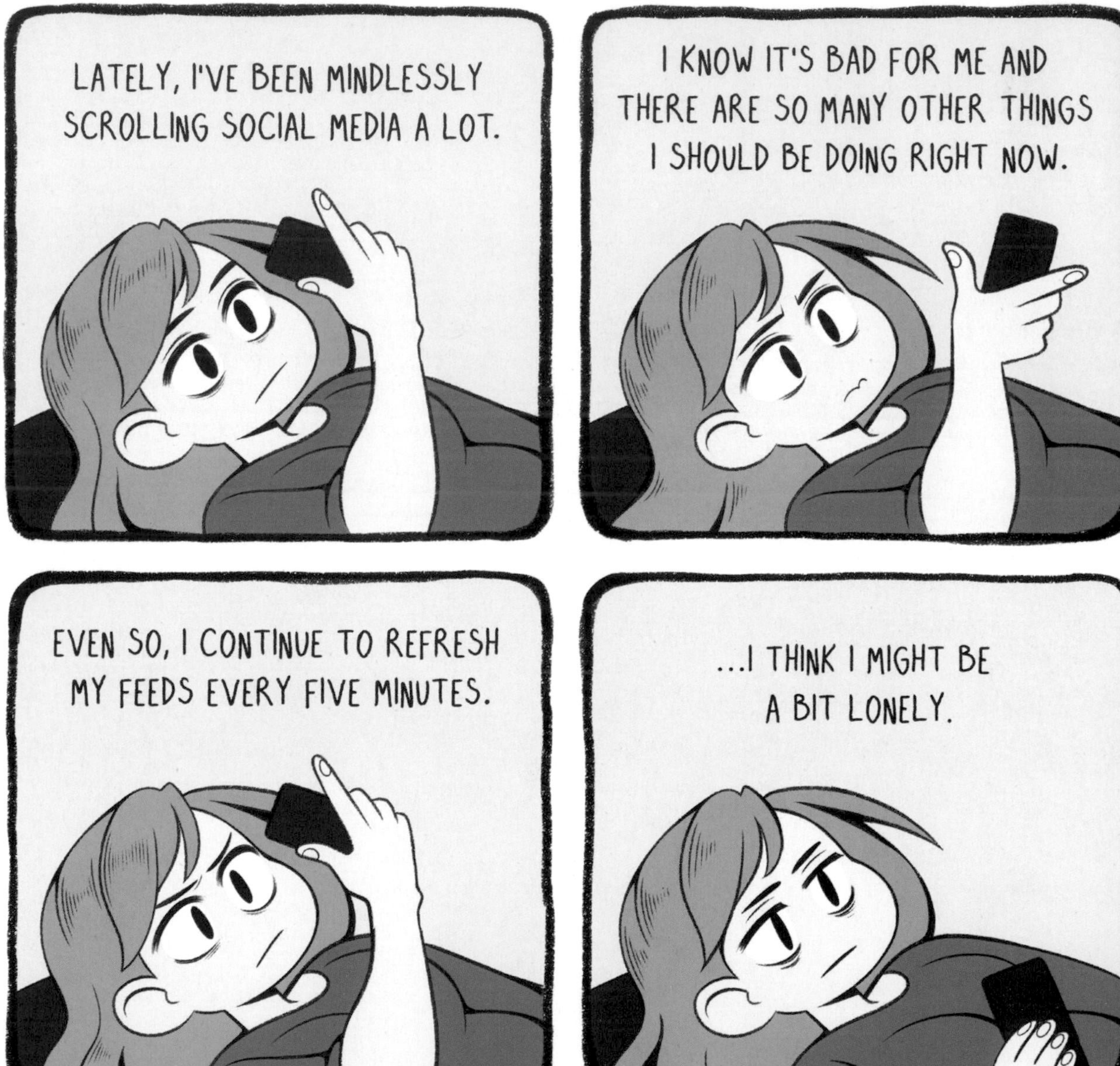
LATELY, I'VE BEEN MINDLESSLY SCROLLING SOCIAL MEDIA A LOT.
I KNOW IT'S BAD FOR ME AND THERE ARE SO MANY OTHER THINGS I SHOULD BE DOING RIGHT NOW.
EVEN SO, I CONTINUE TO REFRESH MY FEEDS EVERY FIVE MINUTES.
...I THINK I MIGHT BE A BIT LONELY.

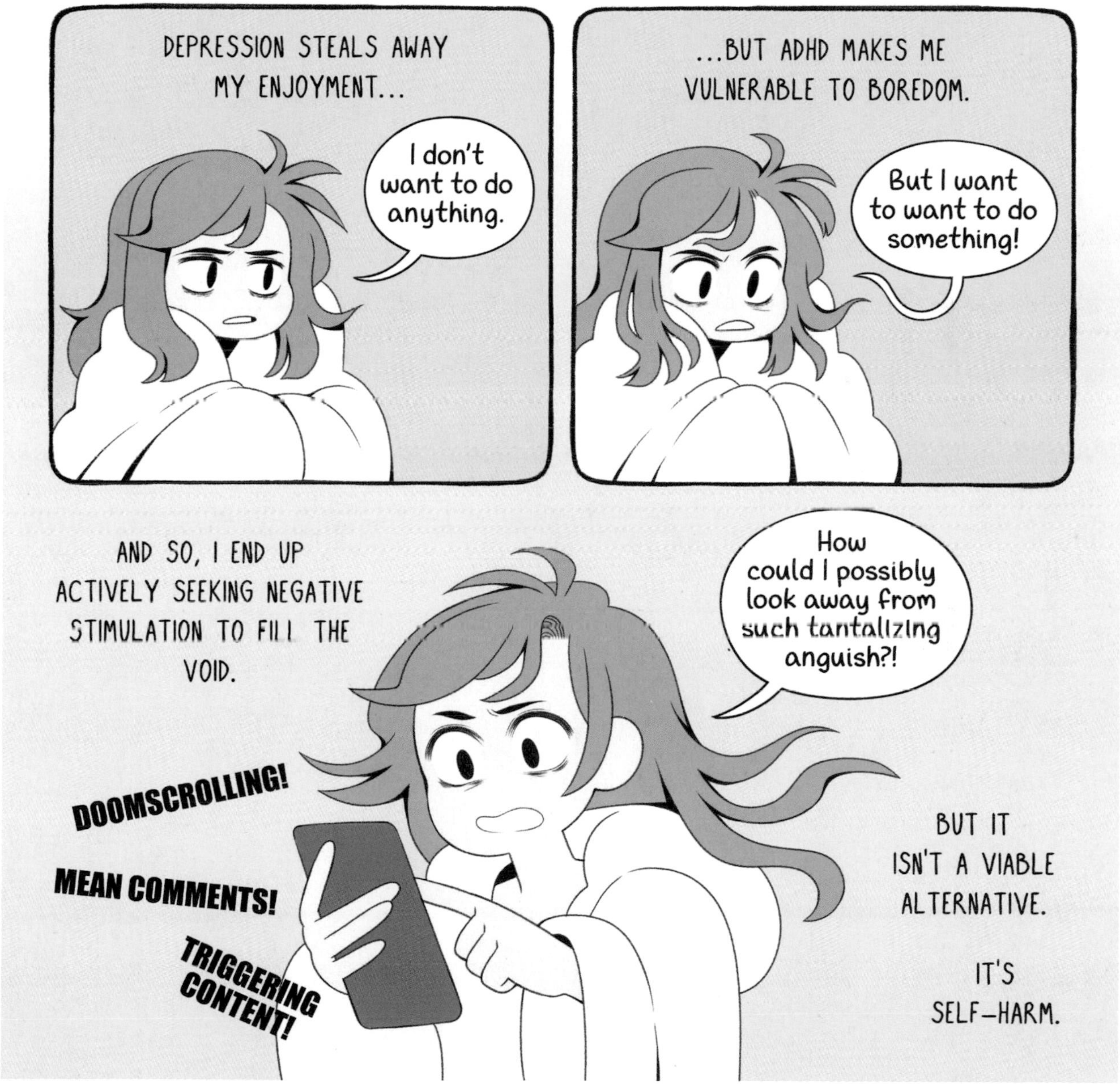
DEPRESSION STEALS AWAY MY ENJOYMENT...
I don't want to do anything.
...BUT ADHD MAKES ME VULNERABLE TO BOREDOM.
But I want to want to do something!
AND SO, I END UP ACTIVELY SEEKING NEGATIVE STIMULATION TO FILL THE VOID.
How could I possibly look away from such tantalizing anguish?!
DOOMSCROLLING!
MEAN COMMENTS!
TRIGGERING CONTENT!
BUT IT ISN'T A VIABLE ALTERNATIVE.
IT'S SELF-HARM.

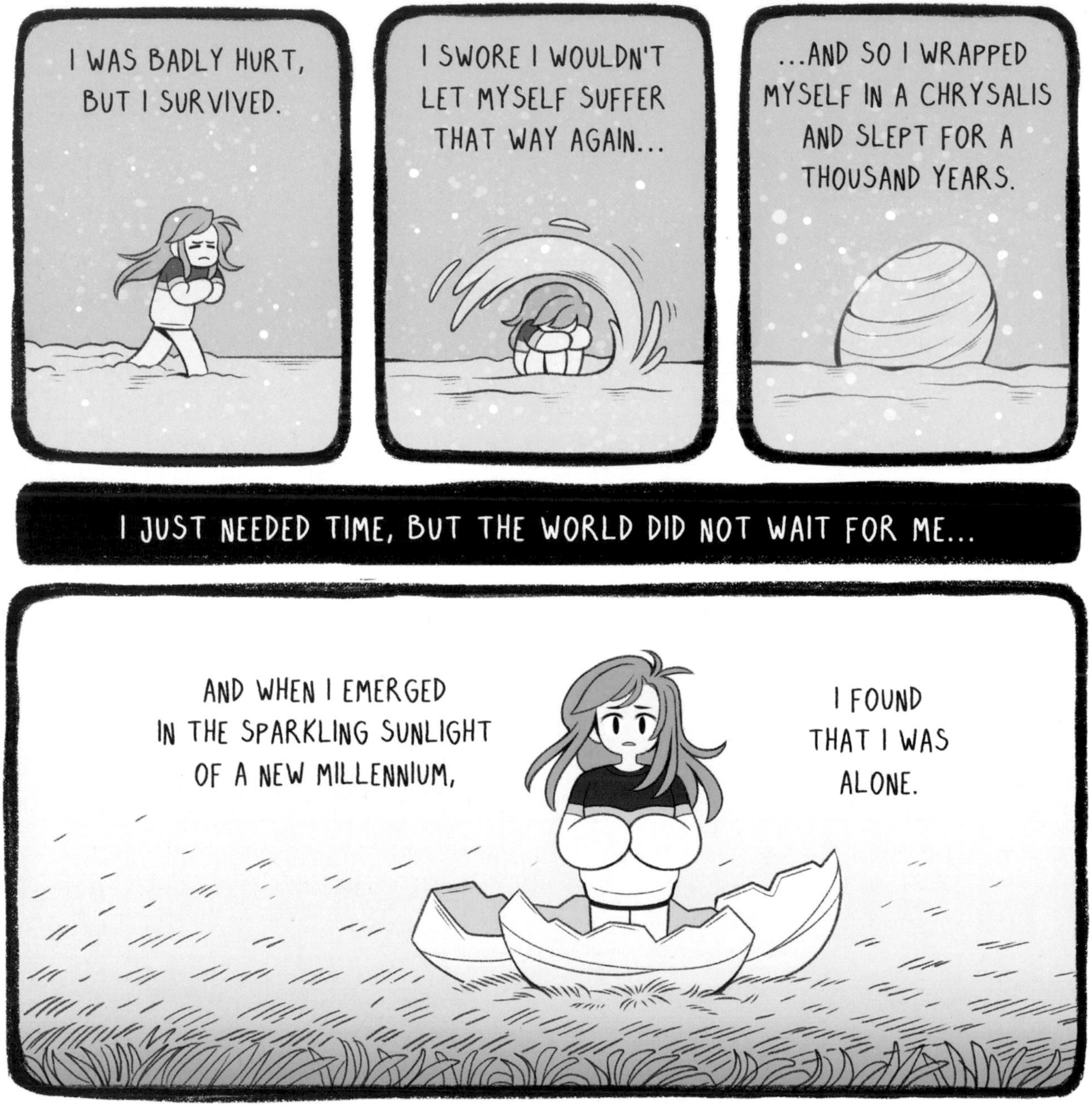

I WAS BADLY HURT, BUT I SURVIVED.
I SWORE I WOULDN'T LET MYSELF SUFFER THAT WAY AGAIN...
...AND SO I WRAPPED MYSELF IN A CHRYSALIS AND SLEPT FOR A THOUSAND YEARS.
I JUST NEEDED TIME, BUT THE WORLD DID NOT WAIT FOR ME...
AND WHEN I EMERGED IN THE SPARKLING SUNLIGHT OF A NEW MILLENNIUM,
I FOUND THAT I WAS ALONE.

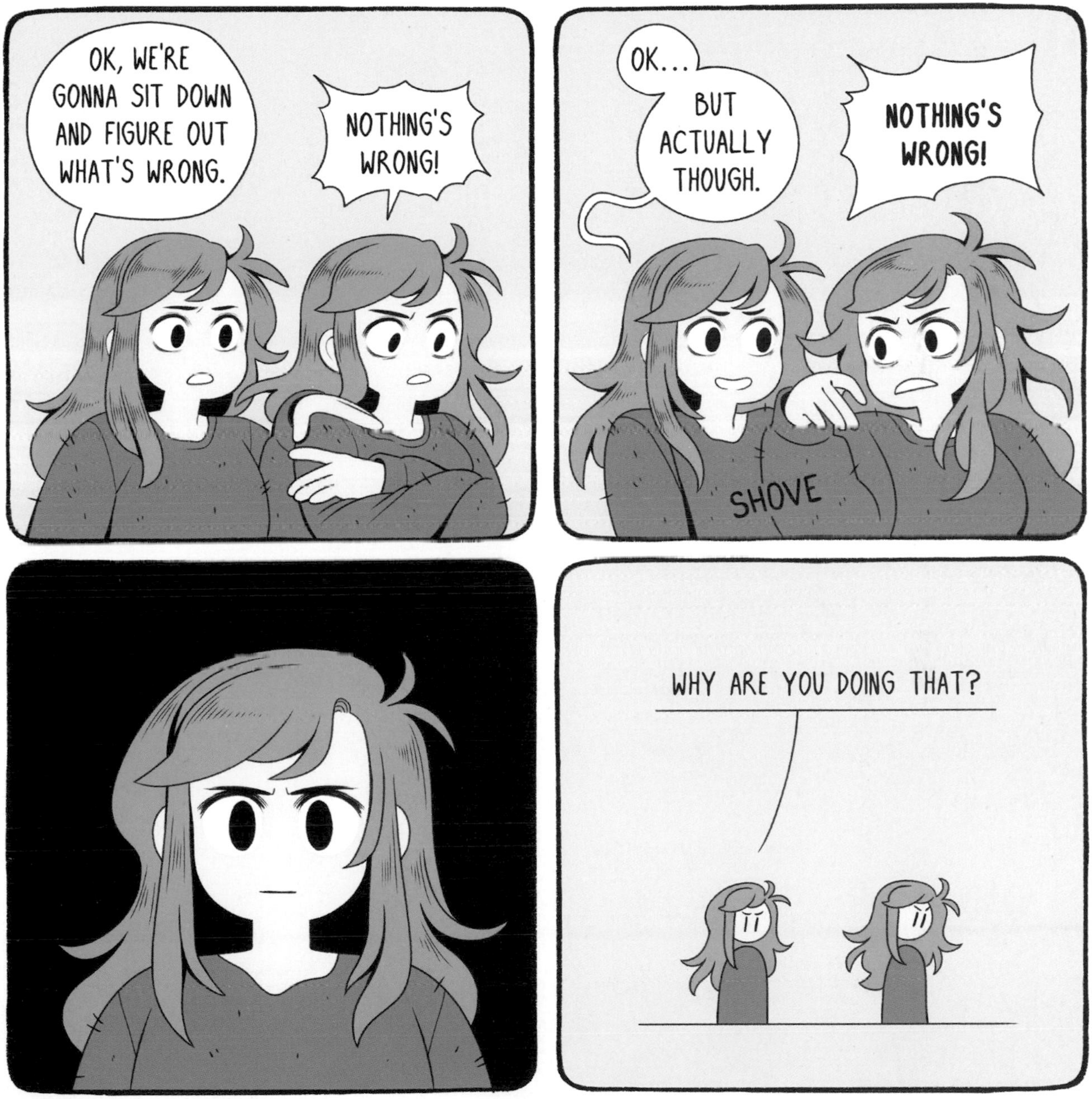
OK, WE'RE GONNA SIT DOWN AND FIGURE OUT WHAT'S WRONG.
NOTHING'S WRONG!
OK...
BUT ACTUALLY THOUGH.
NOTHING'S WRONG!
SHOVE
WHY ARE YOU DOING THAT?

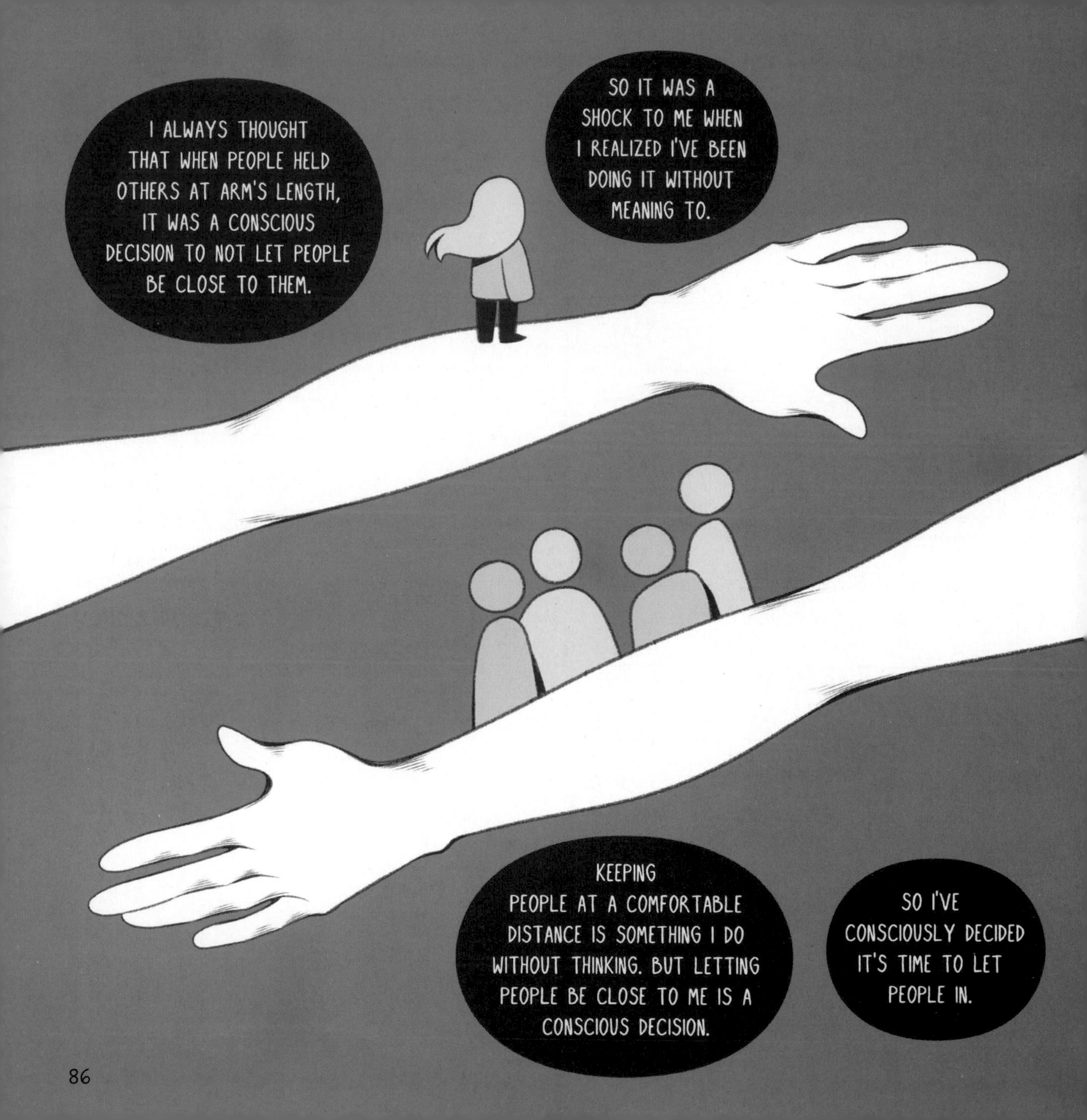
I ALWAYS THOUGHT THAT WHEN PEOPLE HELD OTHERS AT ARM'S LENGTH, IT WAS A CONSCIOUS DECISION TO NOT LET PEOPLE BE CLOSE TO THEM.
SO IT WAS A SHOCK TO ME WHEN I REALIZED I'VE BEEN DOING IT WITHOUT MEANING TO.
KEEPING PEOPLE AT A COMFORTABLE DISTANCE IS SOMETHING I DO WITHOUT THINKING. BUT LETTING PEOPLE BE CLOSE TO ME IS A CONSCIOUS DECISION.
SO I'VE CONSCIOUSLY DECIDED IT'S TIME TO LET PEOPLE IN.

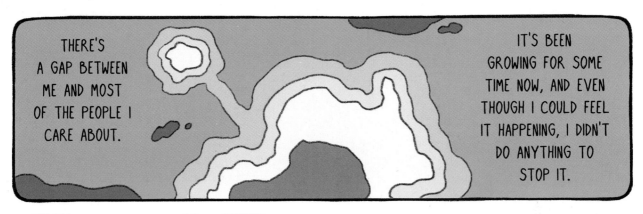

THERE'S A GAP BETWEEN ME AND MOST OF THE PEOPLE I CARE ABOUT.

IT'S BEEN GROWING FOR SOME TIME NOW, AND EVEN THOUGH I COULD FEEL IT HAPPENING, I DIDN'T DO ANYTHING TO STOP IT.

I WAS TOO TIRED FOR TOO LONG.

I DIDN'T ACCEPT THE LIFELINES THAT WERE THROWN TO ME, BUT I DIDN'T RETURN THEM EITHER.

I LET THEM SIT, ASSUMING THEY'D ALWAYS BE THERE.

BUT I CAN FEEL THAT I'M BEING LEFT BEHIND AND I KNOW IT'S MY OWN FAULT.

I WANT TO FIX THIS WHILE I STILL CAN.

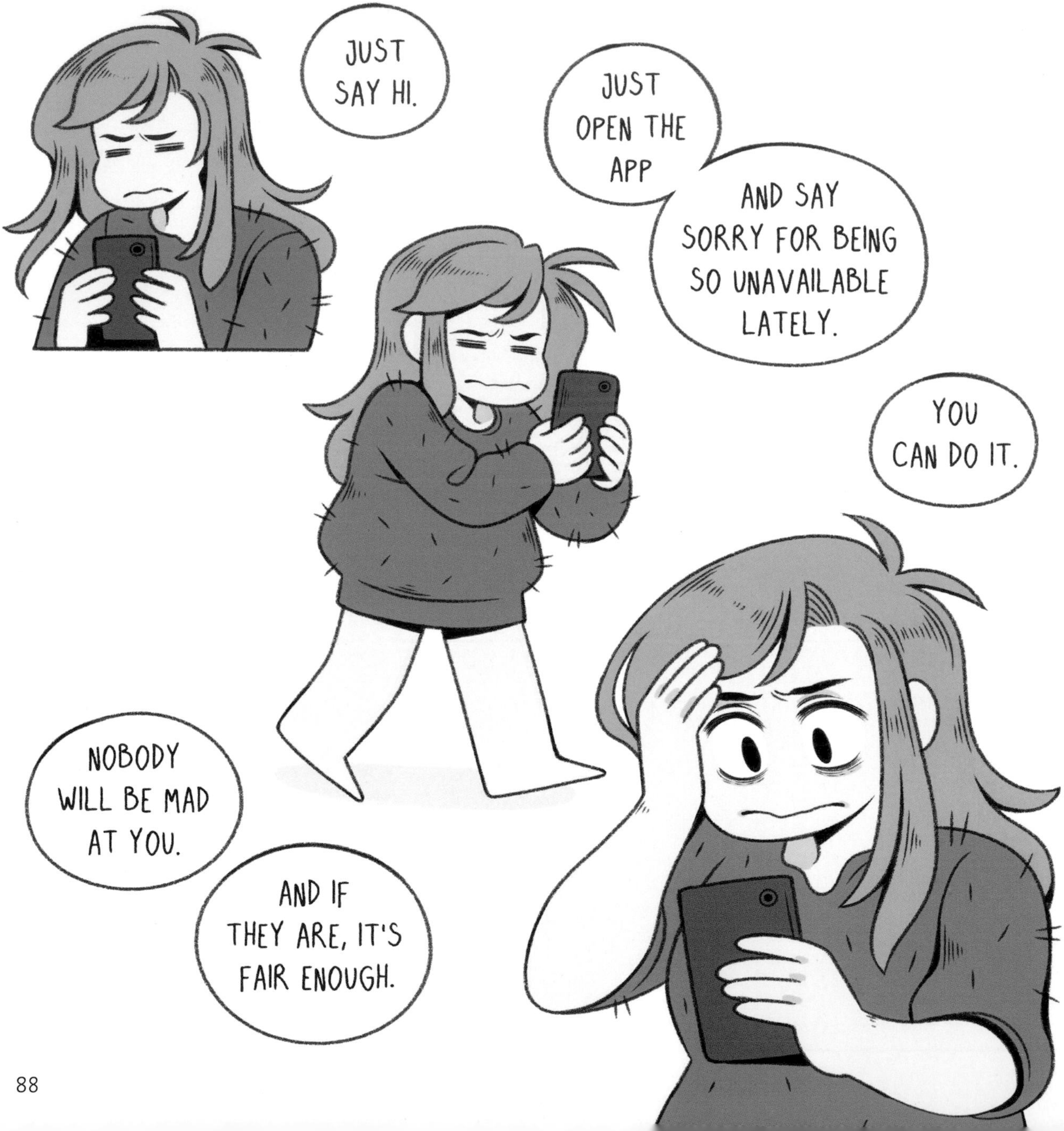
JUST SAY HI.
JUST OPEN THE APP
AND SAY SORRY FOR BEING SO UNAVAILABLE LATELY.
YOU CAN DO IT.
NOBODY WILL BE MAD AT YOU.
AND IF THEY ARE, IT'S FAIR ENOUGH.

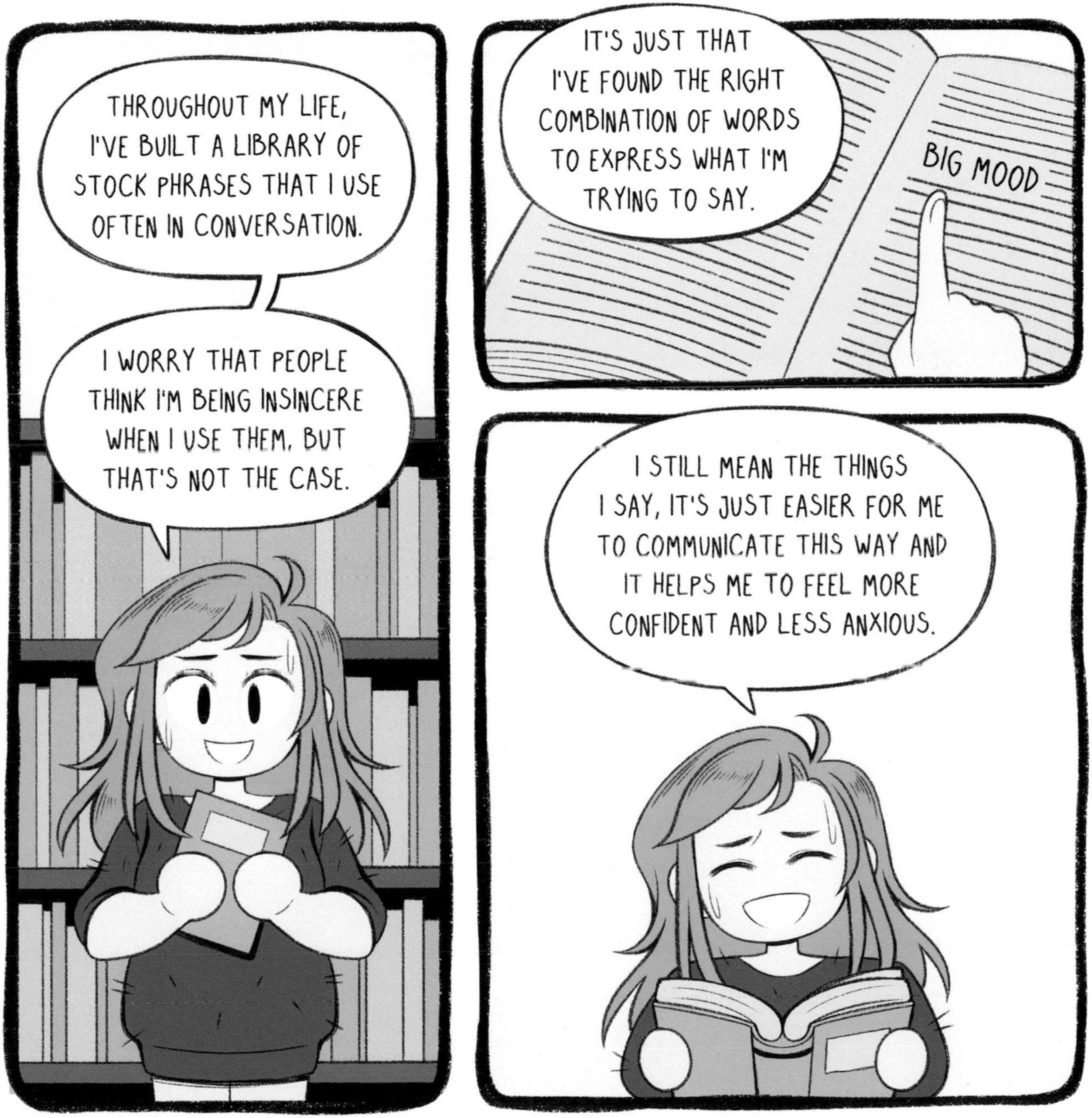
THROUGHOUT MY LIFE, I'VE BUILT A LIBRARY OF STOCK PHRASES THAT I USE OFTEN IN CONVERSATION.
I WORRY THAT PEOPLE THINK I'M BEING INSINCERE WHEN I USE THEM, BUT THAT'S NOT THE CASE.
IT'S JUST THAT I'VE FOUND THE RIGHT COMBINATION OF WORDS TO EXPRESS WHAT I'M TRYING TO SAY.
BIG MOOD
I STILL MEAN THE THINGS I SAY, IT'S JUST EASIER FOR ME TO COMMUNICATE THIS WAY AND IT HELPS ME TO FEEL MORE CONFIDENT AND LESS ANXIOUS.

MY FINGERNAILS PROVIDE A FAIRLY ACCURATE INDICATOR OF HOW I'M DOING IN GENERAL.

WHEN I'M IN A BAD PLACE, I COMPULSIVELY BITE AND CUT MY NAILS AS MUCH AS I CAN.

AT SOME POINT WHEN THINGS ARE GOOD AGAIN, I'LL SUDDENLY REALIZE THEY'VE GROWN BACK.

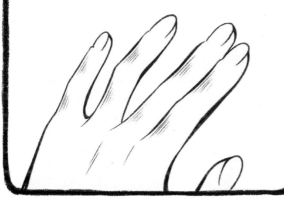

IT'S PRETTY NICE TO HAVE A VISUAL REMINDER THAT I'M OK.

TAP
TAP
TAP

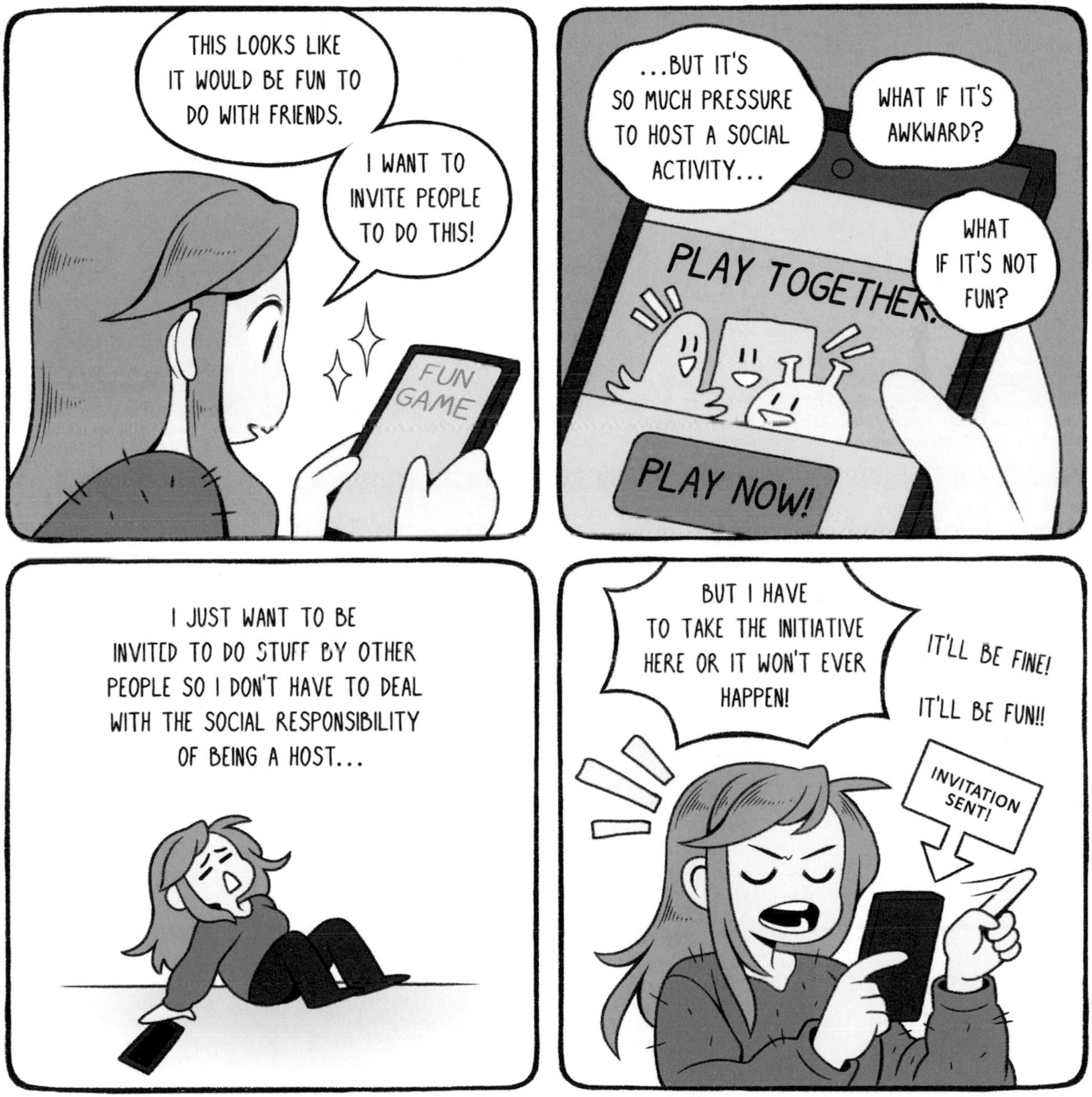

THIS LOOKS LIKE IT WOULD BE FUN TO DO WITH FRIENDS.
I WANT TO INVITE PEOPLE TO DO THIS!
FUN GAME
...BUT IT'S SO MUCH PRESSURE TO HOST A SOCIAL ACTIVITY...
WHAT IF IT'S AWKWARD?
WHAT IF IT'S NOT FUN?
PLAY TOGETHER!
PLAY NOW!
I JUST WANT TO BE INVITED TO DO STUFF BY OTHER PEOPLE SO I DON'T HAVE TO DEAL WITH THE SOCIAL RESPONSIBILITY OF BEING A HOST...
BUT I HAVE TO TAKE THE INITIATIVE HERE OR IT WON'T EVER HAPPEN!
IT'LL BE FINE!
IT'LL BE FUN!!
INVITATION SENT!

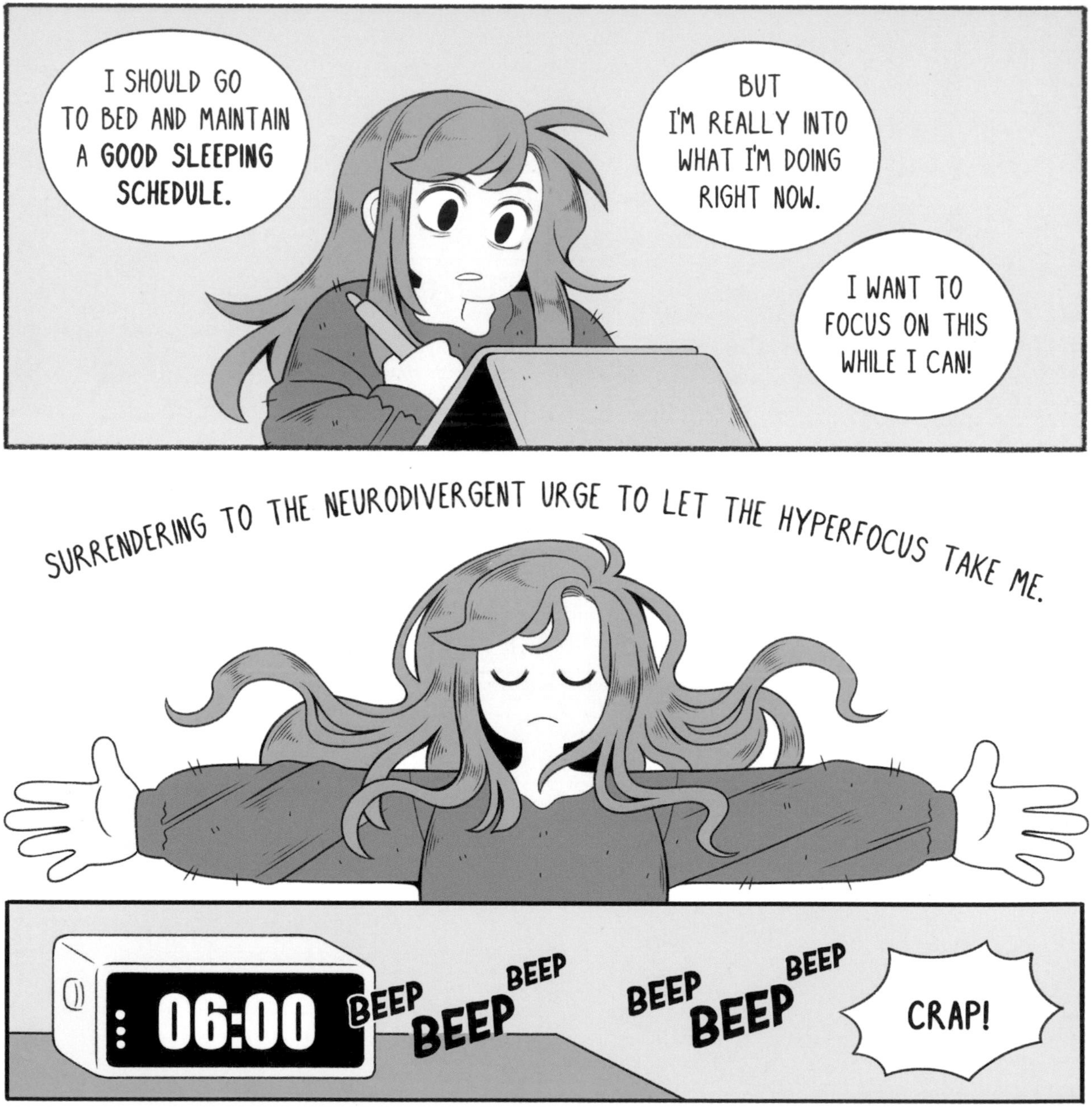
I SHOULD GO TO BED AND MAINTAIN A GOOD SLEEPING SCHEDULE.
BUT I'M REALLY INTO WHAT I'M DOING RIGHT NOW.
I WANT TO FOCUS ON THIS WHILE I CAN!
SURRENDERING TO THE NEURODIVERGENT URGE TO LET THE HYPERFOCUS TAKE ME.
06:00
BEEP BEEP BEEP
BEEP BEEP BEEP
CRAP!

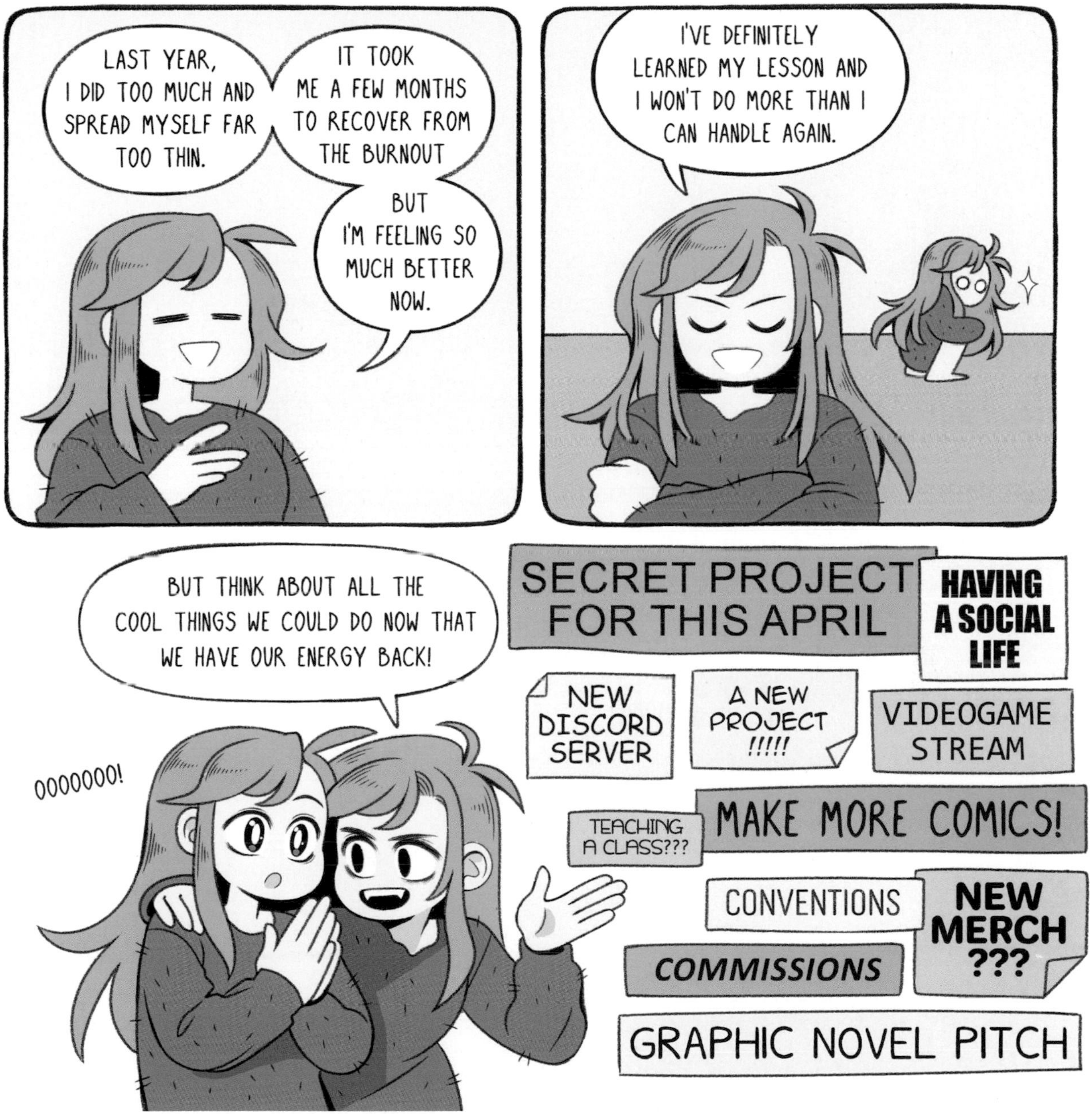
LAST YEAR, I DID TOO MUCH AND SPREAD MYSELF FAR TOO THIN.
IT TOOK ME A FEW MONTHS TO RECOVER FROM THE BURNOUT
BUT I'M FEELING SO MUCH BETTER NOW.
I'VE DEFINITELY LEARNED MY LESSON AND I WON'T DO MORE THAN I CAN HANDLE AGAIN.
BUT THINK ABOUT ALL THE COOL THINGS WE COULD DO NOW THAT WE HAVE OUR ENERGY BACK!
OOOOOOO!
SECRET PROJECT FOR THIS APRIL
HAVING A SOCIAL LIFE
NEW DISCORD SERVER
A NEW PROJECT !!!!!
VIDEOGAME STREAM
TEACHING A CLASS???
MAKE MORE COMICS!
CONVENTIONS
NEW MERCH ???
COMMISSIONS
GRAPHIC NOVEL PITCH

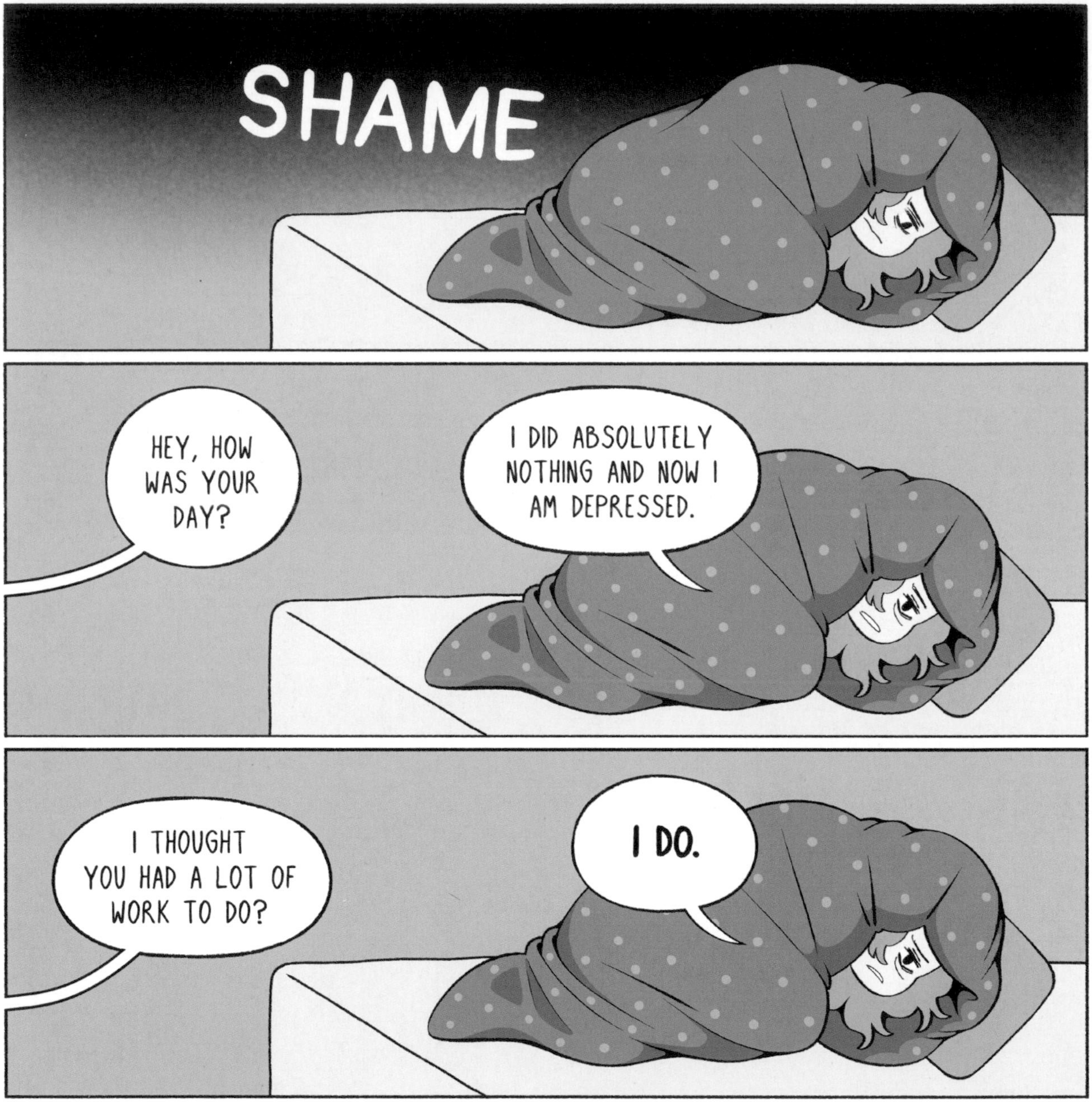
SHAME
HEY, HOW WAS YOUR DAY?
I DID ABSOLUTELY NOTHING AND NOW I AM DEPRESSED.
I THOUGHT YOU HAD A LOT OF WORK TO DO?
I DO.

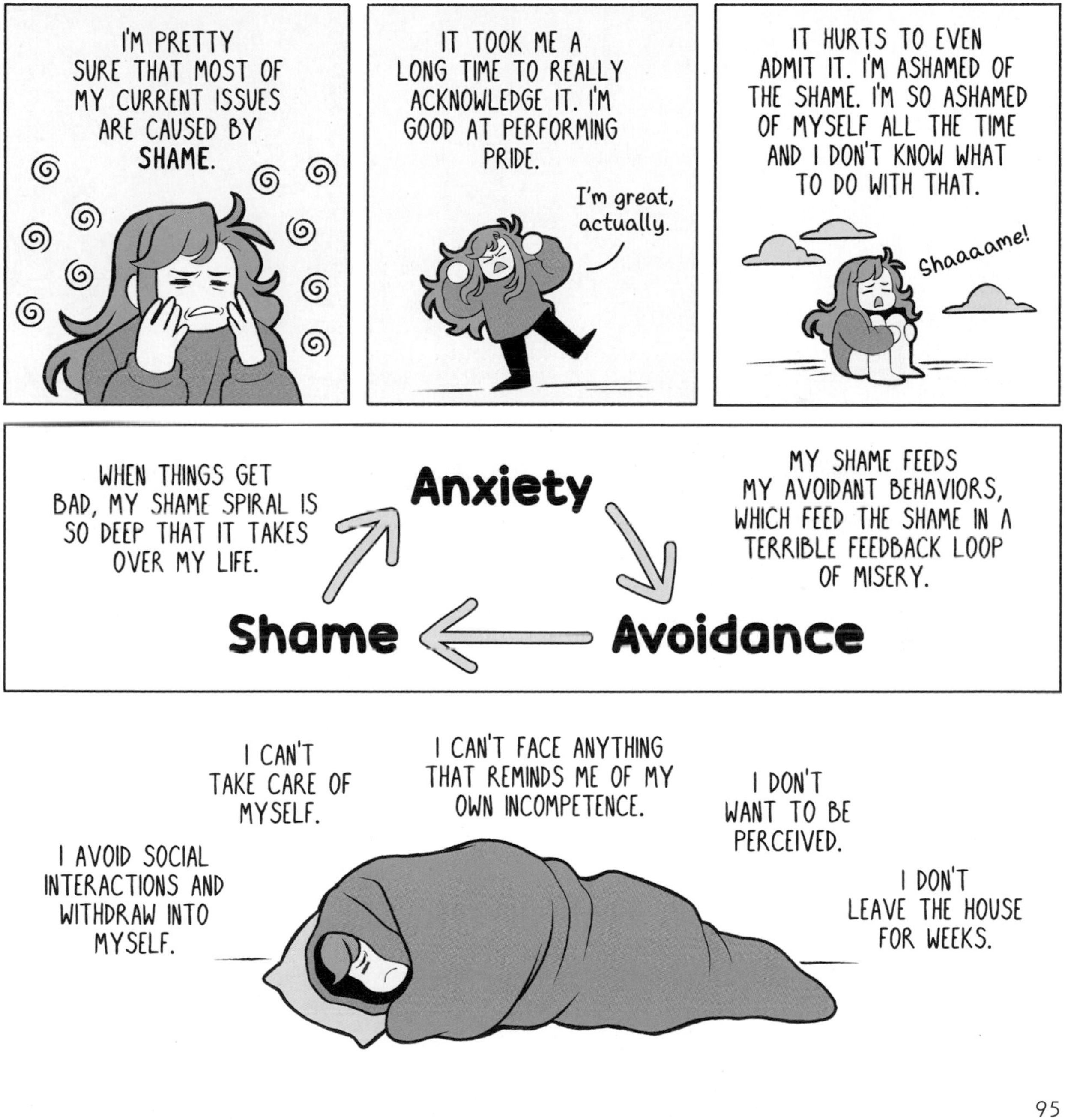
I'M PRETTY SURE THAT MOST OF MY CURRENT ISSUES ARE CAUSED BY SHAME.
IT TOOK ME A LONG TIME TO REALLY ACKNOWLEDGE IT. I'M GOOD AT PERFORMING PRIDE.
I'm great, actually.
IT HURTS TO EVEN ADMIT IT. I'M ASHAMED OF THE SHAME. I'M SO ASHAMED OF MYSELF ALL THE TIME AND I DON'T KNOW WHAT TO DO WITH THAT.
Shaaaame!
WHEN THINGS GET BAD, MY SHAME SPIRAL IS SO DEEP THAT IT TAKES OVER MY LIFE.
Anxiety
Avoidance
Shame
MY SHAME FEEDS MY AVOIDANT BEHAVIORS, WHICH FEED THE SHAME IN A TERRIBLE FEEDBACK LOOP OF MISERY.
I AVOID SOCIAL INTERACTIONS AND WITHDRAW INTO MYSELF.
I CAN'T TAKE CARE OF MYSELF.
I CAN'T FACE ANYTHING THAT REMINDS ME OF MY OWN INCOMPETENCE.
I DON'T WANT TO BE PERCEIVED.
I DON'T LEAVE THE HOUSE FOR WEEKS.

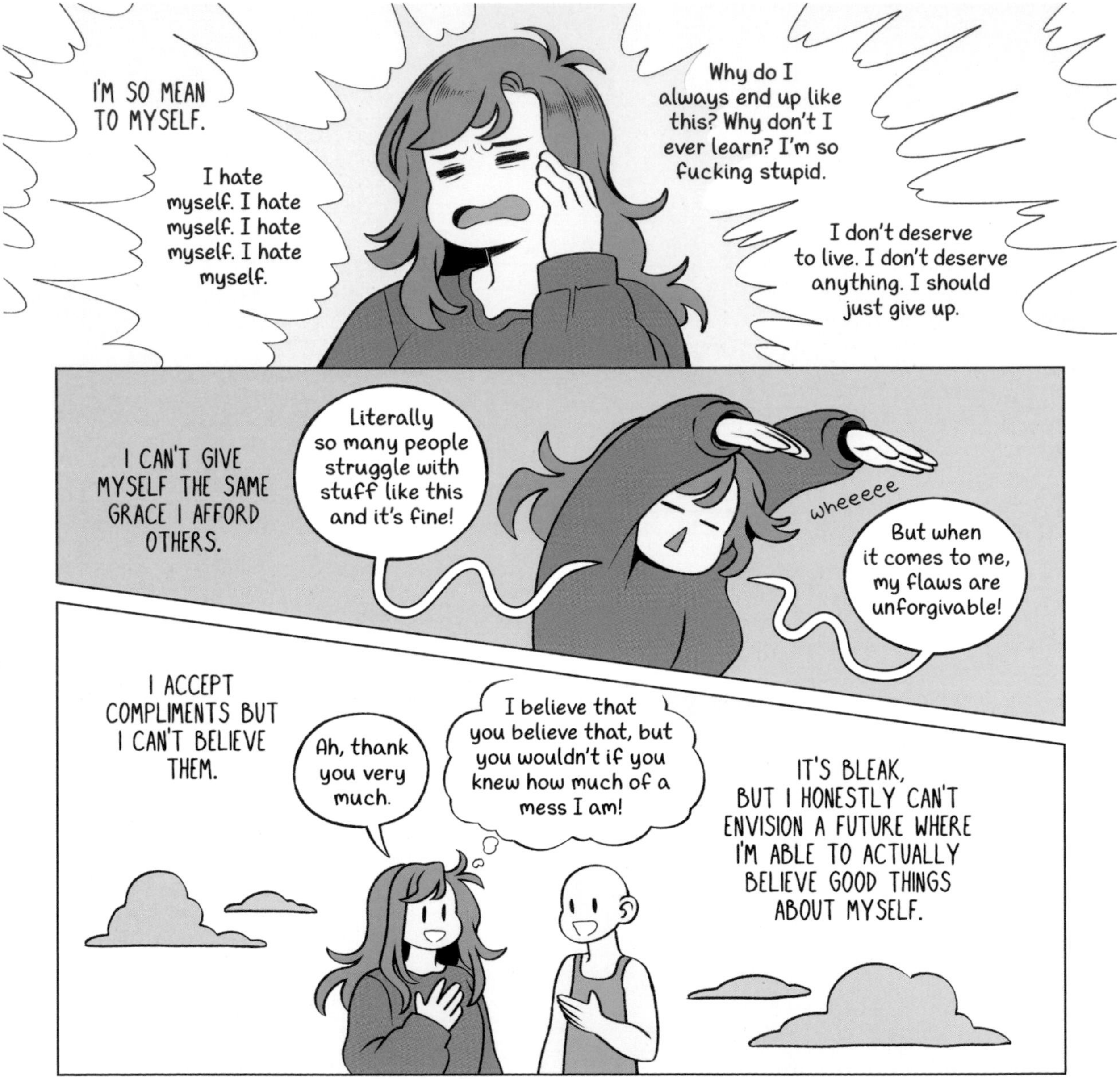
I'M SO MEAN TO MYSELF.
I hate myself. I hate myself. I hate myself. I hate myself.
Why do I always end up like this? Why don't I ever learn? I'm so fucking stupid.
I don't deserve to live. I don't deserve anything. I should just give up.
I CAN'T GIVE MYSELF THE SAME GRACE I AFFORD OTHERS.
Literally so many people struggle with stuff like this and it's fine!
wheeeee
But when it comes to me, my flaws are unforgivable!
I ACCEPT COMPLIMENTS BUT I CAN'T BELIEVE THEM.
Ah, thank you very much.
I believe that you believe that, but you wouldn't if you knew how much of a mess I am!
IT'S BLEAK, BUT I HONESTLY CAN'T ENVISION A FUTURE WHERE I'M ABLE TO ACTUALLY BELIEVE GOOD THINGS ABOUT MYSELF.

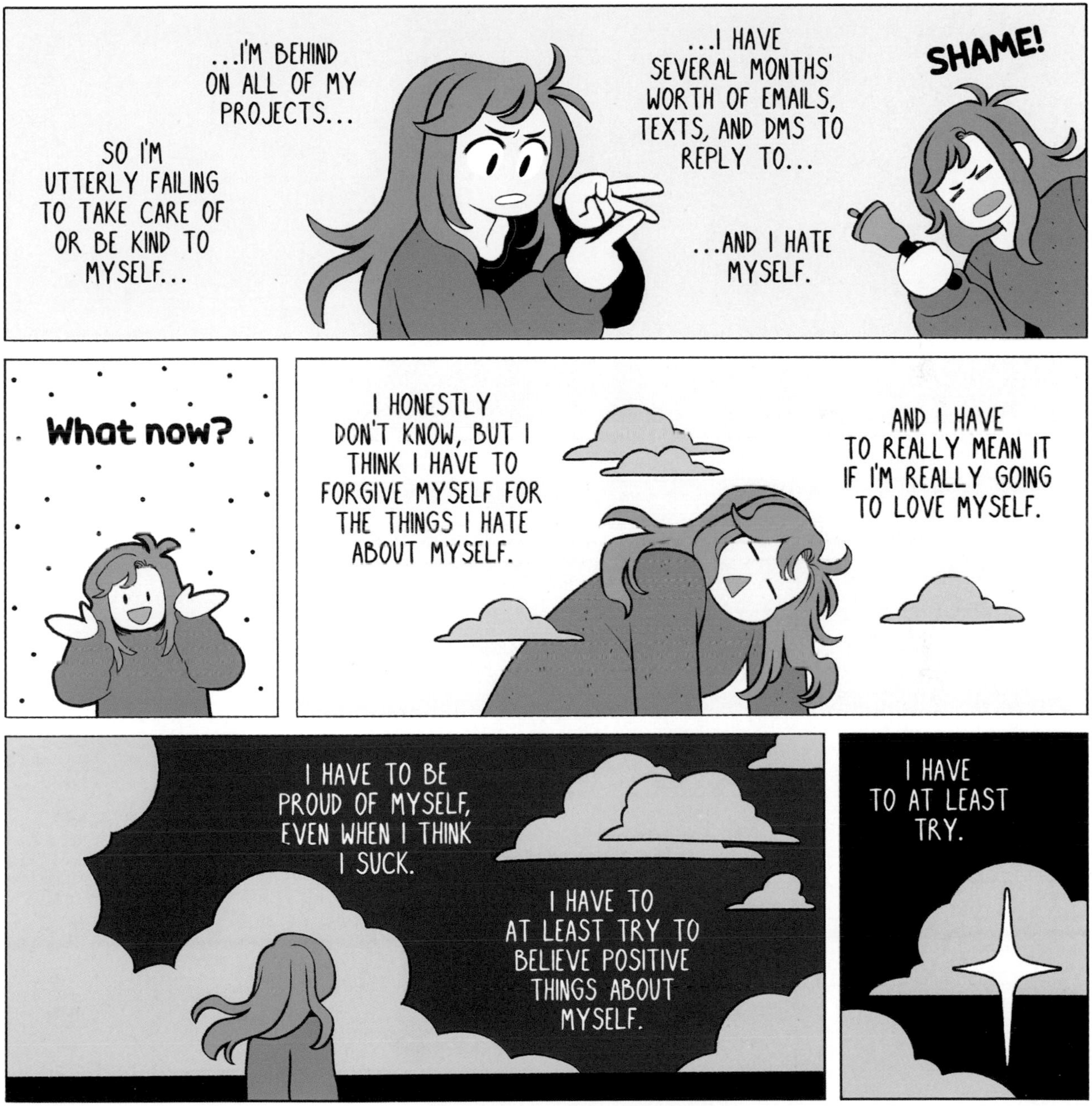

SO I'M UTTERLY FAILING TO TAKE CARE OF OR BE KIND TO MYSELF...
...I'M BEHIND ON ALL OF MY PROJECTS...
...I HAVE SEVERAL MONTHS' WORTH OF EMAILS, TEXTS, AND DMS TO REPLY TO...
...AND I HATE MYSELF.
SHAME!
What now?
I HONESTLY DON'T KNOW, BUT I THINK I HAVE TO FORGIVE MYSELF FOR THE THINGS I HATE ABOUT MYSELF.
AND I HAVE TO REALLY MEAN IT IF I'M REALLY GOING TO LOVE MYSELF.
I HAVE TO BE PROUD OF MYSELF, EVEN WHEN I THINK I SUCK.
I HAVE TO AT LEAST TRY TO BELIEVE POSITIVE THINGS ABOUT MYSELF.
I HAVE TO AT LEAST TRY.

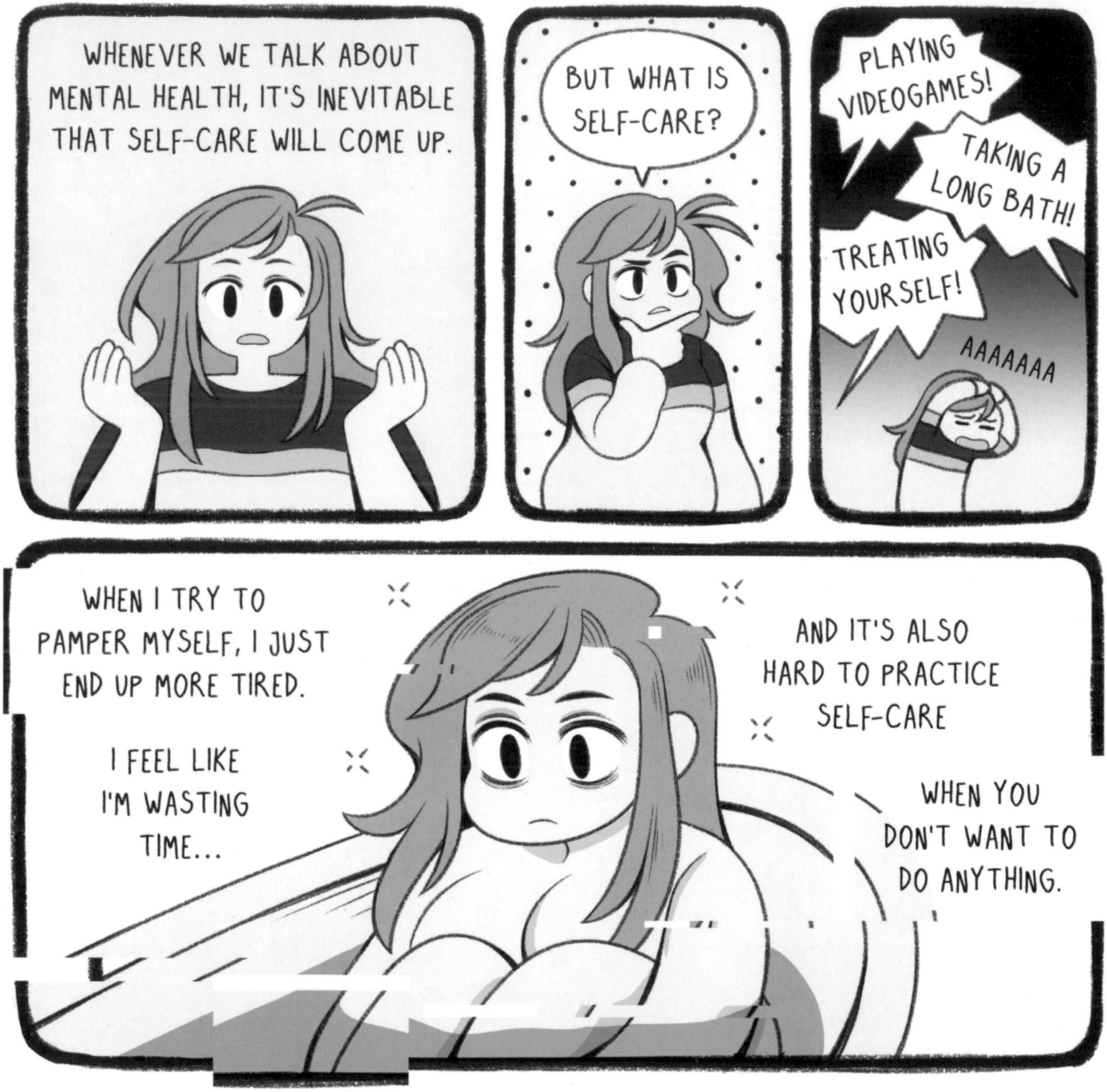

WHENEVER WE TALK ABOUT MENTAL HEALTH, IT'S INEVITABLE THAT SELF-CARE WILL COME UP.
BUT WHAT IS SELF-CARE?
PLAYING VIDEOGAMES!
TAKING A LONG BATH!
TREATING YOURSELF!
AAAAAAA
WHEN I TRY TO PAMPER MYSELF, I JUST END UP MORE TIRED.
I FEEL LIKE I'M WASTING TIME...
AND IT'S ALSO HARD TO PRACTICE SELF-CARE
WHEN YOU DON'T WANT TO DO ANYTHING.

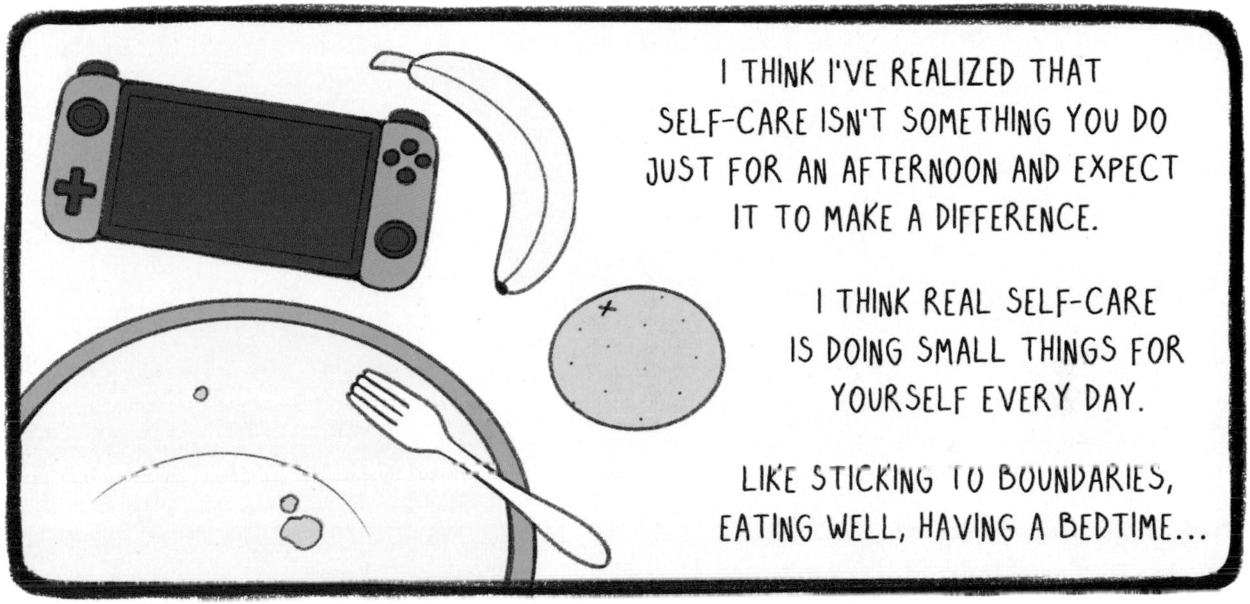
I THINK I'VE REALIZED THAT SELF-CARE ISN'T SOMETHING YOU DO JUST FOR AN AFTERNOON AND EXPECT IT TO MAKE A DIFFERENCE.
I THINK REAL SELF-CARE IS DOING SMALL THINGS FOR YOURSELF EVERY DAY.
LIKE STICKING TO BOUNDARIES, EATING WELL, HAVING A BEDTIME...

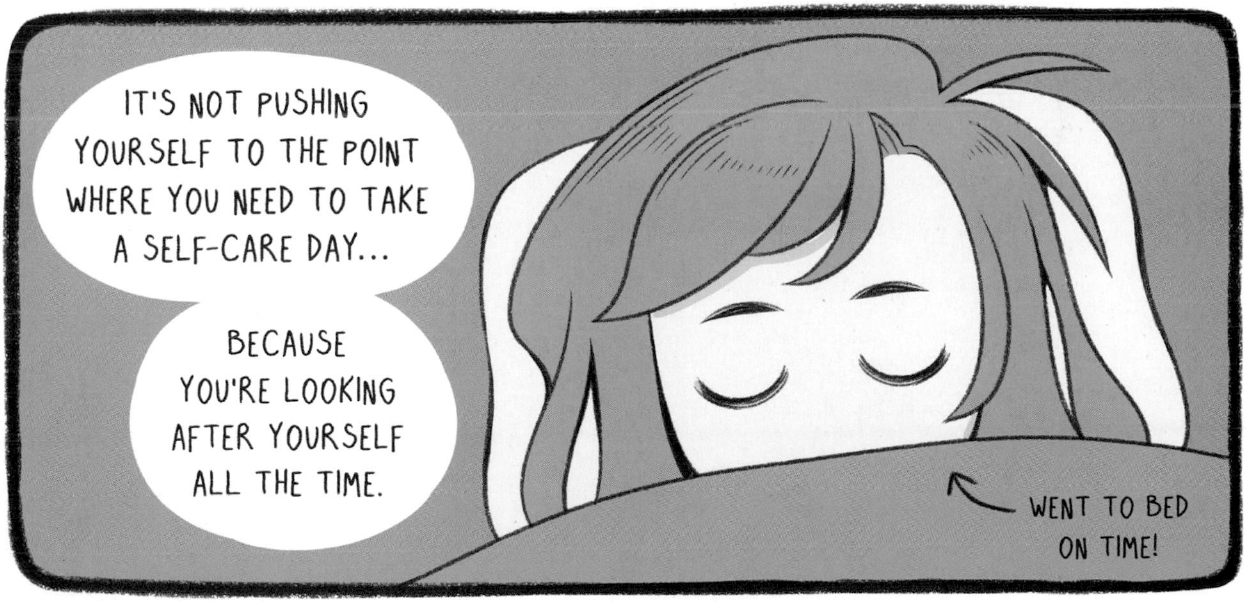
IT'S NOT PUSHING YOURSELF TO THE POINT WHERE YOU NEED TO TAKE A SELF-CARE DAY...
BECAUSE YOU'RE LOOKING AFTER YOURSELF ALL THE TIME.
WENT TO BED ON TIME!

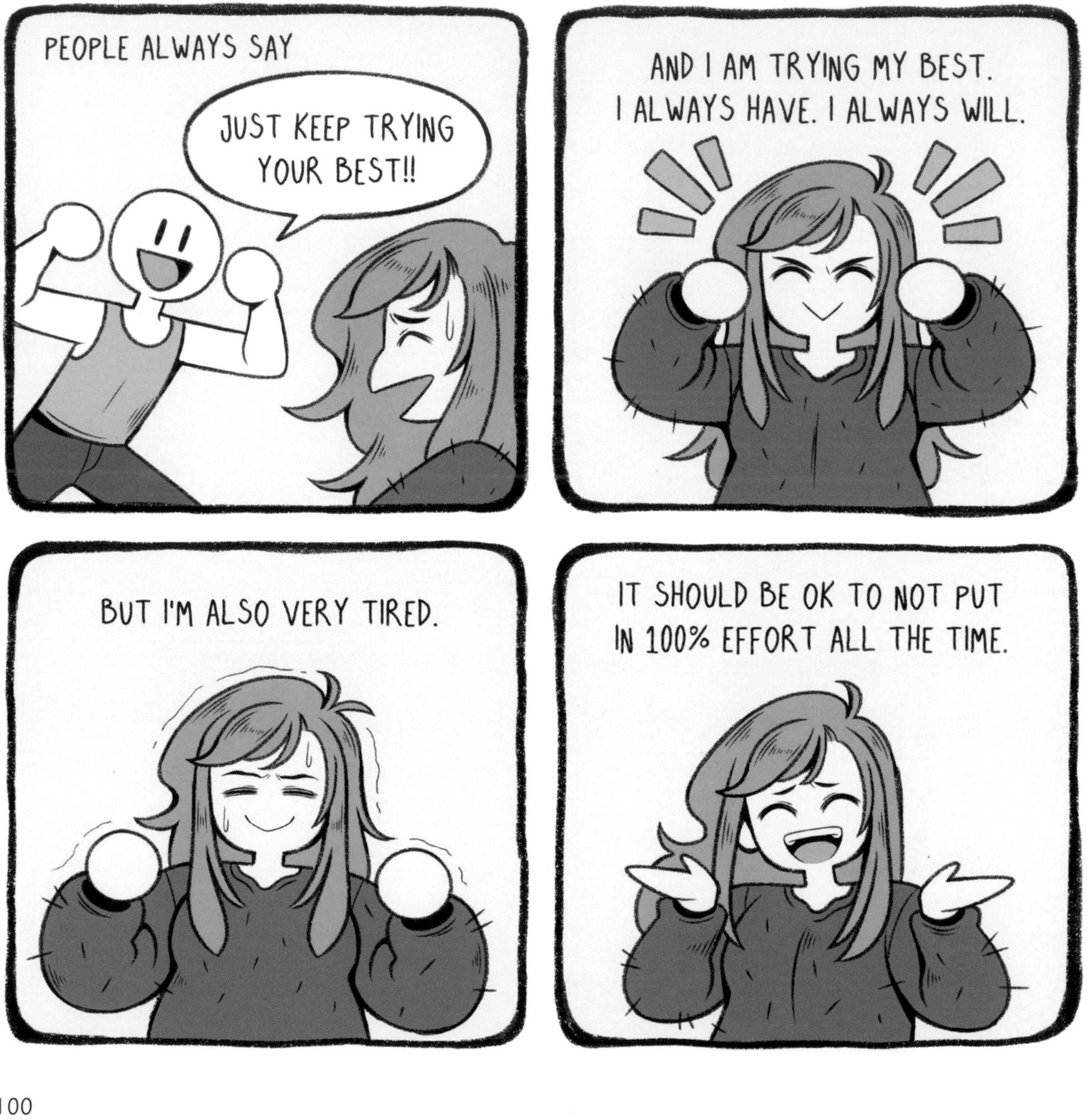
PEOPLE ALWAYS SAY
JUST KEEP TRYING YOUR BEST!!
AND I AM TRYING MY BEST. I ALWAYS HAVE. I ALWAYS WILL.
BUT I'M ALSO VERY TIRED.
IT SHOULD BE OK TO NOT PUT IN 100% EFFORT ALL THE TIME.

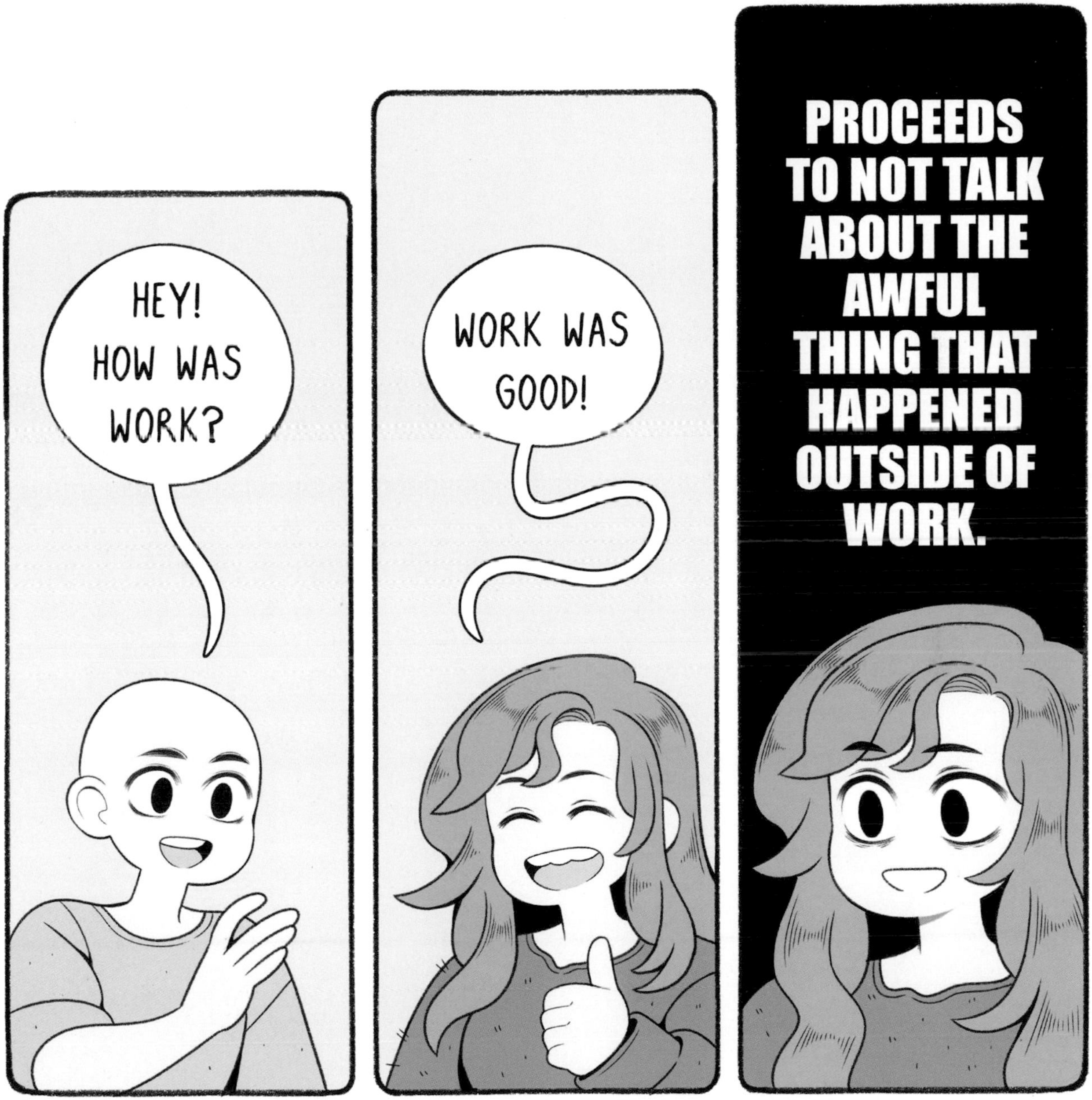
HEY! HOW WAS WORK?
WORK WAS GOOD!
PROCEEDS TO NOT TALK ABOUT THE AWFUL THING THAT HAPPENED OUTSIDE OF WORK.

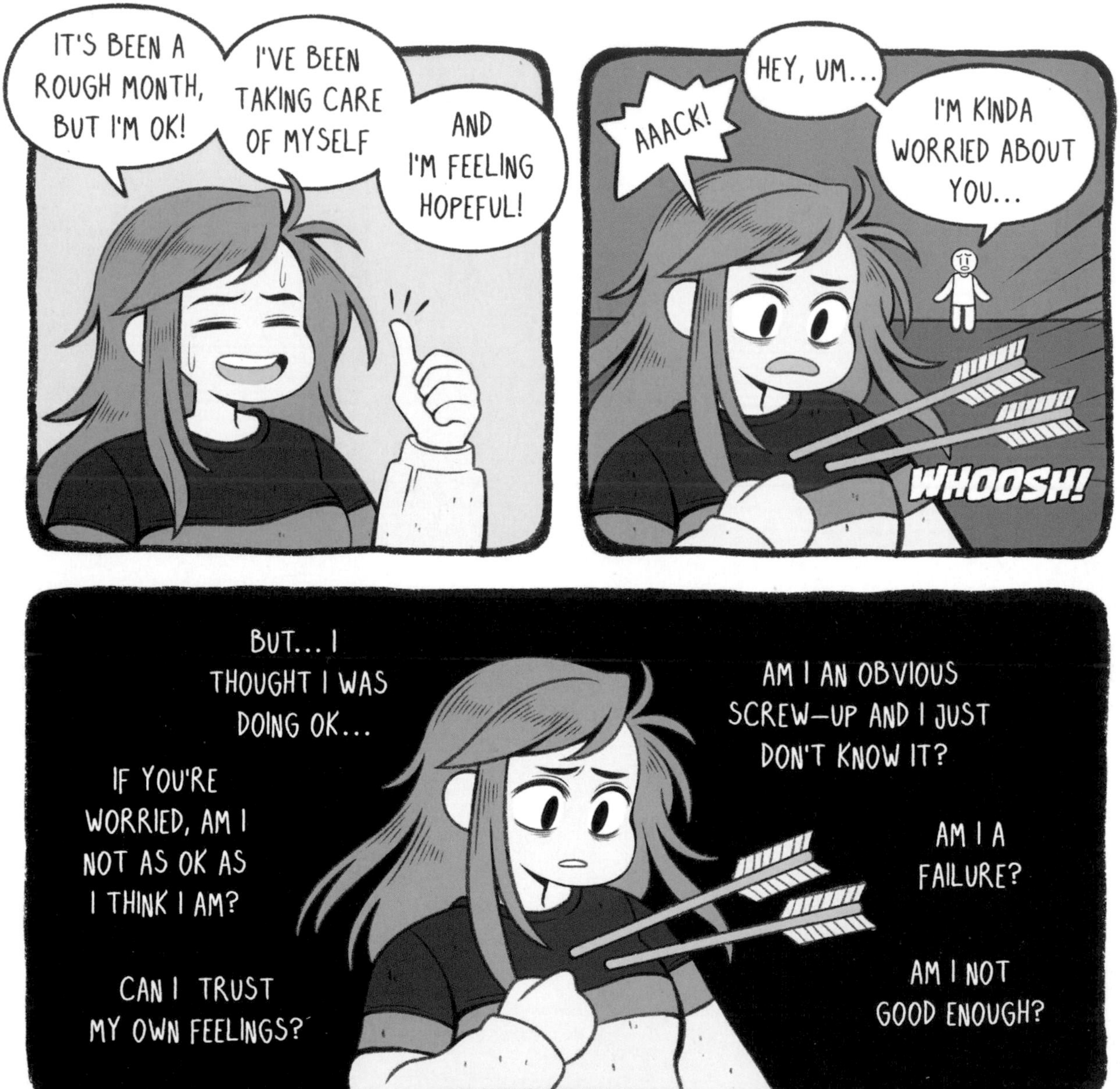
IT'S BEEN A ROUGH MONTH, BUT I'M OK!
I'VE BEEN TAKING CARE OF MYSELF
AND I'M FEELING HOPEFUL!
AAACK!
HEY, UM...
I'M KINDA WORRIED ABOUT YOU...
WHOOSH!
BUT... I THOUGHT I WAS DOING OK...
IF YOU'RE WORRIED, AM I NOT AS OK AS I THINK I AM?
CAN I TRUST MY OWN FEELINGS?
AM I AN OBVIOUS SCREW-UP AND I JUST DON'T KNOW IT?
AM I A FAILURE?
AM I NOT GOOD ENOUGH?

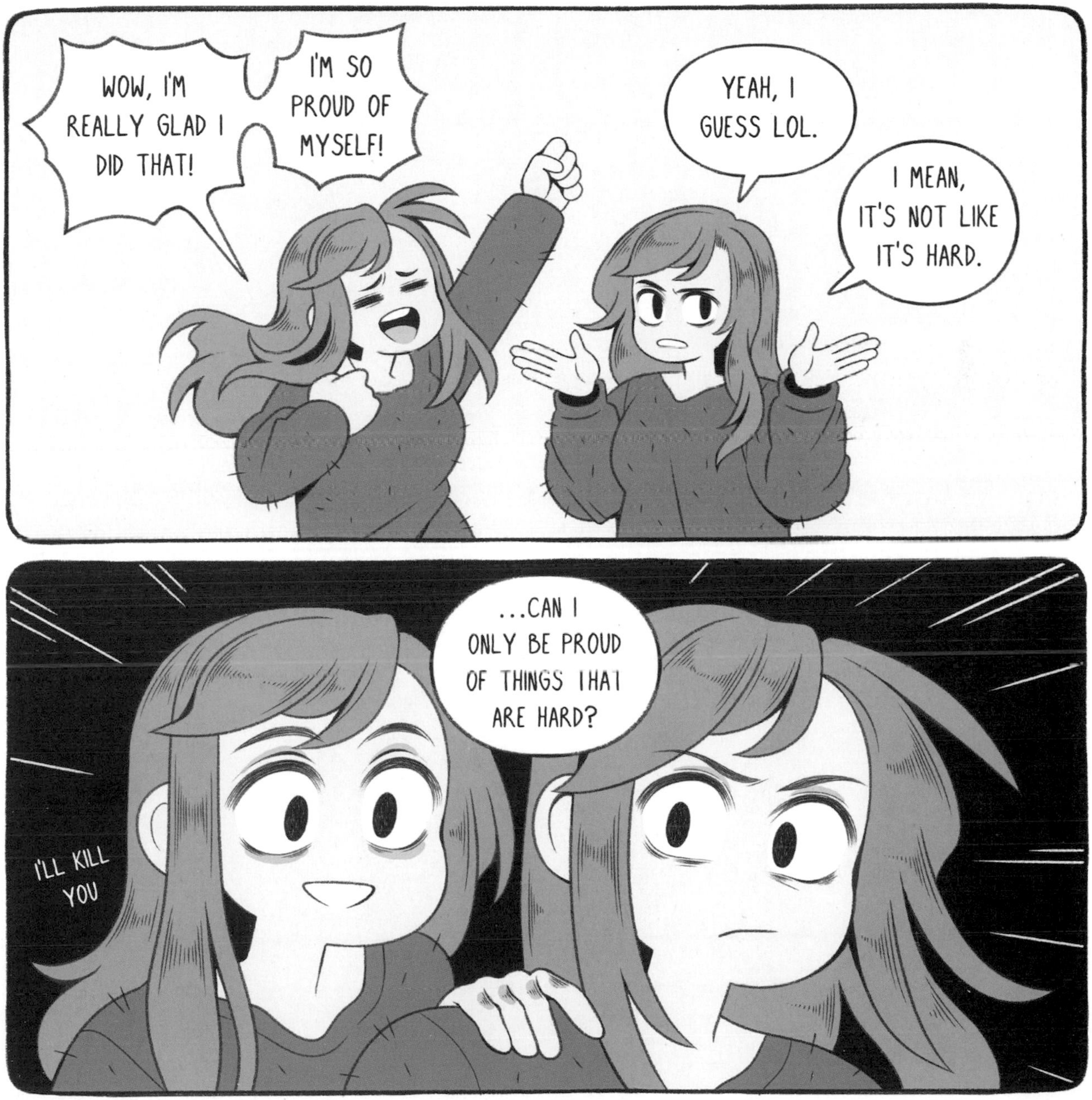
WOW, I'M REALLY GLAD I DID THAT!
I'M SO PROUD OF MYSELF!
YEAH, I GUESS LOL.
I MEAN, IT'S NOT LIKE IT'S HARD.
...CAN I ONLY BE PROUD OF THINGS THAT ARE HARD?
I'LL KILL YOU

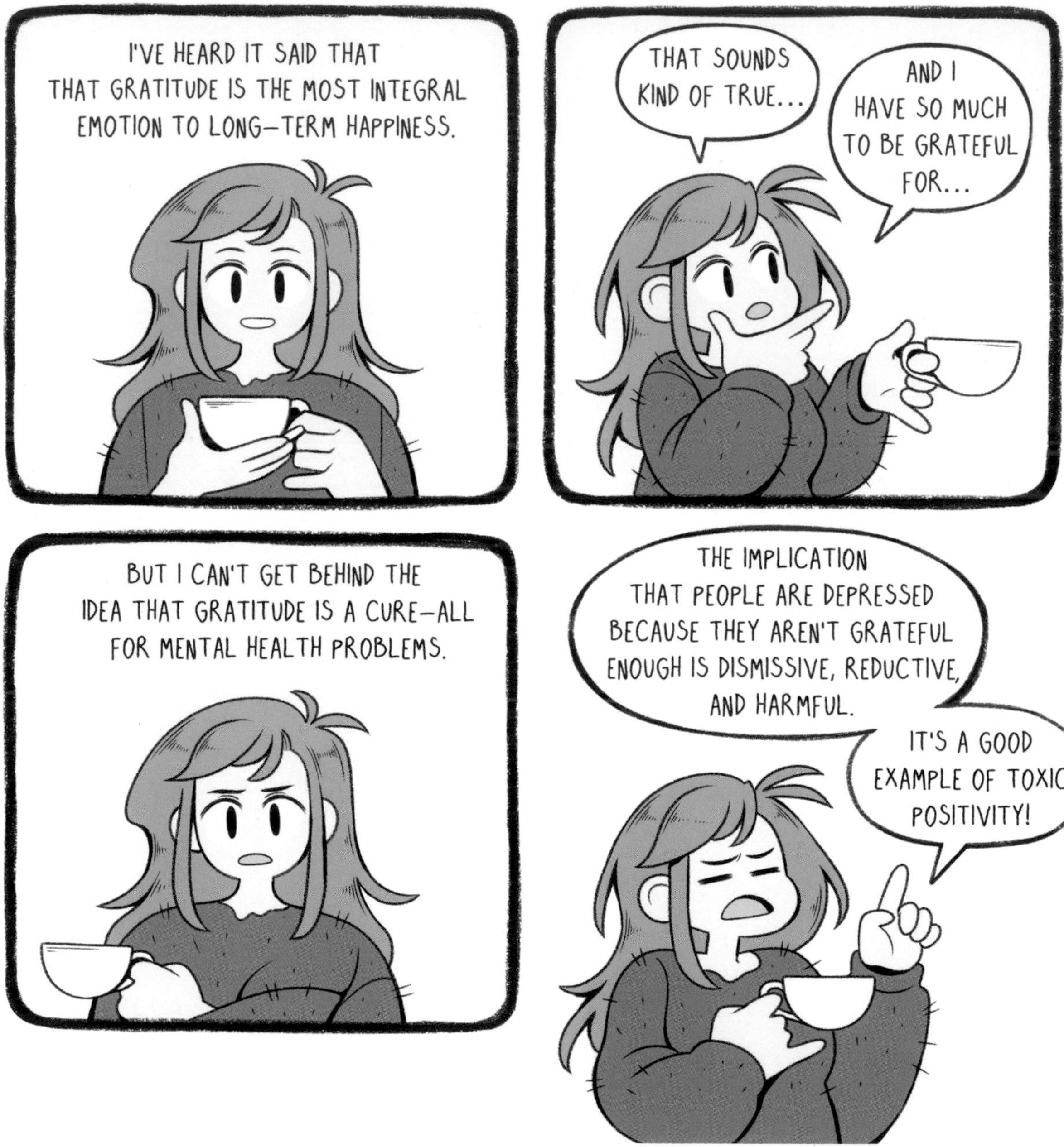
I'VE HEARD IT SAID THAT THAT GRATITUDE IS THE MOST INTEGRAL EMOTION TO LONG-TERM HAPPINESS.
THAT SOUNDS KIND OF TRUE...
AND I HAVE SO MUCH TO BE GRATEFUL FOR...
BUT I CAN'T GET BEHIND THE IDEA THAT GRATITUDE IS A CURE-ALL FOR MENTAL HEALTH PROBLEMS.
THE IMPLICATION THAT PEOPLE ARE DEPRESSED BECAUSE THEY AREN'T GRATEFUL ENOUGH IS DISMISSIVE, REDUCTIVE, AND HARMFUL.
IT'S A GOOD EXAMPLE OF TOXIC POSITIVITY!

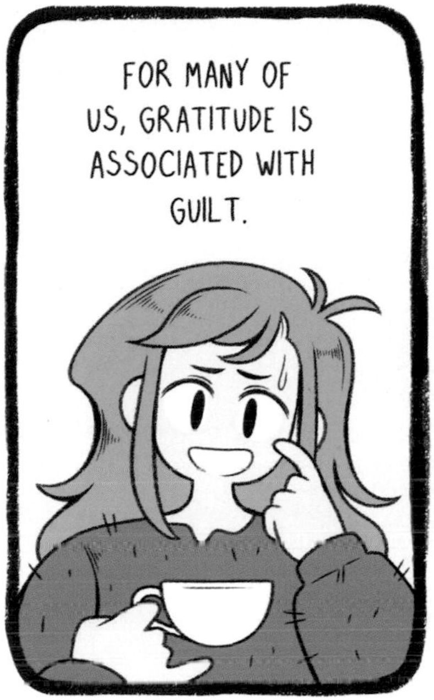
FOR MANY OF US, GRATITUDE IS ASSOCIATED WITH GUILT.

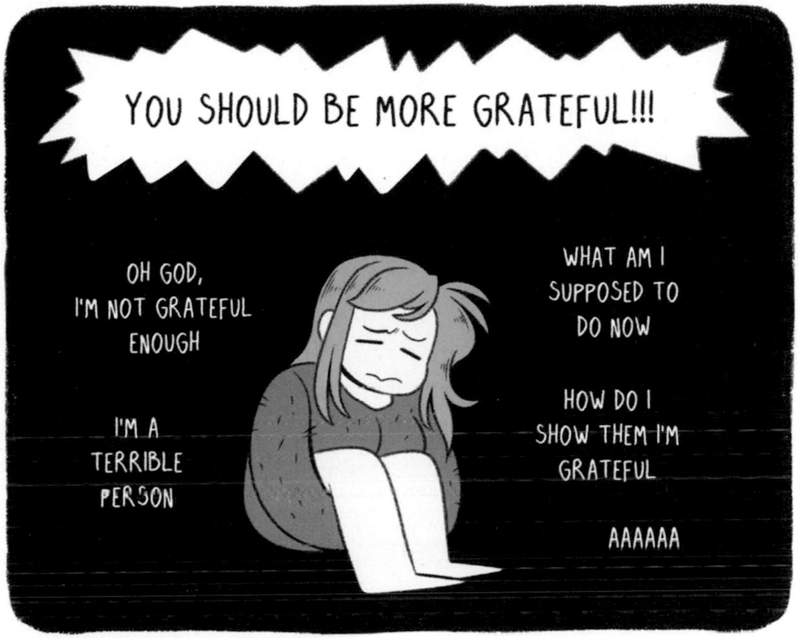
YOU SHOULD BE MORE GRATEFUL!!!
OH GOD, I'M NOT GRATEFUL ENOUGH
I'M A TERRIBLE PERSON
WHAT AM I SUPPOSED TO DO NOW
HOW DO I SHOW THEM I'M GRATEFUL
AAAAAA

MENTAL HEALTH SPIRALS ARE USUALLY ALL-CONSUMING AND BEYOND OUR IMMEDIATE CONTROL.

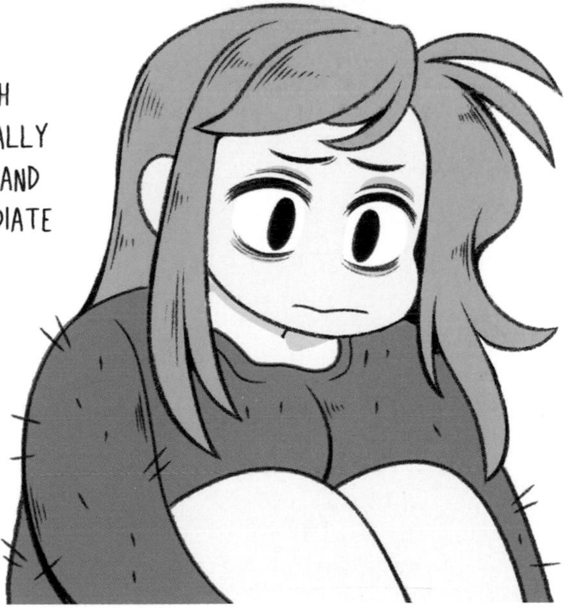

AND JUST BECAUSE WE CAN'T FOCUS ON THE GOOD THINGS IN THOSE MOMENTS DOESN'T MEAN WE DON'T APPRECIATE THEM WHEN WE'RE MORE ABLE TO.

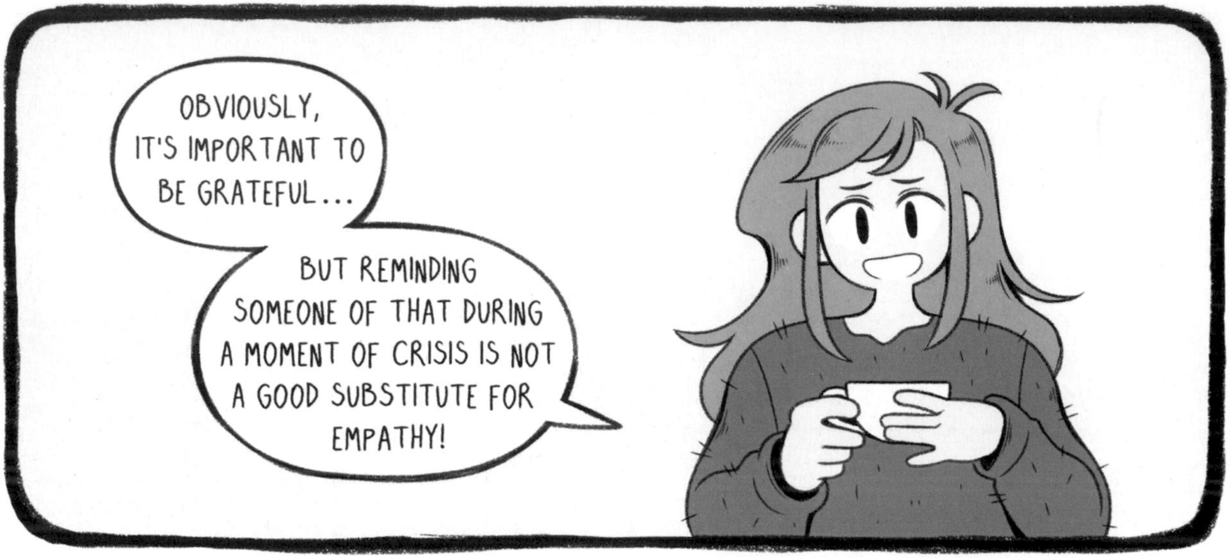
OBVIOUSLY, IT'S IMPORTANT TO BE GRATEFUL...
BUT REMINDING SOMEONE OF THAT DURING A MOMENT OF CRISIS IS NOT A GOOD SUBSTITUTE FOR EMPATHY!

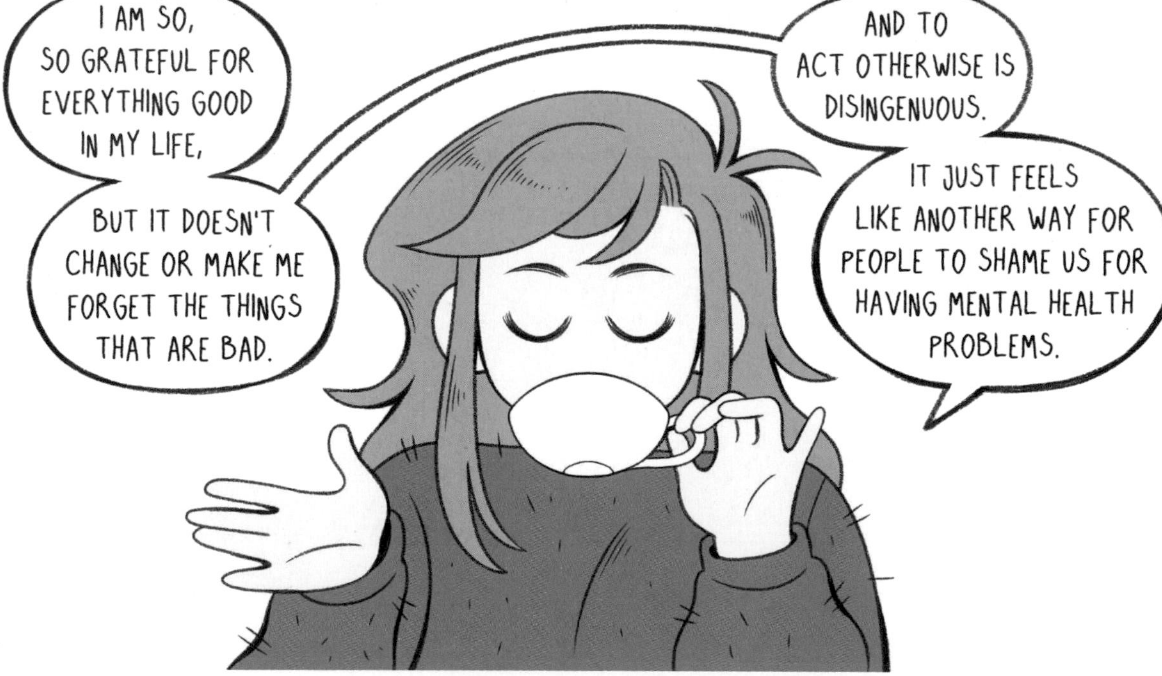
I AM SO, SO GRATEFUL FOR EVERYTHING GOOD IN MY LIFE,
BUT IT DOESN'T CHANGE OR MAKE ME FORGET THE THINGS THAT ARE BAD.
AND TO ACT OTHERWISE IS DISINGENUOUS.
IT JUST FEELS LIKE ANOTHER WAY FOR PEOPLE TO SHAME US FOR HAVING MENTAL HEALTH PROBLEMS.

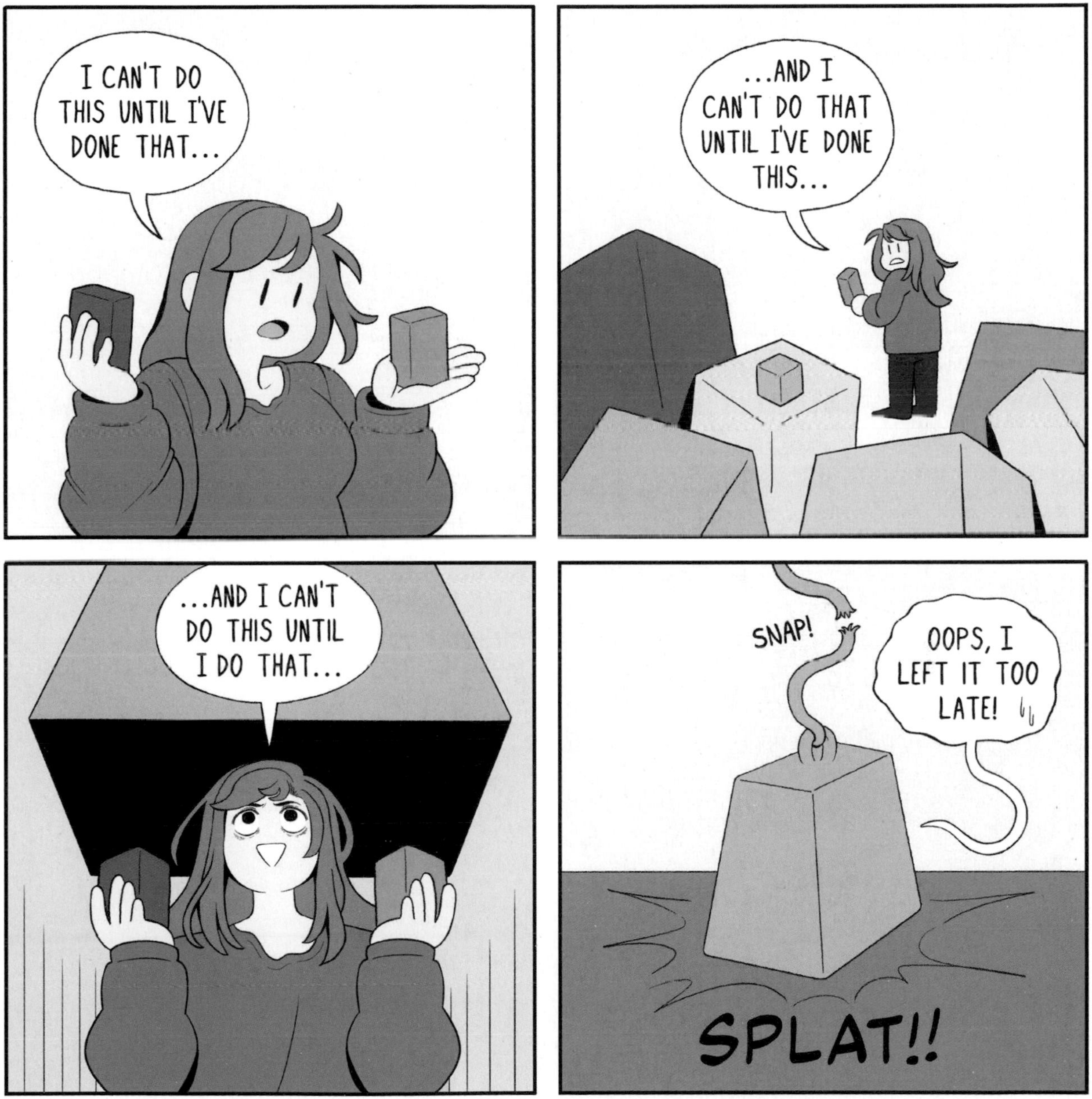
I CAN'T DO THIS UNTIL I'VE DONE THAT...
...AND I CAN'T DO THAT UNTIL I'VE DONE THIS...
...AND I CAN'T DO THIS UNTIL I DO THAT...
SNAP!
OOPS, I LEFT IT TOO LATE!
SPLAT!!

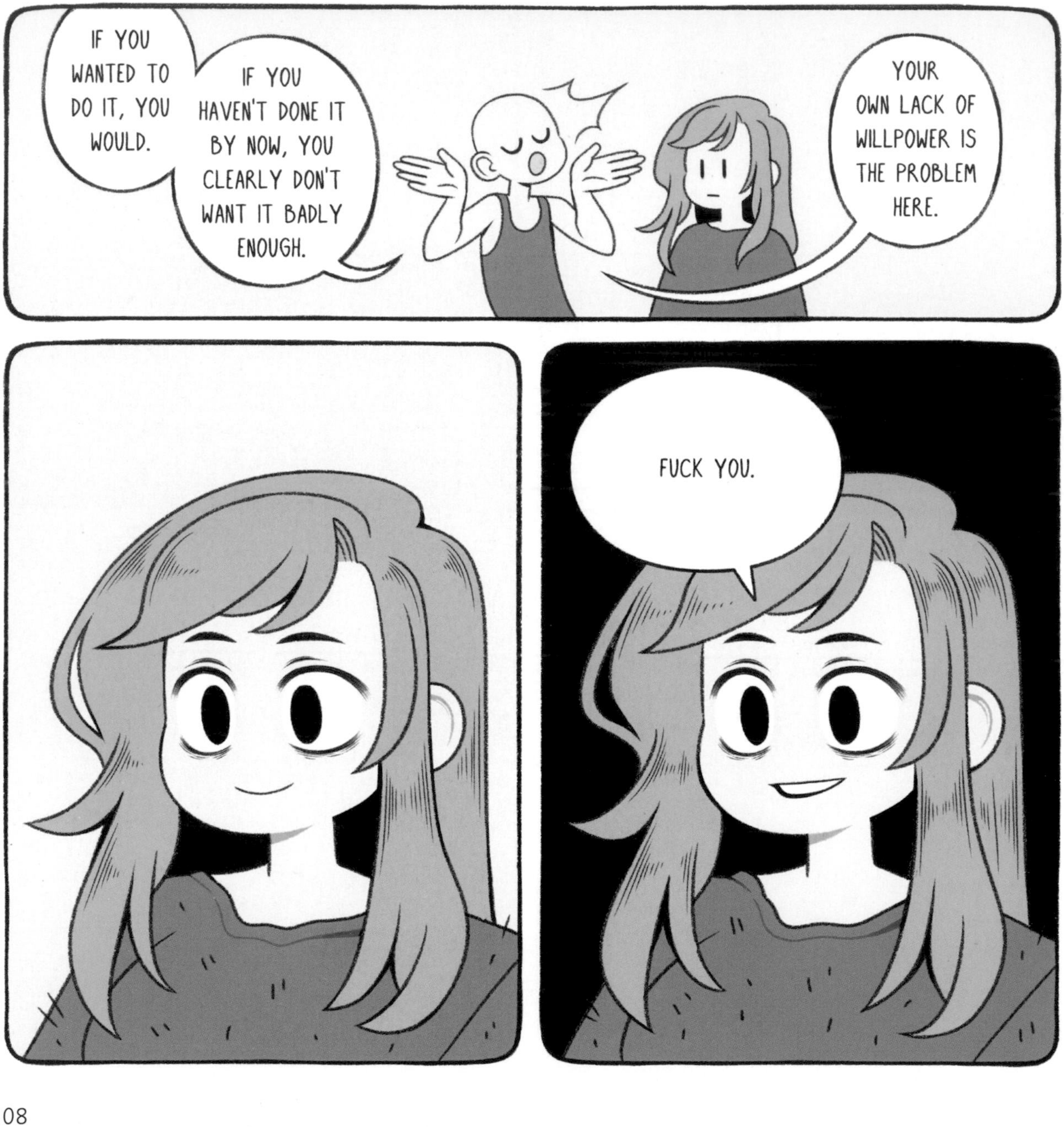
IF YOU WANTED TO DO IT, YOU WOULD.
IF YOU HAVEN'T DONE IT BY NOW, YOU CLEARLY DON'T WANT IT BADLY ENOUGH.
YOUR OWN LACK OF WILLPOWER IS THE PROBLEM HERE.
FUCK YOU.

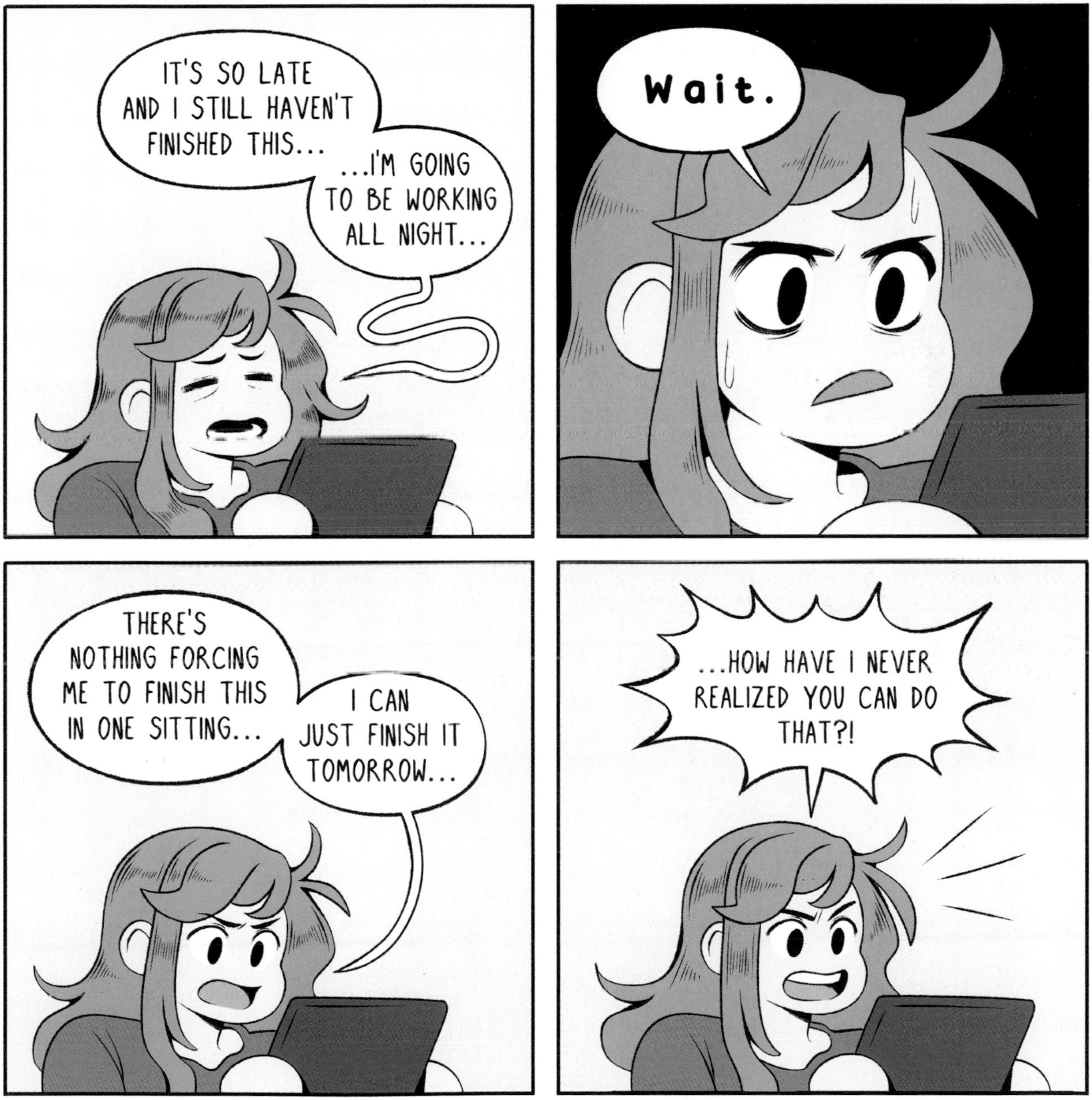
IT'S SO LATE AND I STILL HAVEN'T FINISHED THIS...
...I'M GOING TO BE WORKING ALL NIGHT...
Wait.
THERE'S NOTHING FORCING ME TO FINISH THIS IN ONE SITTING...
I CAN JUST FINISH IT TOMORROW...
...HOW HAVE I NEVER REALIZED YOU CAN DO THAT?!

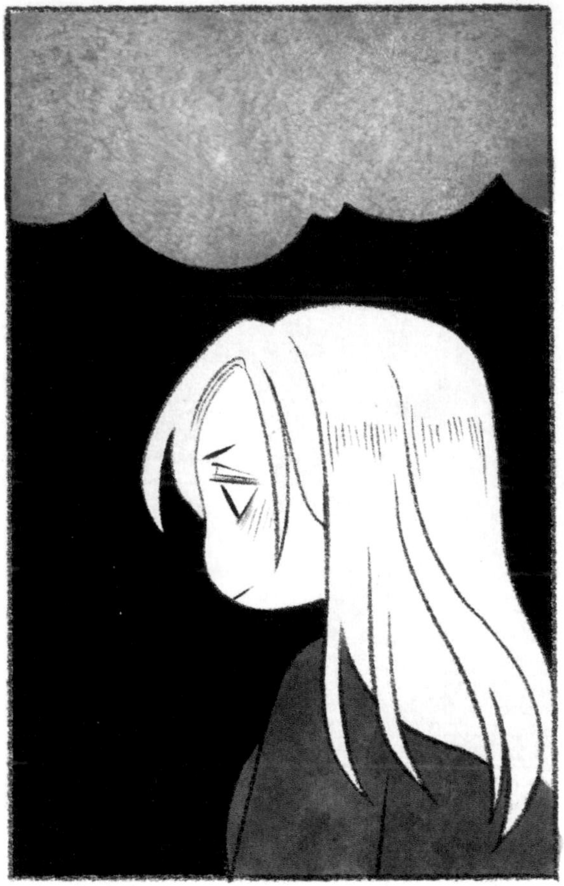

I OVERCAME SO MUCH AND WORKED SO HARD AND I JUST WANT SOMEONE TO TELL ME THEY'RE PROUD OF ME FOR GETTING HERE.

WHY DO I ALWAYS PUT MYSELF DOWN? WHEN DID I BECOME THIS DESPERATE TO BE ACKNOWLEDGED BY OTHERS IN MY VICINITY?

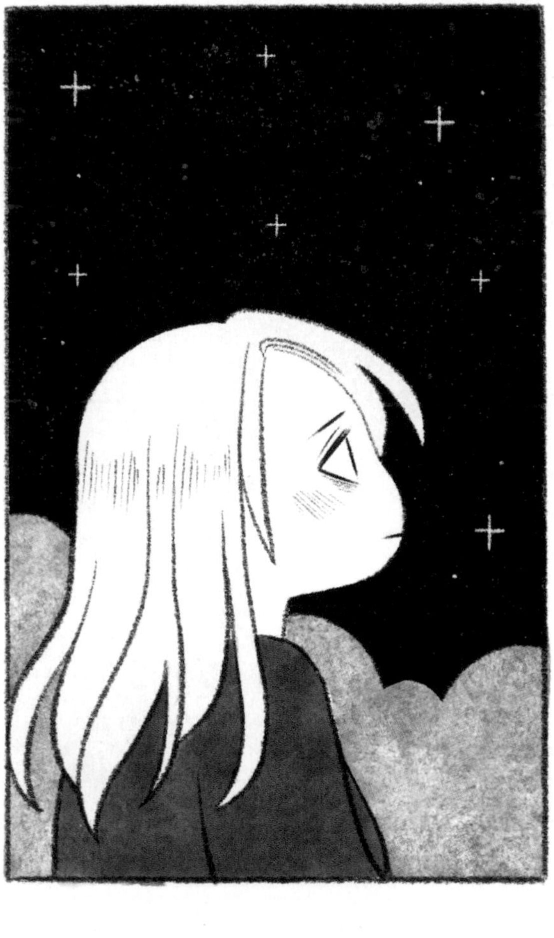

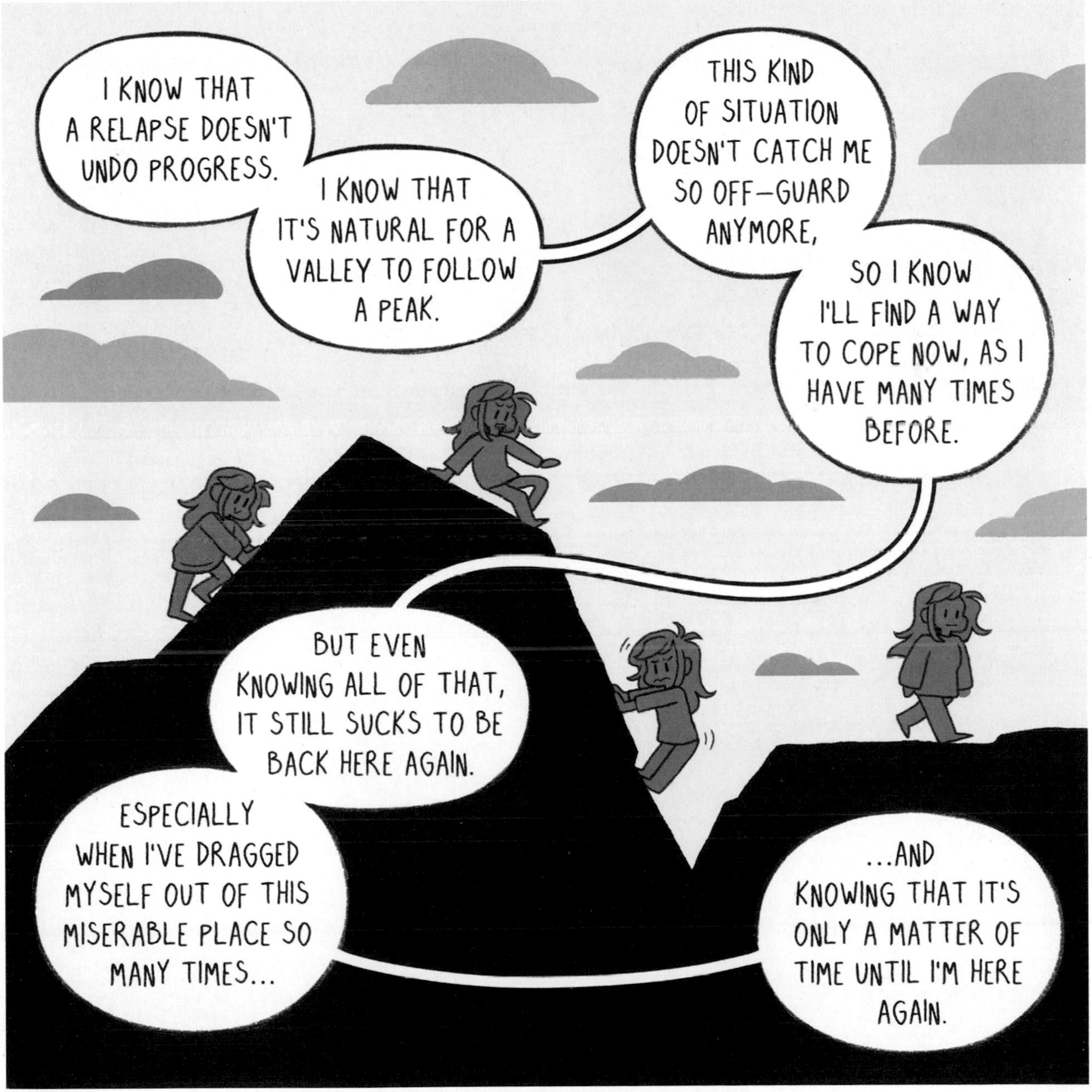
I KNOW THAT A RELAPSE DOESN'T UNDO PROGRESS.
I KNOW THAT IT'S NATURAL FOR A VALLEY TO FOLLOW A PEAK.
THIS KIND OF SITUATION DOESN'T CATCH ME SO OFF-GUARD ANYMORE,
SO I KNOW I'LL FIND A WAY TO COPE NOW, AS I HAVE MANY TIMES BEFORE.
BUT EVEN KNOWING ALL OF THAT, IT STILL SUCKS TO BE BACK HERE AGAIN.
ESPECIALLY WHEN I'VE DRAGGED MYSELF OUT OF THIS MISERABLE PLACE SO MANY TIMES...
...AND KNOWING THAT IT'S ONLY A MATTER OF TIME UNTIL I'M HERE AGAIN.

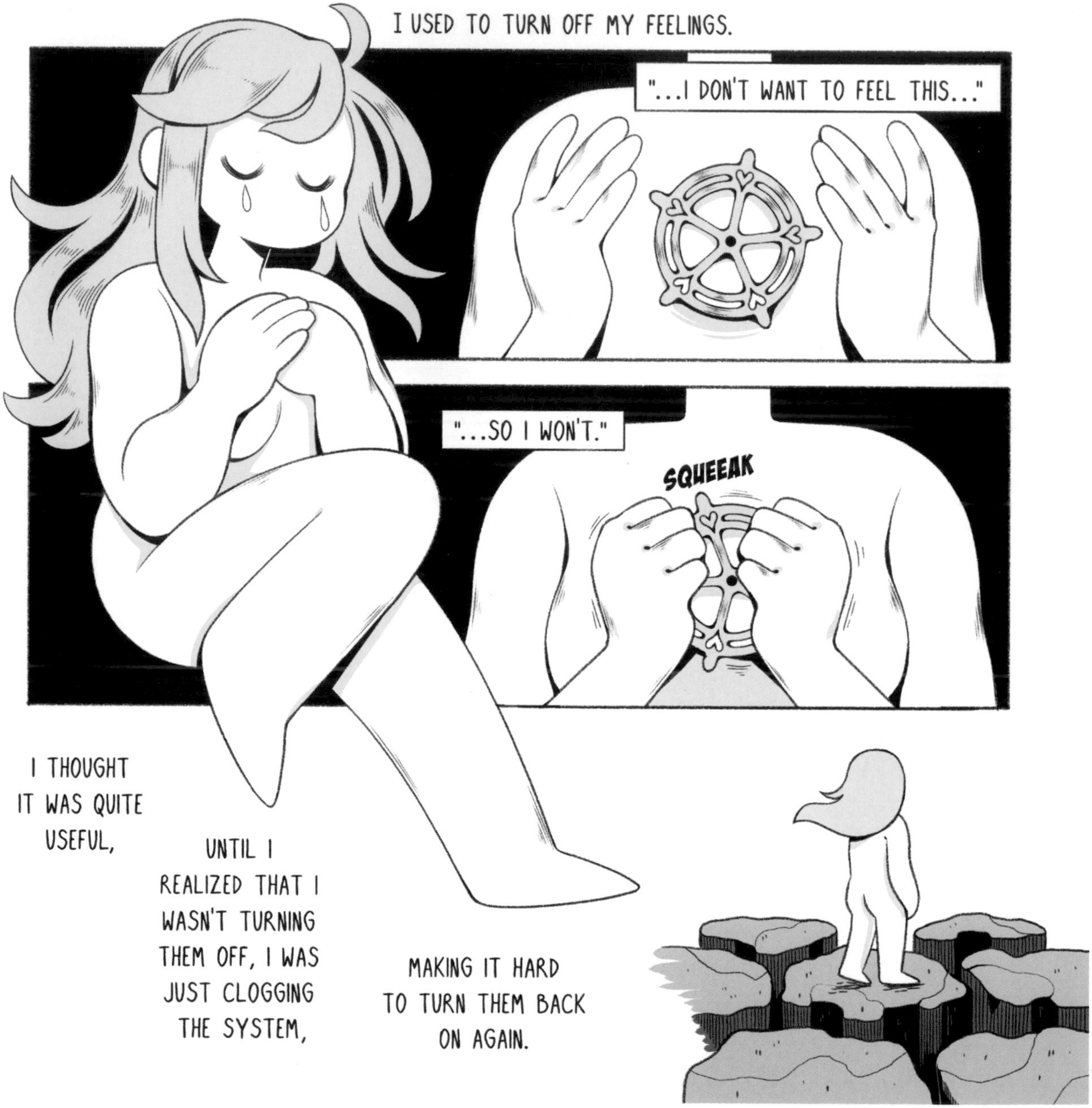
I USED TO TURN OFF MY FEELINGS.
"...I DON'T WANT TO FEEL THIS..."
"...SO I WON'T."
SQUEEAK
I THOUGHT IT WAS QUITE USEFUL,
UNTIL I REALIZED THAT I WASN'T TURNING THEM OFF, I WAS JUST CLOGGING THE SYSTEM,
MAKING IT HARD TO TURN THEM BACK ON AGAIN.

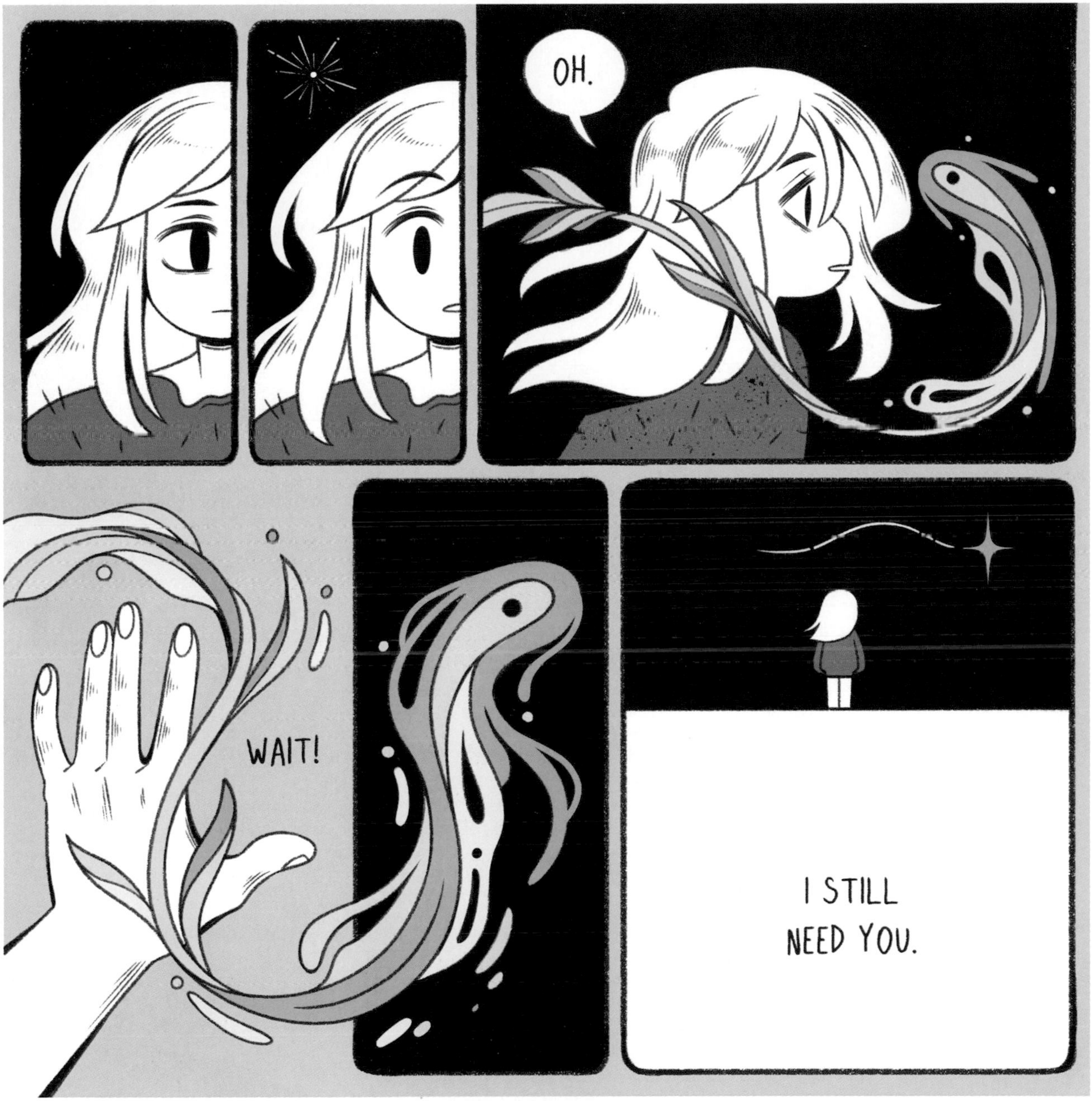
OH.
WAIT!
I STILL
NEED YOU.

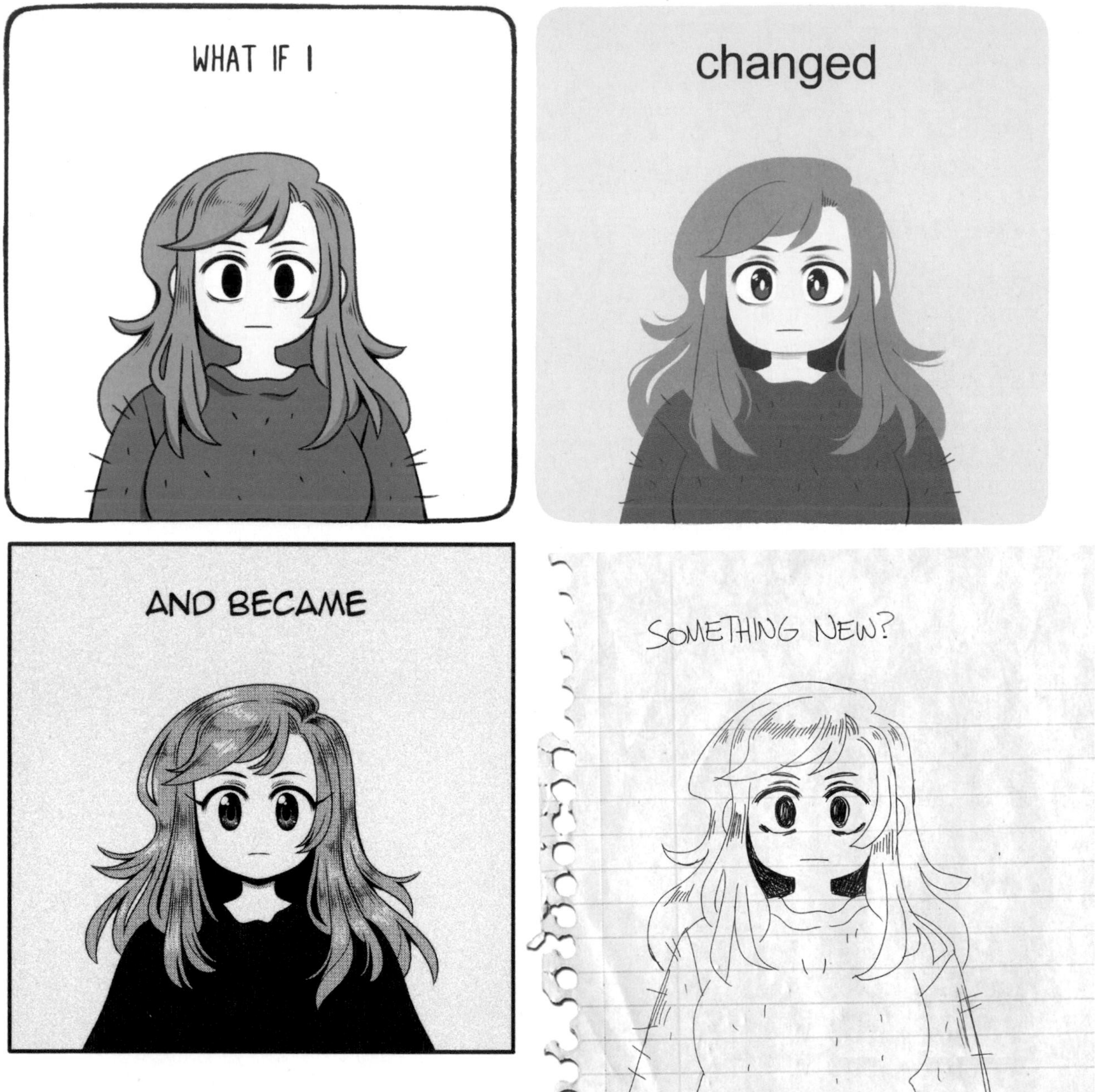
WHAT IF I
changed
AND BECAME
SOMETHING NEW?

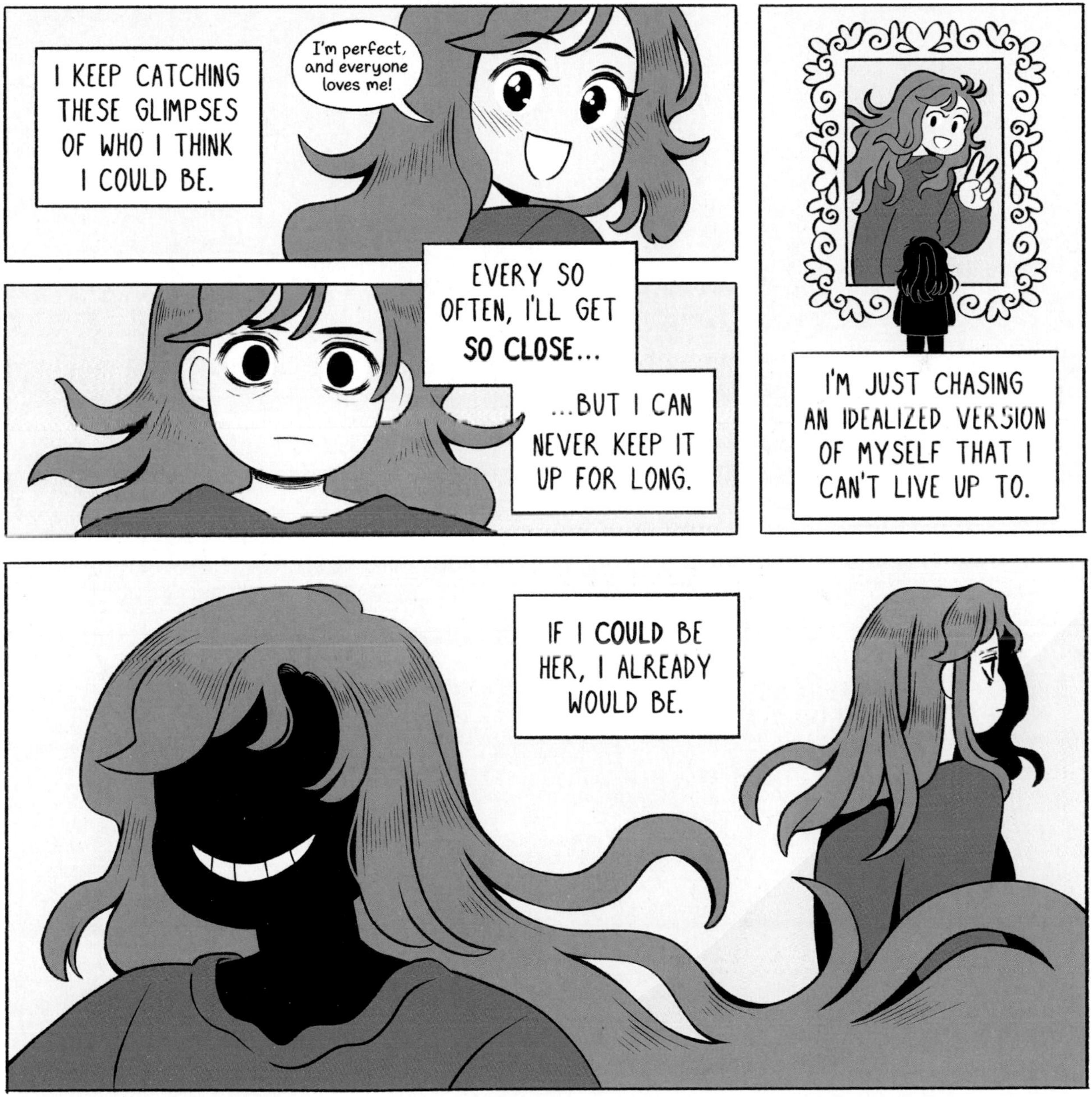
I KEEP CATCHING THESE GLIMPSES OF WHO I THINK I COULD BE.
I'm perfect, and everyone loves me!
EVERY SO OFTEN, I'LL GET **SO CLOSE**...
...BUT I CAN NEVER KEEP IT UP FOR LONG.
I'M JUST CHASING AN IDEALIZED VERSION OF MYSELF THAT I CAN'T LIVE UP TO.
IF I **COULD** BE HER, I ALREADY WOULD BE.

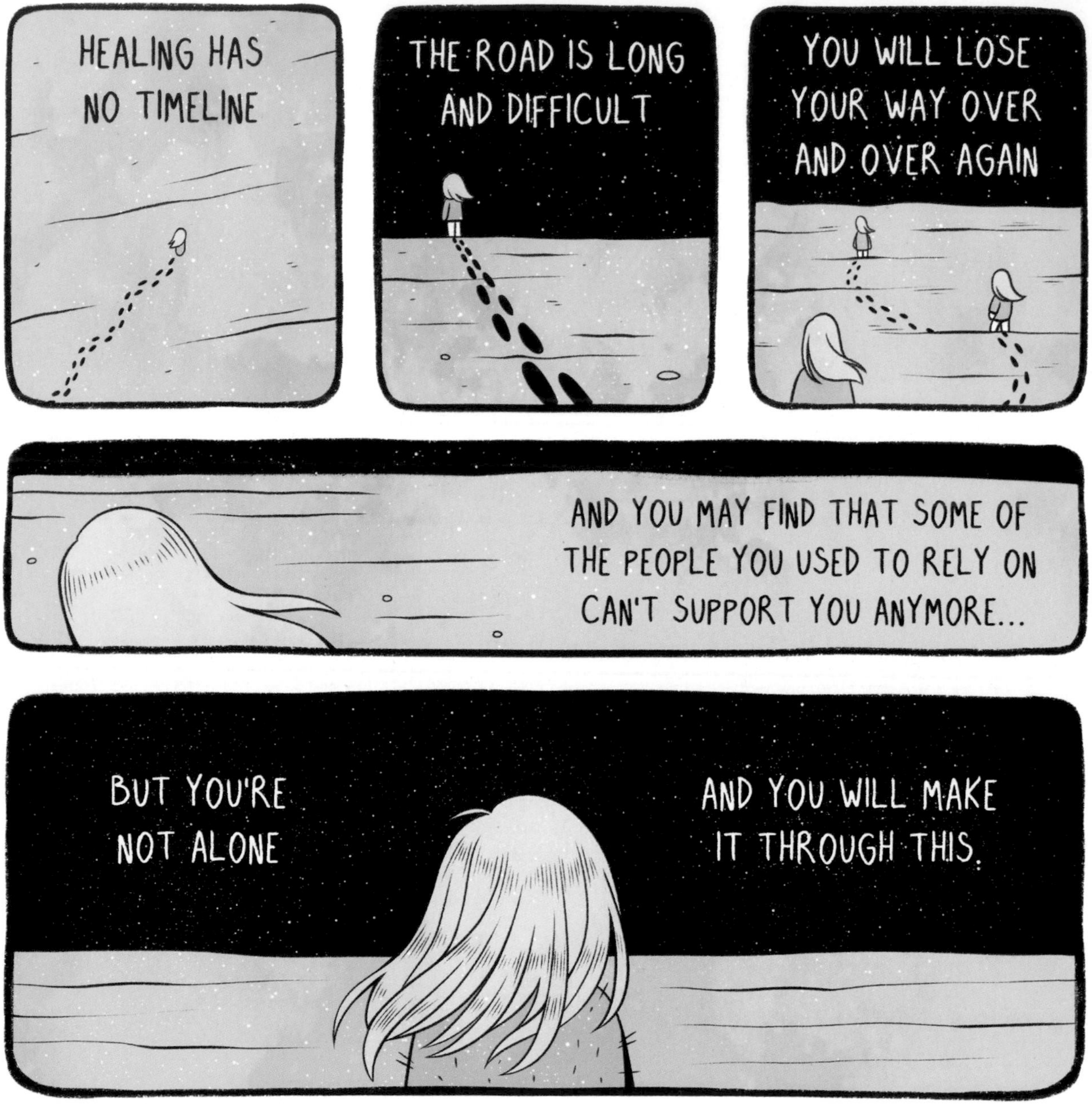
HEALING HAS NO TIMELINE
THE ROAD IS LONG AND DIFFICULT
YOU WILL LOSE YOUR WAY OVER AND OVER AGAIN
AND YOU MAY FIND THAT SOME OF THE PEOPLE YOU USED TO RELY ON CAN'T SUPPORT YOU ANYMORE...
BUT YOU'RE NOT ALONE
AND YOU WILL MAKE IT THROUGH THIS.

I'VE LEARNED FROM THE MISTAKES OF MY PAST

BUT IF I COULD DO IT ALL AGAIN, OR IF I WERE TESTED...

WOULD I REALLY BE ABLE TO SHOW IMPROVEMENT?

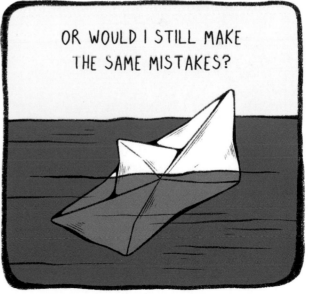

OR WOULD I STILL MAKE THE SAME MISTAKES?

I OFTEN FEEL LIKE I'M SO FAR BEHIND EVERYONE ELSE.

BUT EVEN IF WE'RE THE SAME AGE, WE HAVEN'T NECESSARILY HAD THE SAME TIME.

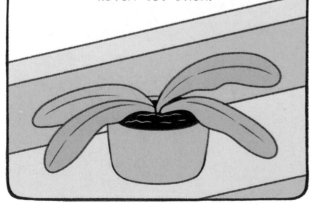

DISABILITY, TRAUMA, AND RECOVERY HAVE TAKEN SO MUCH TIME FROM ME THAT I'LL NEVER GET BACK.

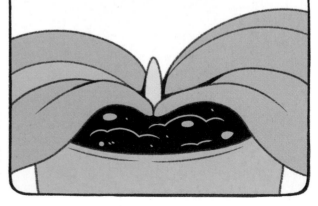

I'VE GROWN AT MY OWN PACE AND I'M FOLLOWING MY OWN PATH.

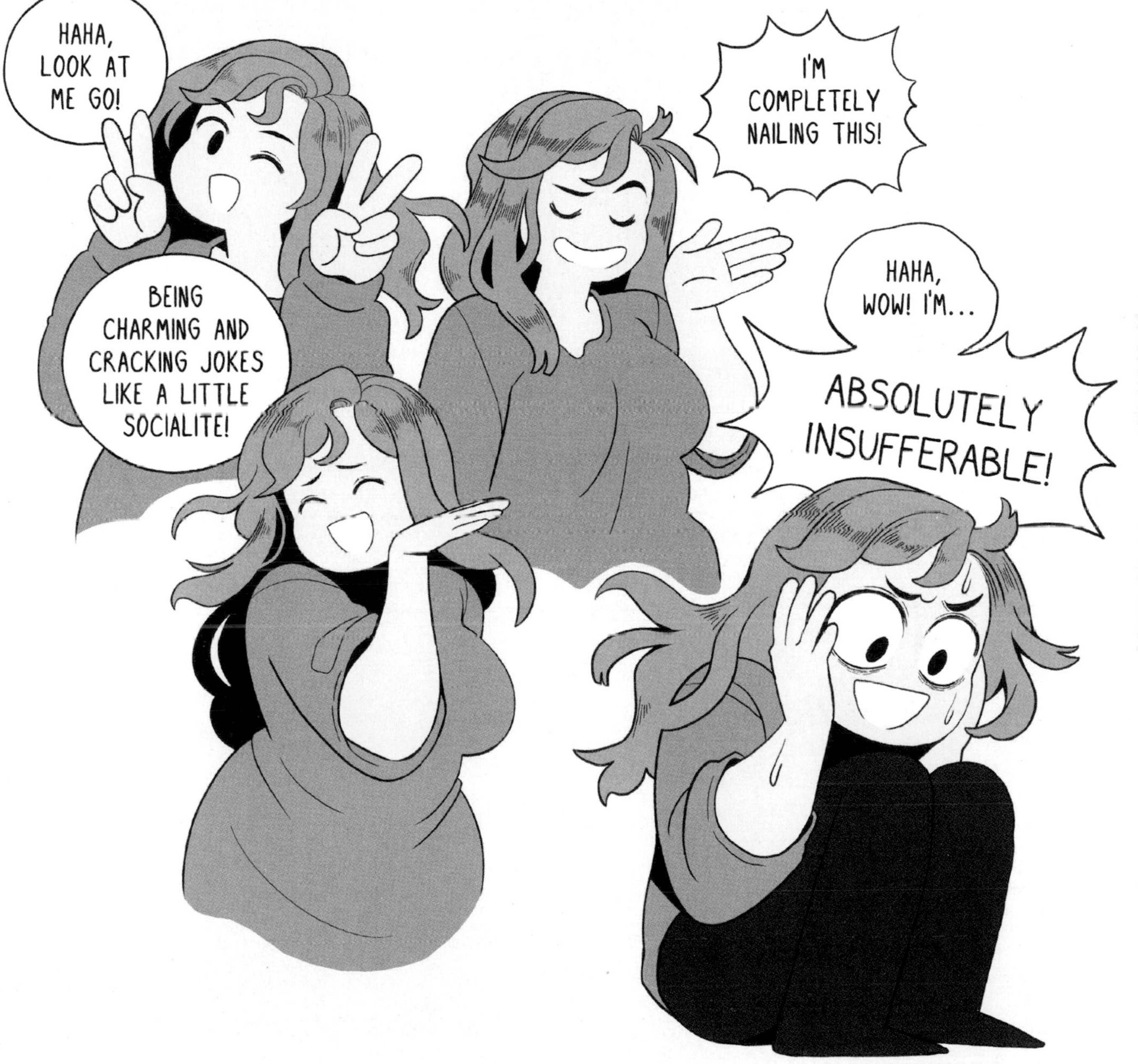
HAHA, LOOK AT ME GO!
I'M COMPLETELY NAILING THIS!
BEING CHARMING AND CRACKING JOKES LIKE A LITTLE SOCIALITE!
HAHA, WOW! I'M...
ABSOLUTELY INSUFFERABLE!

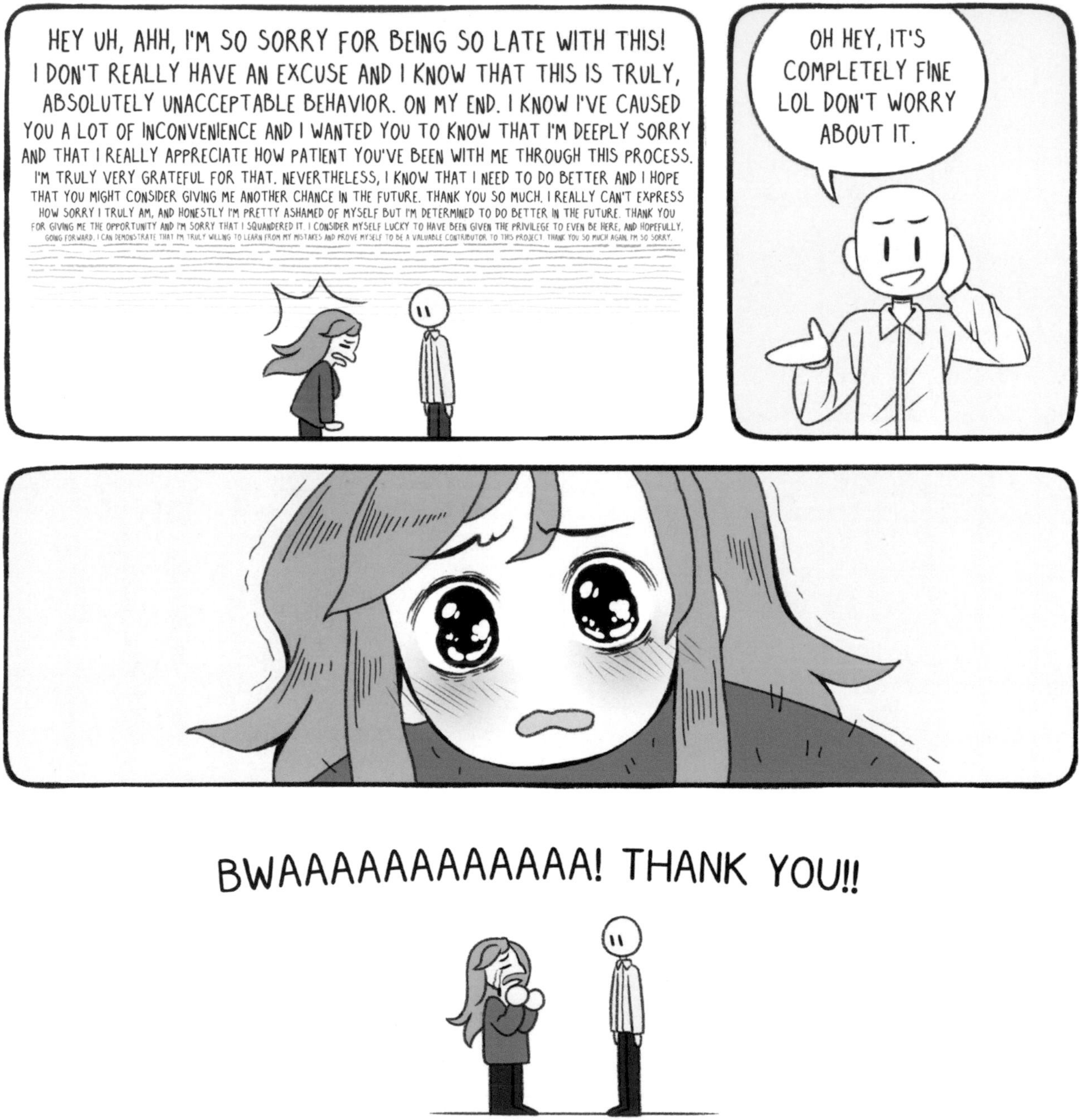
HEY UH, AHH, I'M SO SORRY FOR BEING SO LATE WITH THIS! I DON'T REALLY HAVE AN EXCUSE AND I KNOW THAT THIS IS TRULY, ABSOLUTELY UNACCEPTABLE BEHAVIOR. ON MY END. I KNOW I'VE CAUSED YOU A LOT OF INCONVENIENCE AND I WANTED YOU TO KNOW THAT I'M DEEPLY SORRY AND THAT I REALLY APPRECIATE HOW PATIENT YOU'VE BEEN WITH ME THROUGH THIS PROCESS. I'M TRULY VERY GRATEFUL FOR THAT. NEVERTHELESS, I KNOW THAT I NEED TO DO BETTER AND I HOPE THAT YOU MIGHT CONSIDER GIVING ME ANOTHER CHANCE IN THE FUTURE. THANK YOU SO MUCH. I REALLY CAN'T EXPRESS HOW SORRY I TRULY AM, AND HONESTLY I'M PRETTY ASHAMED OF MYSELF BUT I'M DETERMINED TO DO BETTER IN THE FUTURE. THANK YOU FOR GIVING ME THE OPPORTUNITY AND I'M SORRY THAT I SQUANDERED IT. I CONSIDER MYSELF LUCKY TO HAVE BEEN GIVEN THE PRIVILEGE TO EVEN BE HERE, AND HOPEFULLY, GOING FORWARD, I CAN DEMONSTRATE THAT I'M TRULY WILLING TO LEARN FROM MY MISTAKES AND PROVE MYSELF TO BE A VALUABLE CONTRIBUTOR TO THIS PROJECT. THANK YOU SO MUCH AGAIN. I'M SO SORRY.
OH HEY, IT'S COMPLETELY FINE LOL DON'T WORRY ABOUT IT.
BWAAAAAAAAAAAA! THANK YOU!!

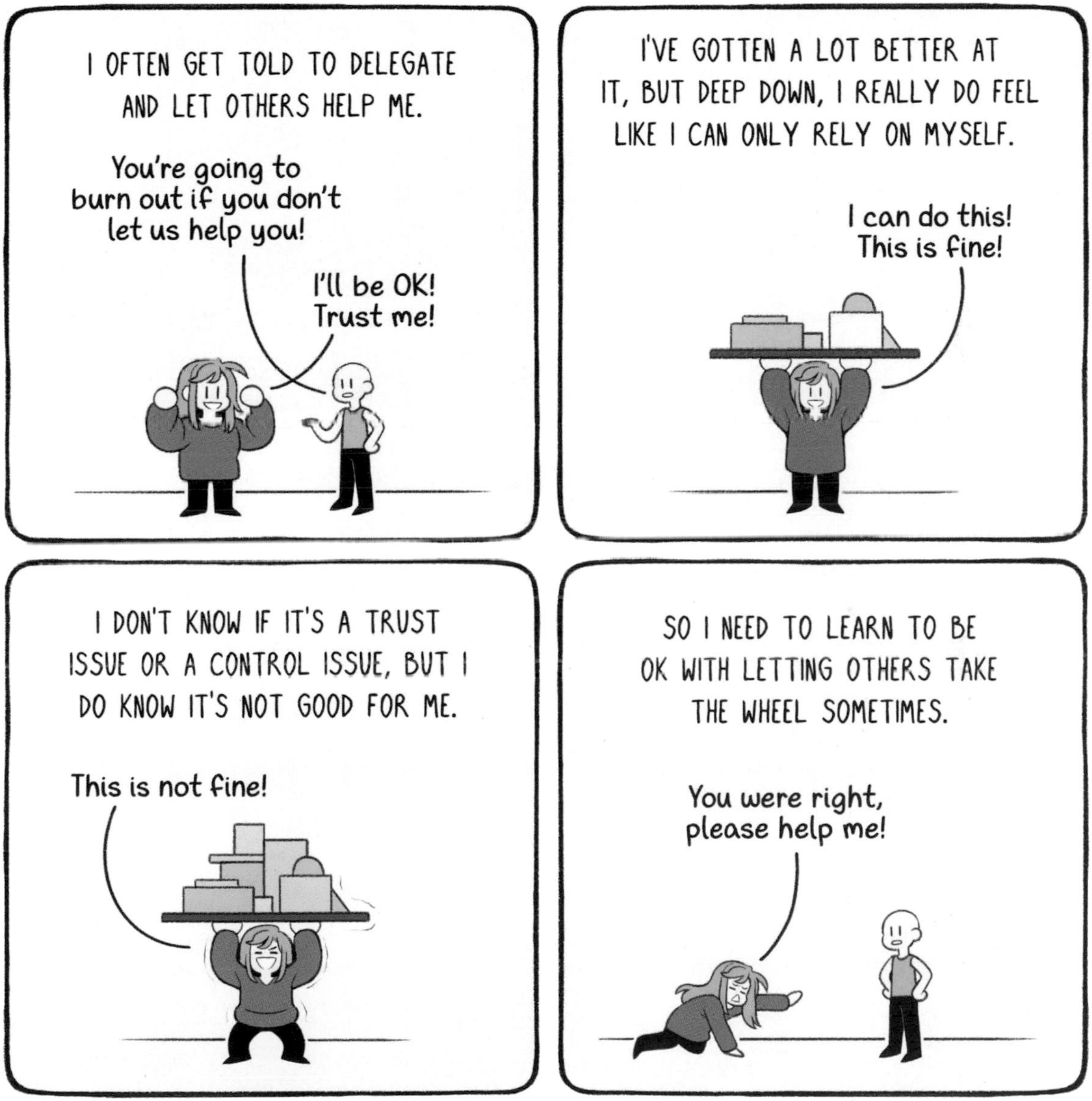
I OFTEN GET TOLD TO DELEGATE AND LET OTHERS HELP ME.
You're going to burn out if you don't let us help you!
I'll be OK! Trust me!
I'VE GOTTEN A LOT BETTER AT IT, BUT DEEP DOWN, I REALLY DO FEEL LIKE I CAN ONLY RELY ON MYSELF.
I can do this! This is fine!
I DON'T KNOW IF IT'S A TRUST ISSUE OR A CONTROL ISSUE, BUT I DO KNOW IT'S NOT GOOD FOR ME.
This is not fine!
SO I NEED TO LEARN TO BE OK WITH LETTING OTHERS TAKE THE WHEEL SOMETIMES.
You were right, please help me!

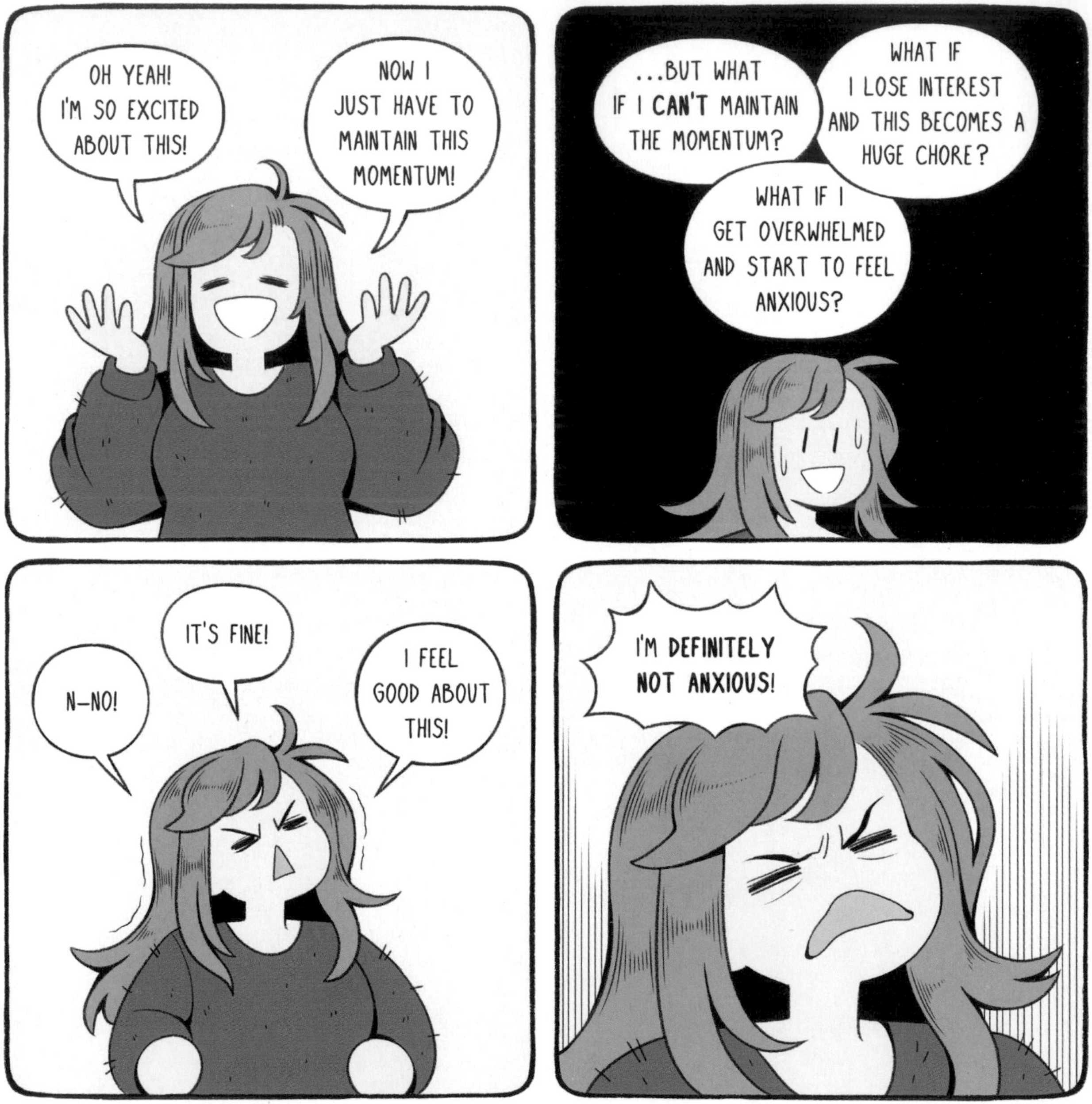

OH YEAH! I'M SO EXCITED ABOUT THIS!
NOW I JUST HAVE TO MAINTAIN THIS MOMENTUM!
...BUT WHAT IF I **CAN'T** MAINTAIN THE MOMENTUM?
WHAT IF I LOSE INTEREST AND THIS BECOMES A HUGE CHORE?
WHAT IF I GET OVERWHELMED AND START TO FEEL ANXIOUS?
N–NO!
IT'S FINE!
I FEEL GOOD ABOUT THIS!
I'M **DEFINITELY NOT ANXIOUS!**

# FINALLY OVERCOMING ANXIETY

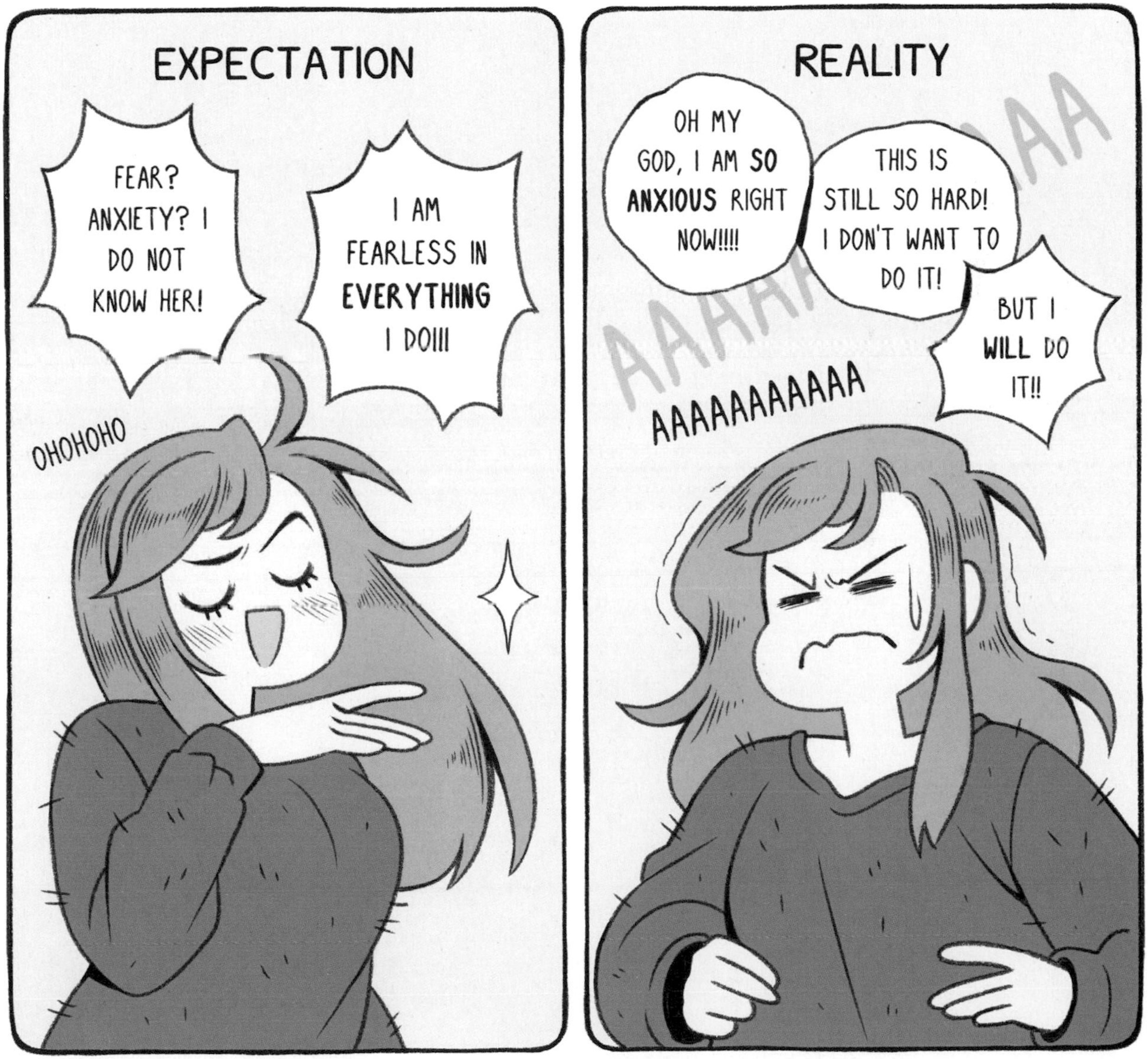
EXPECTATION
FEAR? ANXIETY? I DO NOT KNOW HER!
I AM FEARLESS IN **EVERYTHING** I DO!!!
OHOHOHO
REALITY
OH MY GOD, I AM **SO ANXIOUS** RIGHT NOW!!!!
THIS IS STILL SO HARD! I DON'T WANT TO DO IT!
BUT I **WILL** DO IT!!
AAAAAAAAAA

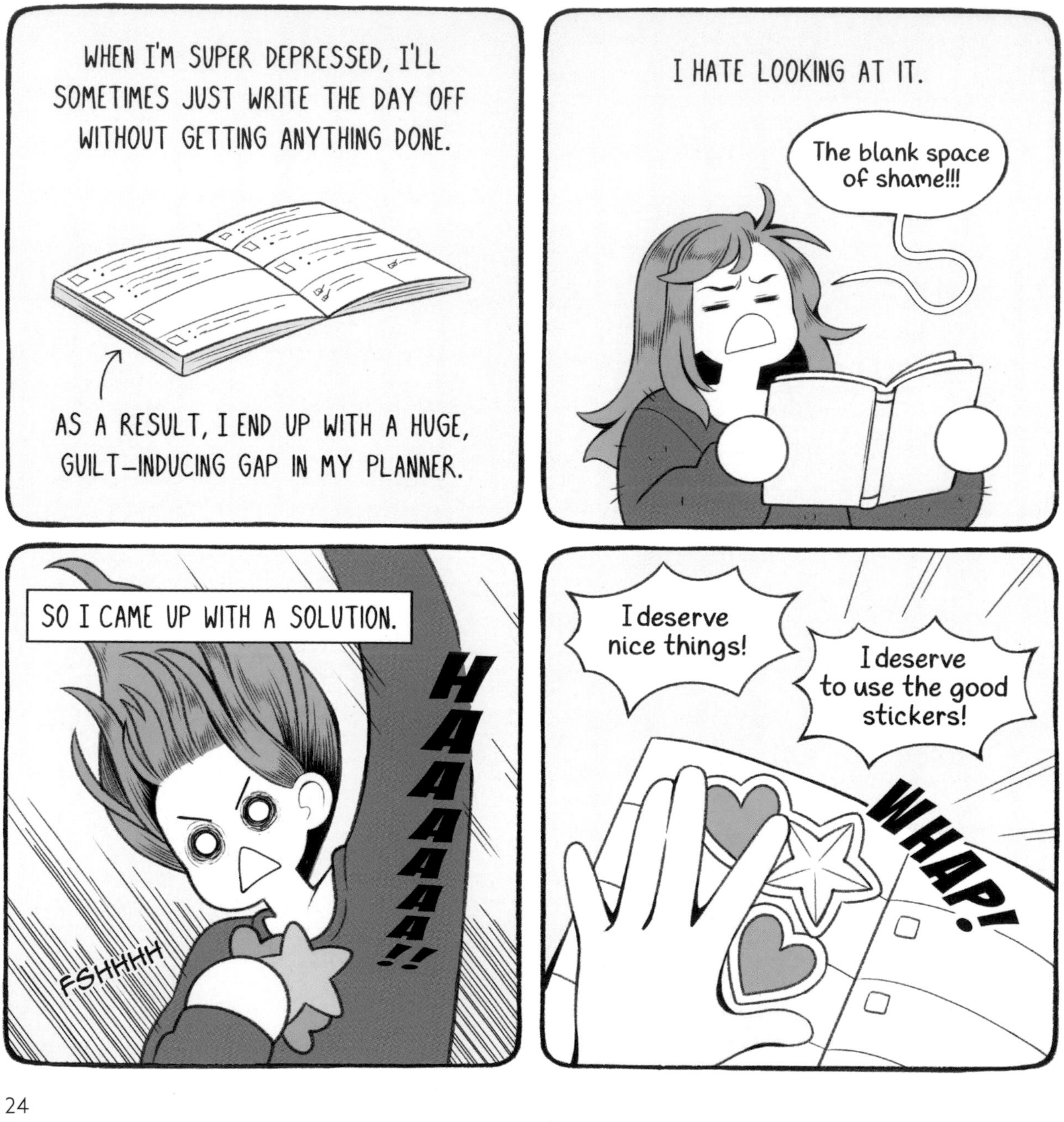
WHEN I'M SUPER DEPRESSED, I'LL SOMETIMES JUST WRITE THE DAY OFF WITHOUT GETTING ANYTHING DONE.
AS A RESULT, I END UP WITH A HUGE, GUILT-INDUCING GAP IN MY PLANNER.
I HATE LOOKING AT IT.
The blank space of shame!!!
SO I CAME UP WITH A SOLUTION.
HAAAAAAAA!!
FSHHHH
I deserve nice things!
I deserve to use the good stickers!
WHAP!

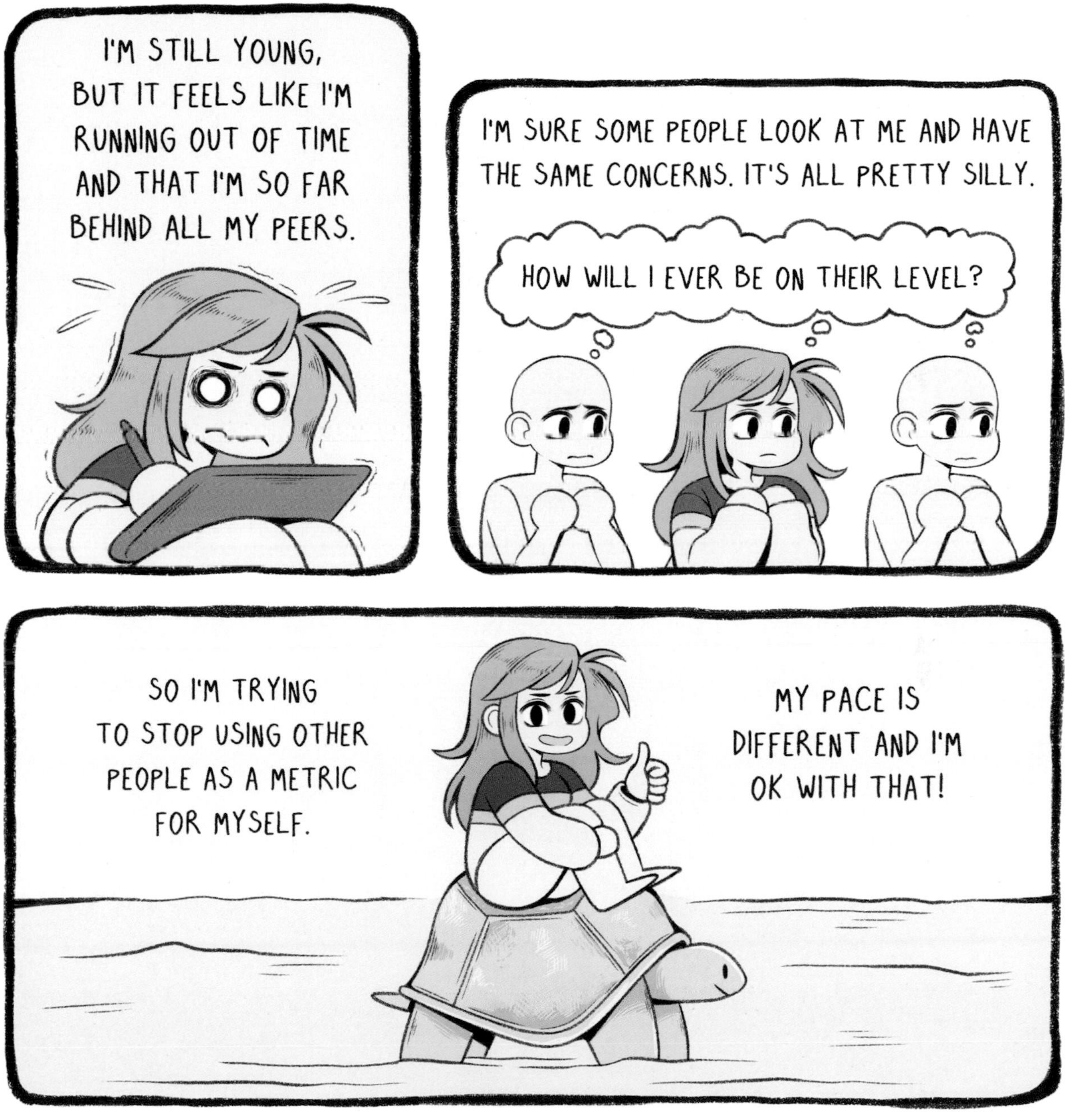
I'M STILL YOUNG, BUT IT FEELS LIKE I'M RUNNING OUT OF TIME AND THAT I'M SO FAR BEHIND ALL MY PEERS.
I'M SURE SOME PEOPLE LOOK AT ME AND HAVE THE SAME CONCERNS. IT'S ALL PRETTY SILLY.
HOW WILL I EVER BE ON THEIR LEVEL?
SO I'M TRYING TO STOP USING OTHER PEOPLE AS A METRIC FOR MYSELF.
MY PACE IS DIFFERENT AND I'M OK WITH THAT!

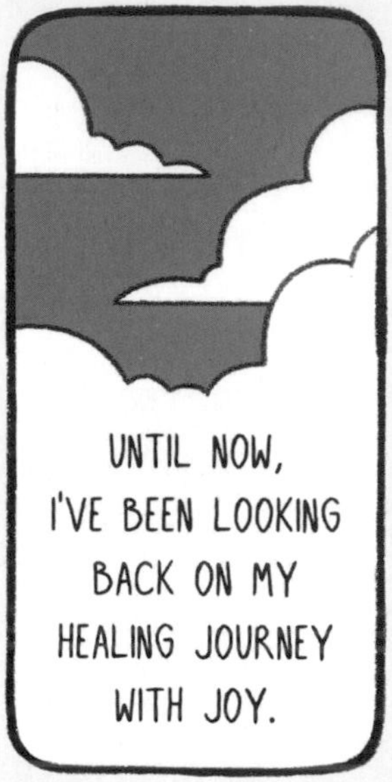
UNTIL NOW, I'VE BEEN LOOKING BACK ON MY HEALING JOURNEY WITH JOY.

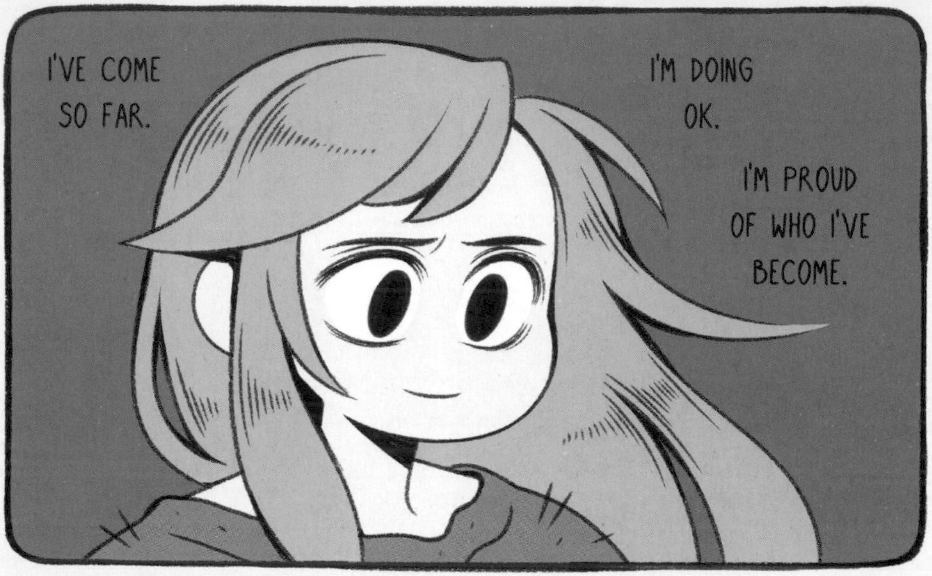
I'VE COME SO FAR.
I'M DOING OK.
I'M PROUD OF WHO I'VE BECOME.

IT'S BECOME HARD FOR ME TO THINK OF ME AND MY PAST SELVES AS BEING THE SAME PERSON.

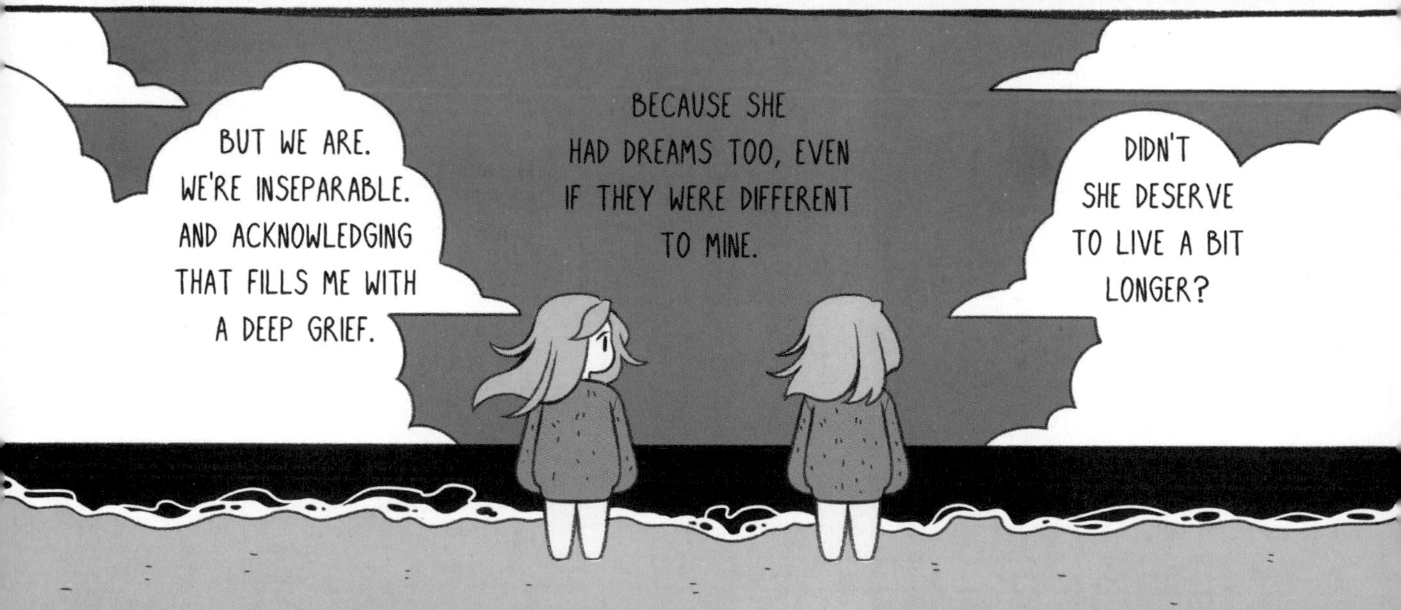
BUT WE ARE. WE'RE INSEPARABLE. AND ACKNOWLEDGING THAT FILLS ME WITH A DEEP GRIEF.
BECAUSE SHE HAD DREAMS TOO, EVEN IF THEY WERE DIFFERENT TO MINE.
DIDN'T SHE DESERVE TO LIVE A BIT LONGER?

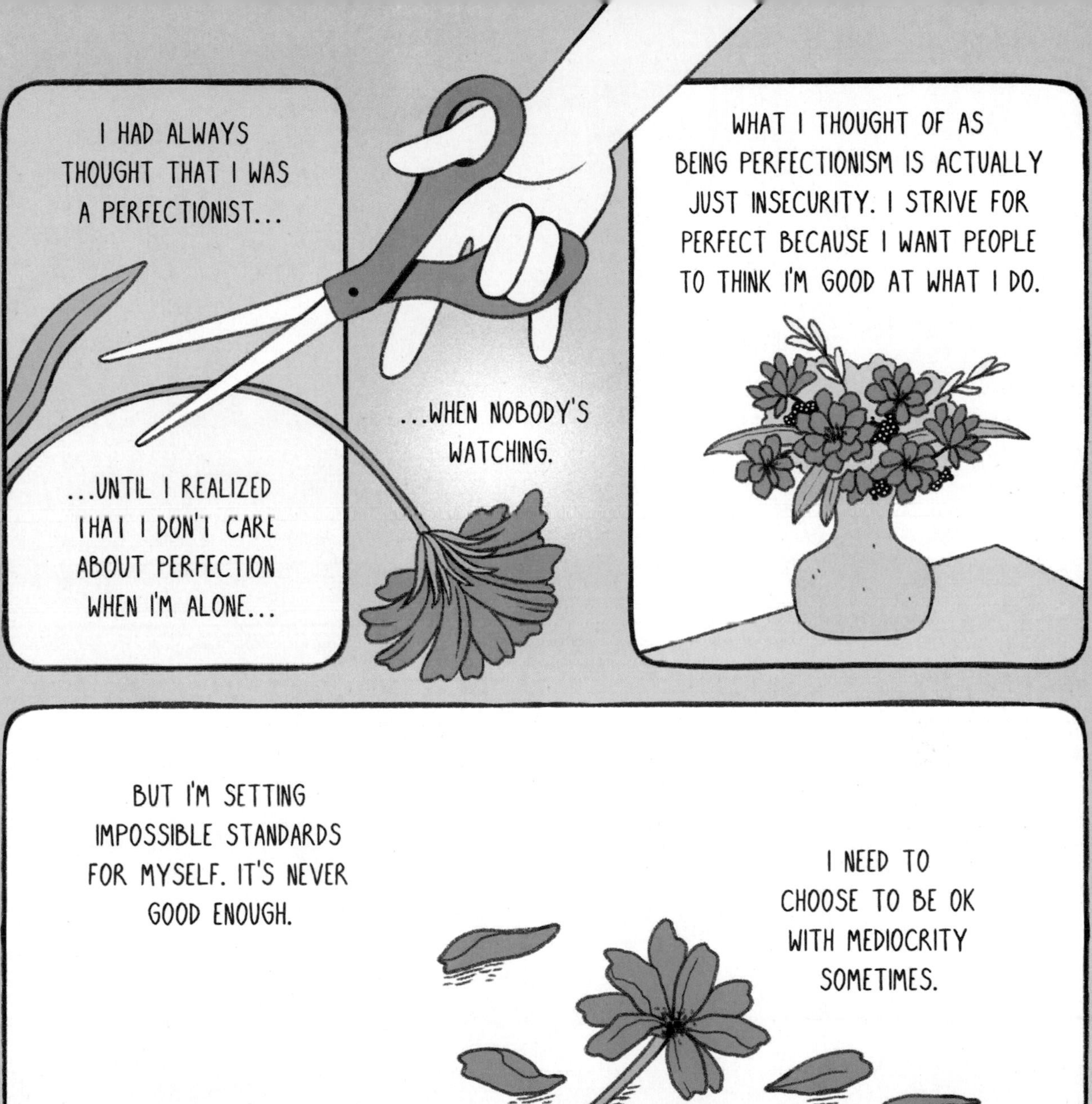
I HAD ALWAYS THOUGHT THAT I WAS A PERFECTIONIST...
...UNTIL I REALIZED THAT I DON'T CARE ABOUT PERFECTION WHEN I'M ALONE...
...WHEN NOBODY'S WATCHING.
WHAT I THOUGHT OF AS BEING PERFECTIONISM IS ACTUALLY JUST INSECURITY. I STRIVE FOR PERFECT BECAUSE I WANT PEOPLE TO THINK I'M GOOD AT WHAT I DO.
BUT I'M SETTING IMPOSSIBLE STANDARDS FOR MYSELF. IT'S NEVER GOOD ENOUGH.
I NEED TO CHOOSE TO BE OK WITH MEDIOCRITY SOMETIMES.

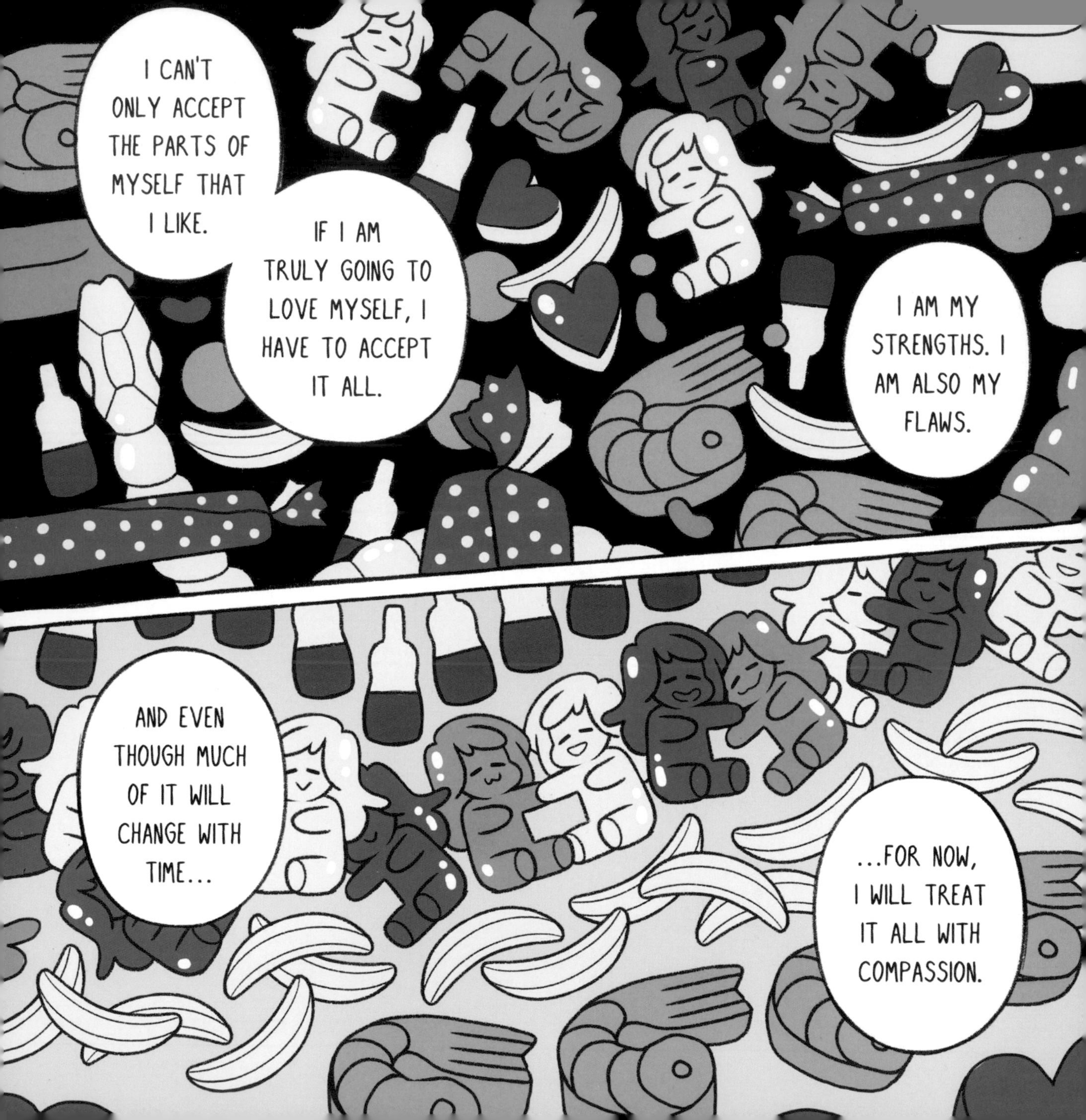
I CAN'T ONLY ACCEPT THE PARTS OF MYSELF THAT I LIKE.
IF I AM TRULY GOING TO LOVE MYSELF, I HAVE TO ACCEPT IT ALL.
I AM MY STRENGTHS. I AM ALSO MY FLAWS.
AND EVEN THOUGH MUCH OF IT WILL CHANGE WITH TIME...
...FOR NOW, I WILL TREAT IT ALL WITH COMPASSION.

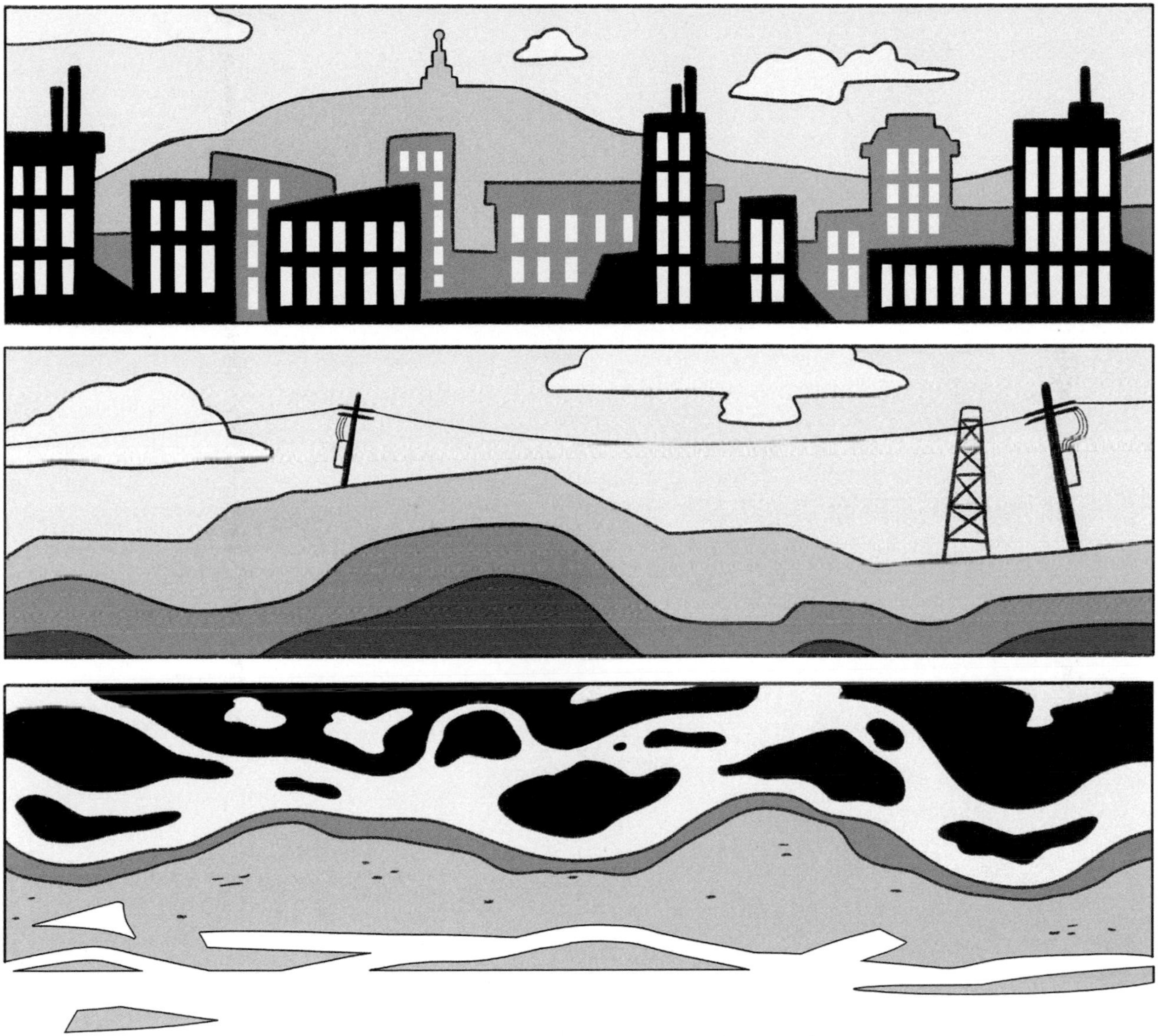

ONE DAY, I WILL MAKE ALL OF THIS RIGHT.

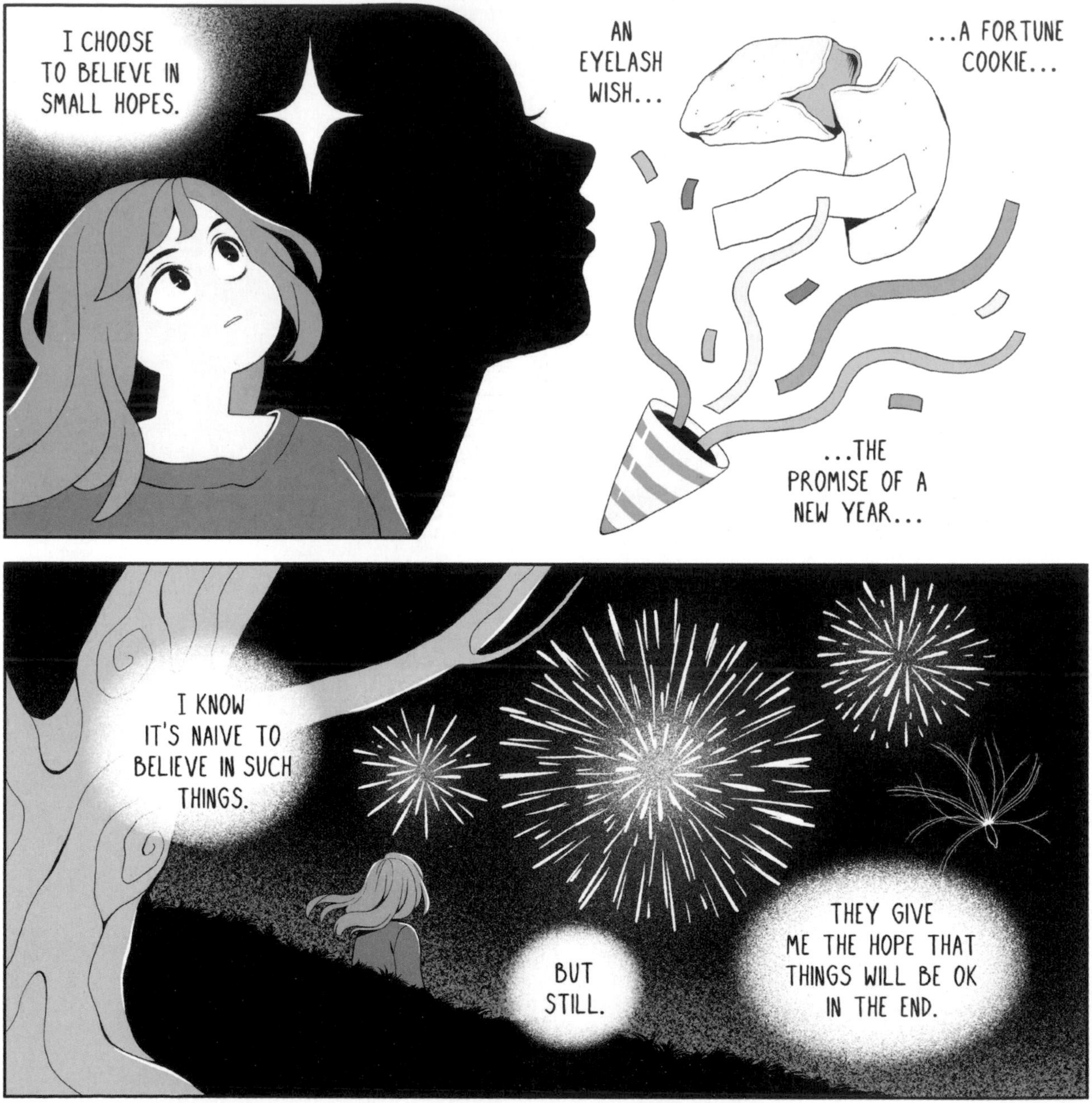
I CHOOSE TO BELIEVE IN SMALL HOPES.
AN EYELASH WISH...
...A FORTUNE COOKIE...
...THE PROMISE OF A NEW YEAR...
I KNOW IT'S NAIVE TO BELIEVE IN SUCH THINGS.
BUT STILL.
THEY GIVE ME THE HOPE THAT THINGS WILL BE OK IN THE END.

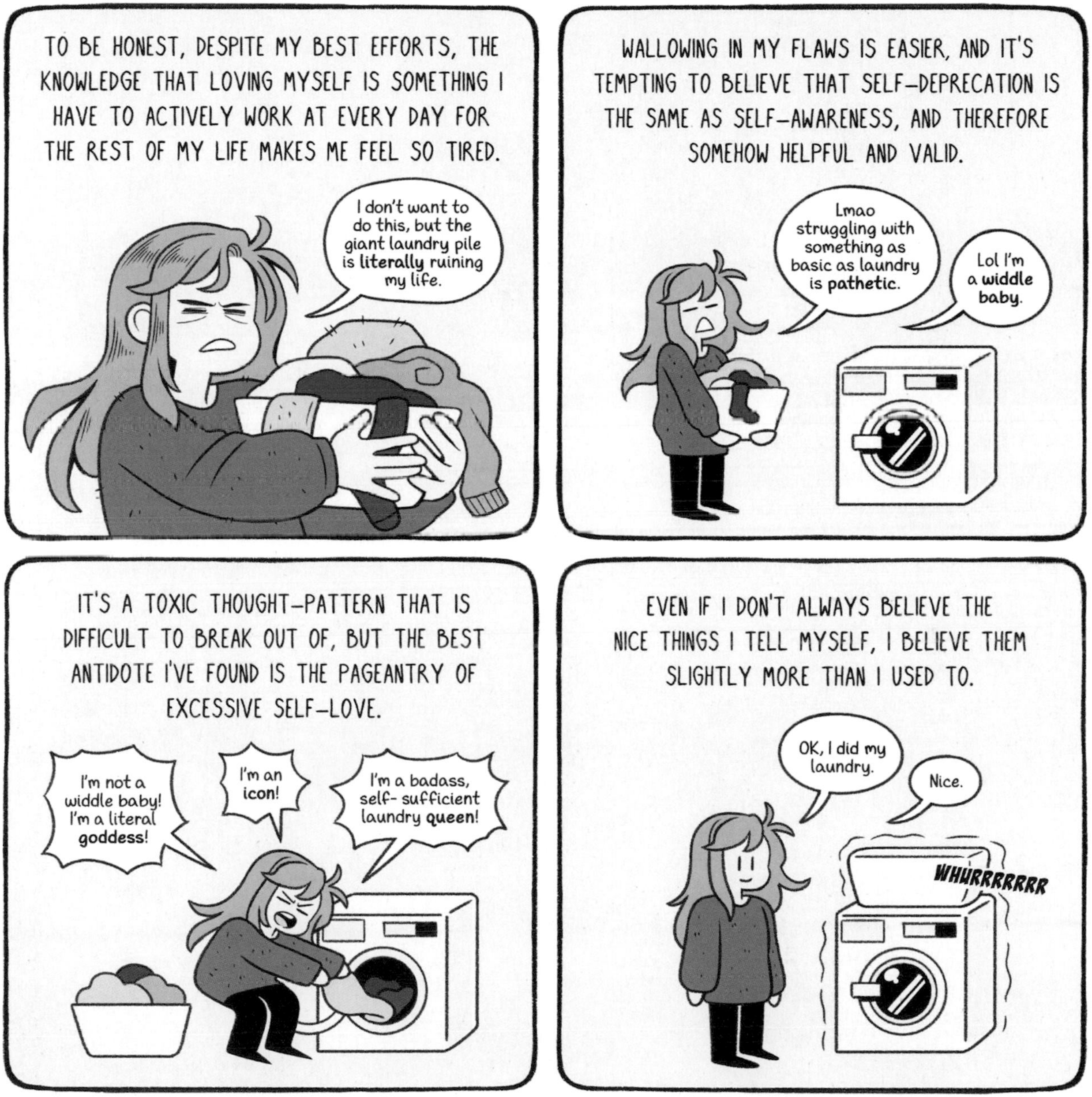
TO BE HONEST, DESPITE MY BEST EFFORTS, THE KNOWLEDGE THAT LOVING MYSELF IS SOMETHING I HAVE TO ACTIVELY WORK AT EVERY DAY FOR THE REST OF MY LIFE MAKES ME FEEL SO TIRED.
I don't want to do this, but the giant laundry pile is **literally** ruining my life.
WALLOWING IN MY FLAWS IS EASIER, AND IT'S TEMPTING TO BELIEVE THAT SELF-DEPRECATION IS THE SAME AS SELF-AWARENESS, AND THEREFORE SOMEHOW HELPFUL AND VALID.
Lmao struggling with something as basic as laundry is **pathetic**.
Lol I'm a **widdle baby**.
IT'S A TOXIC THOUGHT-PATTERN THAT IS DIFFICULT TO BREAK OUT OF, BUT THE BEST ANTIDOTE I'VE FOUND IS THE PAGEANTRY OF EXCESSIVE SELF-LOVE.
I'm not a widdle baby! I'm a literal **goddess**!
I'm an **icon**!
I'm a badass, self- sufficient laundry **queen**!
EVEN IF I DON'T ALWAYS BELIEVE THE NICE THINGS I TELL MYSELF, I BELIEVE THEM SLIGHTLY MORE THAN I USED TO.
OK, I did my laundry.
Nice.
WHURRRRRRR

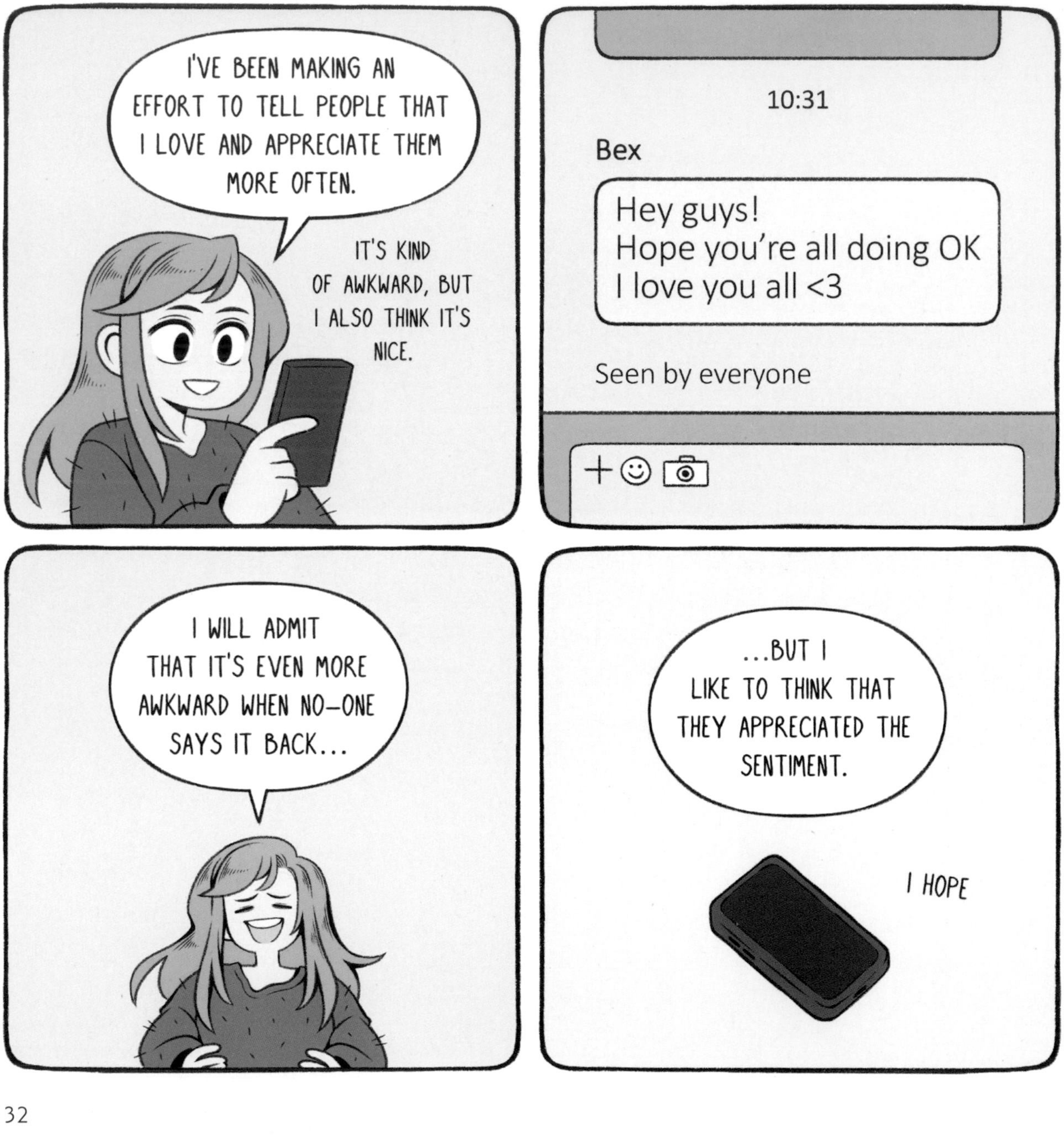
I'VE BEEN MAKING AN EFFORT TO TELL PEOPLE THAT I LOVE AND APPRECIATE THEM MORE OFTEN.
IT'S KIND OF AWKWARD, BUT I ALSO THINK IT'S NICE.
10:31
Bex
Hey guys!
Hope you're all doing OK
I love you all <3
Seen by everyone
I WILL ADMIT THAT IT'S EVEN MORE AWKWARD WHEN NO-ONE SAYS IT BACK...
...BUT I LIKE TO THINK THAT THEY APPRECIATED THE SENTIMENT.
I HOPE

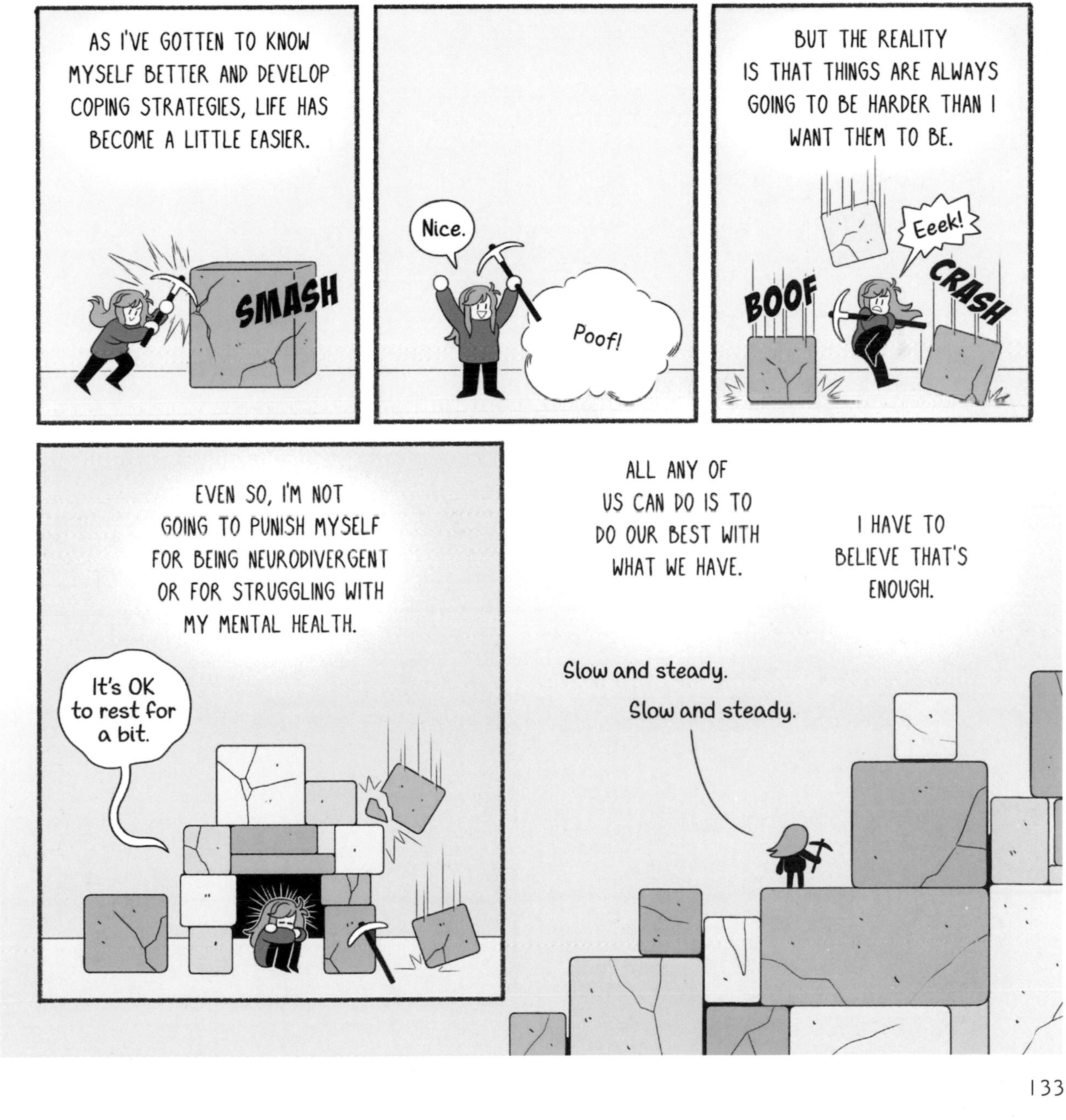
AS I'VE GOTTEN TO KNOW MYSELF BETTER AND DEVELOP COPING STRATEGIES, LIFE HAS BECOME A LITTLE EASIER.
SMASH
Nice.
Poof!
BUT THE REALITY IS THAT THINGS ARE ALWAYS GOING TO BE HARDER THAN I WANT THEM TO BE.
Eeek!
BOOF
CRASH
EVEN SO, I'M NOT GOING TO PUNISH MYSELF FOR BEING NEURODIVERGENT OR FOR STRUGGLING WITH MY MENTAL HEALTH.
It's OK to rest for a bit.
ALL ANY OF US CAN DO IS TO DO OUR BEST WITH WHAT WE HAVE.
I HAVE TO BELIEVE THAT'S ENOUGH.
Slow and steady.
Slow and steady.

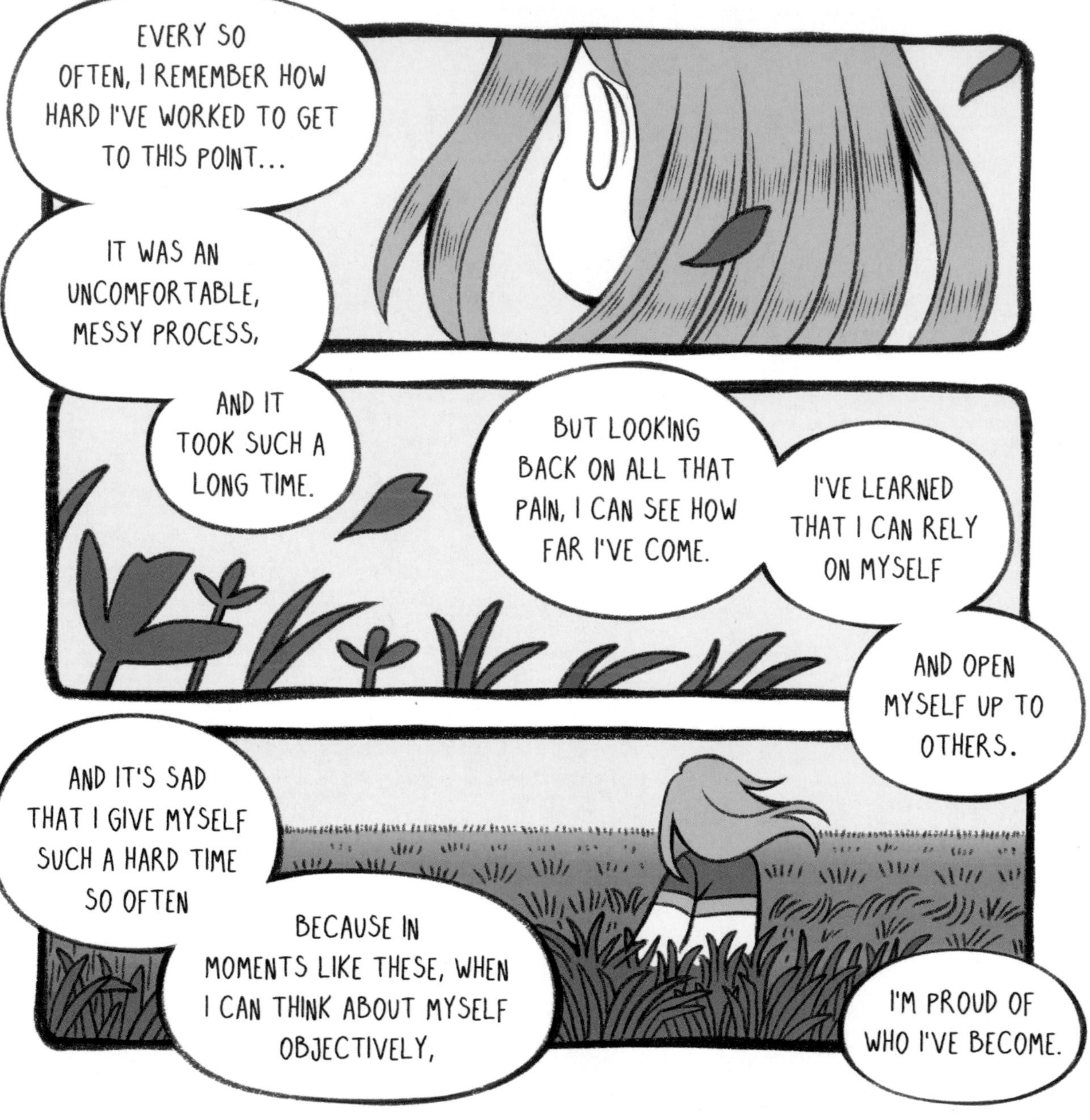
EVERY SO OFTEN, I REMEMBER HOW HARD I'VE WORKED TO GET TO THIS POINT...
IT WAS AN UNCOMFORTABLE, MESSY PROCESS,
AND IT TOOK SUCH A LONG TIME.
BUT LOOKING BACK ON ALL THAT PAIN, I CAN SEE HOW FAR I'VE COME.
I'VE LEARNED THAT I CAN RELY ON MYSELF
AND OPEN MYSELF UP TO OTHERS.
AND IT'S SAD THAT I GIVE MYSELF SUCH A HARD TIME SO OFTEN
BECAUSE IN MOMENTS LIKE THESE, WHEN I CAN THINK ABOUT MYSELF OBJECTIVELY,
I'M PROUD OF WHO I'VE BECOME.

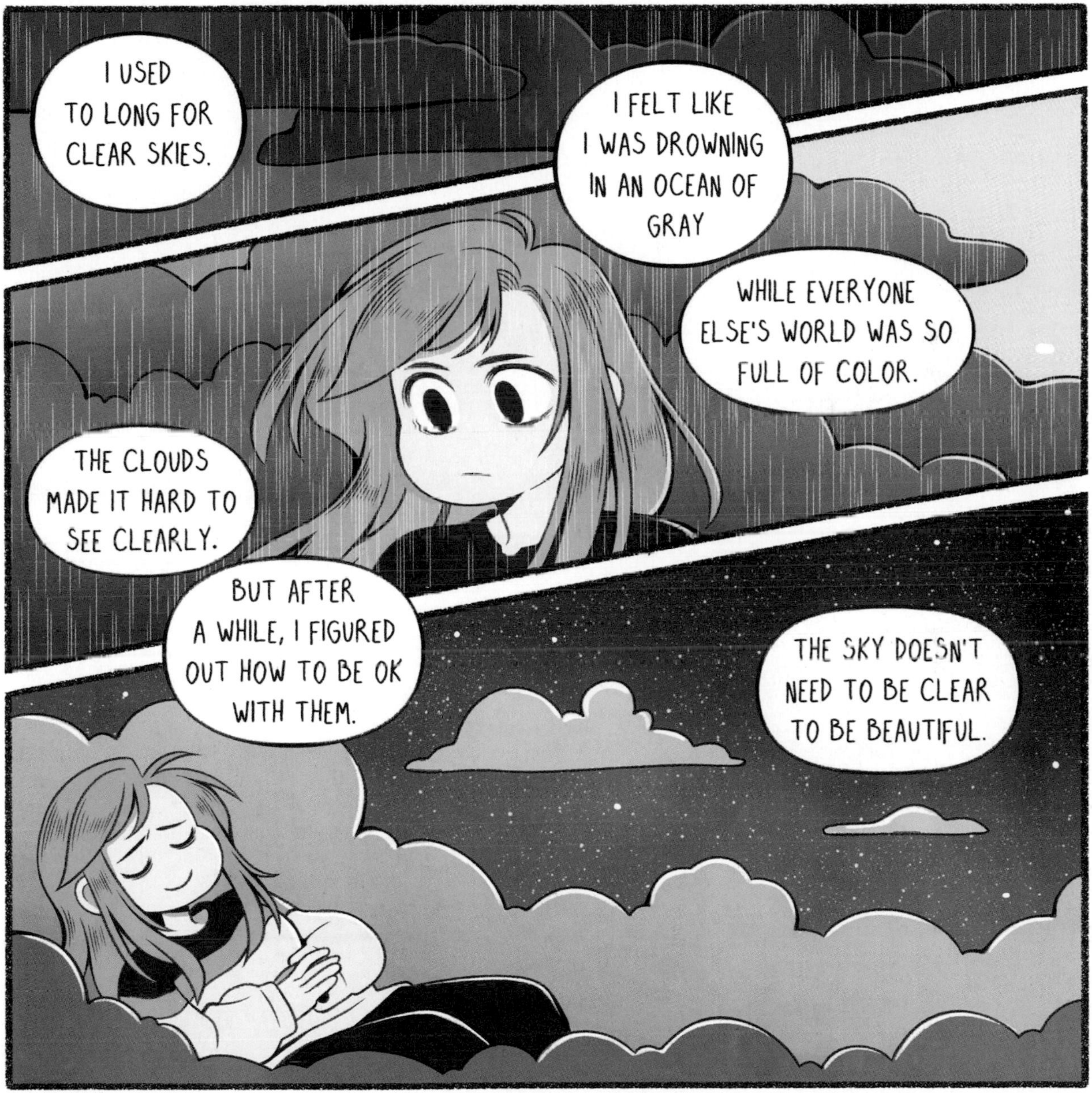
I USED TO LONG FOR CLEAR SKIES.
I FELT LIKE I WAS DROWNING IN AN OCEAN OF GRAY
WHILE EVERYONE ELSE'S WORLD WAS SO FULL OF COLOR.
THE CLOUDS MADE IT HARD TO SEE CLEARLY.
BUT AFTER A WHILE, I FIGURED OUT HOW TO BE OK WITH THEM.
THE SKY DOESN'T NEED TO BE CLEAR TO BE BEAUTIFUL.

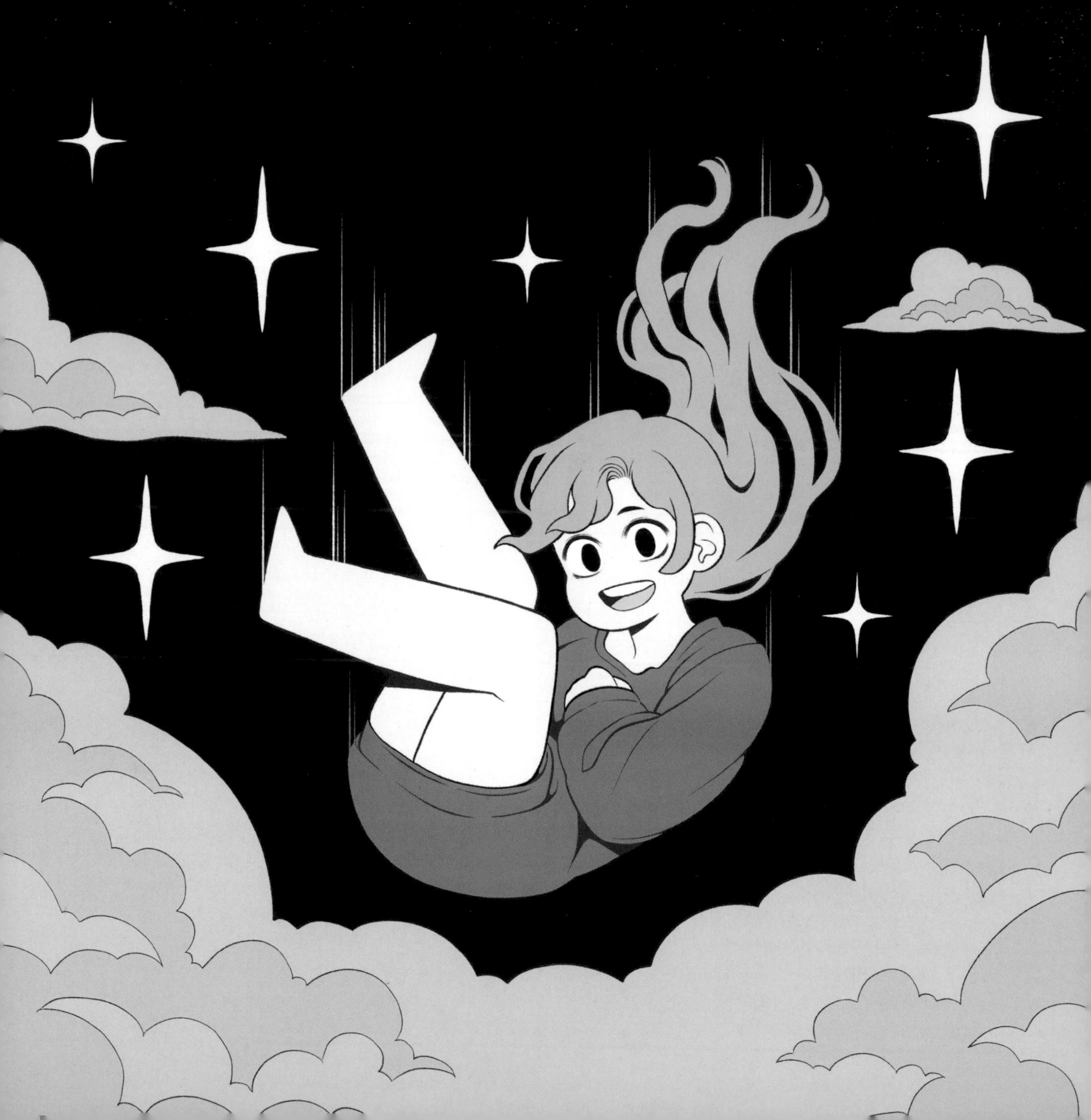

# Acknowledgments

I started making these comics during a time where I felt directionless and lost, but as I kept drawing, I was slowly able to find myself and who I want to be. Putting yourself out into the world is scary, but if not for making these comics and sharing them with the world, I know I would be worse off now. This whole process has been extremely meaningful for me, and I would like to say some words of thanks to the people who helped me on my journey.

I want to start off by thanking my partner, Luke Culver. Our quiet, daily life is all I've ever wanted, and while I have intentionally left that out of this book, it takes precedence in my heart. Your love and encouragement fill me with strength and give me a home. Thank you so much for always being by my side and for going out of your way to support me. Thank you for being strong when I couldn't be. Thank you so much for helping me to become the person I am today. I could never have done any of this without you.

I'd like to thank my parents, Jill and Eric Ollerton, for being a stable source of support throughout this project. I have always felt that no-matter what I do, even if I crash and burn, I will always have you to support me, and I am endlessly grateful for that. Thank you both for being in my corner and for letting me know that I can rely on you for anything. Thank you for being my cheerleaders and for giving me the tools to follow my dreams.

Thank you to Sarah Culver, for allowing me to stay at your place while I was making a lot of these comics, for always having a bubbly and positive attitude, and for taking care of me. You've done so much for me over the years and never asked for anything in return, and I hope that I can repay the huge kindness that you've shown me someday.

I started making *Lavender Clouds* as a way to put my feelings out into the world without having to talk to anyone about them, but through making these comics, I found people to talk to. Thank you to all of my readers, fans, and patrons, not only for engaging in my work, but for engaging with me as a person. Because of you, I've been able to grow into someone who can talk about things, and I know so much more about myself because of you. You taught me that I wasn't alone, and I don't think you'll ever be able to truly know how much that means to me. Thank you.

I'd like to thank Julie Mapes, Lucinda Wilson, and Shona Heaney, for your steadfast encouragement and friendship. Julie, your passion for everything I do fills me with so much life, and your feedback is completely invaluable. I'm always so excited to talk craft with you, and simply put, I wouldn't be the creator I am today without you. I feel extremely fortunate that you're such a big part of my life; we have so much fun together!

Luci, your perspective and wisdom have informed much of my work, along with who I am today. Your ability to confidently live life unapologetically on your own terms and seize a happiness that is truly yours inspires me on such a deep level and has helped me to grow. You often take a different approach to me, and I am enriched by our friendship.

Sho, you were hugely influential in inspiring me to create comics in the first place. Your incredible work has inspired me since we met, and probably will for the rest of my life. I have endless admiration for your unstoppable passion for what you do. Thank you for always bringing the fun and giving me something to laugh with you about. You are a bright light, and I treasure our friendship deeply.

Thank you so much to my wonderful agent, Tara Gilbert, for believing in my comics and for being so pleasant to work with. I sincerely appreciate everything you've done to help me along my path and your kindness and empathy in the face of my disorganization!

Thank you so much to the team at Andrews McMeel for helping me to make this book a reality. I was blown away by your extremely thorough edits—I learned that I've been doing ellipses wrong for years!—and I really enjoyed working together. Thank you for believing in my book and for letting me have so much creative freedom with it.

On top of that, I would like to specifically thank my editor, Lucas Wetzel, whose bright, bubbly emails always left me with a smile. I have nothing but good things to say about you! Working together was such a genuine joy for me: thank you so much for your enthusiasm, but also especially for your kindness and patience as my health waned during the final hurdle. Thank you for trusting that I would come through and for never making me feel pressured. You've been an absolutely ideal partner and I am so grateful.

Last, but not least, I want to thank my late grandmother, Iris Haselden. You were my biggest fan, and even though you never got to read these comics, I know that you would have been so proud of me. I wish so badly that you could see how far I've come, from a shy and moody girl with potential, to a confident woman with strength and skill. You gave me the greatest and most important gift of my life: a belief in myself so fierce and deep that even when it is obscured by anxiety, overwhelm, and all other kinds of unpleasant things, even in the hardest of times, it never goes out. Because of you, I know that one way or another, I'll always find a way through if I don't give up. Thank you so much for your love, I keep you in my heart always, and I will always miss you.

BEX OLLERTON IS AN EISNER—NOMINATED COMIC CREATOR FROM MANCHESTER, UK. SHE CREATES INTROSPECTIVE COMICS ABOUT MENTAL HEALTH, TRAUMA, NEURODIVERGENCE, AND THE GENERAL STRUGGLES OF BEING A HUMAN BEING IN AN OVERWHELMING WORLD; MOST NOTABLY, *SENSORY: LIFE ON THE SPECTRUM*. OLLERTON TELLS STORIES THAT CONVEY AN EMOTIONAL TRUTH AND USES THE MEDIUM TO RAISE AWARENESS OF THINGS THAT CAN BE HARD TO TALK ABOUT.